Planning for Public Transport

The Built Environment Series

Series Editors:

Michael J. Bruton, *Head of the School of Planning and Landscape, City of Birmingham Polytechnic*

John Ratcliffe, *Senior Lecturer in Planning, The Polytechnic of Central London*

The Spirit and Purpose of Planning   Edited by *Michael J. Bruton*
Introduction to Transportation Planning   *Michael J. Bruton*
Introduction to Town and Country Planning   *John Ratcliffe*
Introduction to Regional Planning   *John Glasson*
Introduction to Town Planning Techniques   *Margaret Roberts*
Citizens in Conflict   *James Simmie*
An Introduction to the Sociology of Town Planning   *James Simmie*
The Dynamics of Urbanism   *Peter F. Smith*

In association with the Open University Press

The Future of Cities   Edited by *Andrew Blowers Chris Hamnett* and *Philip Sarre*
Man-Made Futures   Edited by *Nigel Cross, David Elliott* and *Robin Roy*

Planning for Public Transport

Peter R. White M.C.I.T.

Senior Lecturer in Public Transport Systems in the Transport Studies Group at the Polytechnic of Central London

Hutchinson of London

Hutchinson & Co (Publishers) Ltd
3 Fitzroy Square, London W1

London Melbourne Sydney Auckland
Wellington Johannesburg and agencies
throughout the world

First published 1976
© Peter R. White 1976

Set in Monotype Times
Printed in Great Britain by The Anchor Press Ltd
and bound by Wm Brendon & Son Ltd, both of
Tiptree, Essex

ISBN 0 09 126850 8 (cased)
      0 09 126851 6 (paper)

Contents

Preface

My intention in writing this book has been to provide a basic text-book on public transport planning which will also appeal to the interested layman, and offer suggestions on policy as well as purely factual matters.

The British transport system is taken as the context, since many aspects of transport systems – regulation, organization, historical development – are largely unique to the countries in which they function. A text which claimed to relate, for example, to all developed countries of Western Europe would inevitably contain many general-izations of little relevance to specific cases. In particular, public transport in rural areas and small towns varies greatly from one country to another in importance and structure. In this respect the British network is exceptionally intensive and requires separate treatment. However, experience of other countries in intercity and metropolitan systems is of some relevance, and examples are quoted.

At the time of writing, a wide range of material on public trans-port systems is available. Much of this exists in the form of official reports, papers in journals and reports of conferences, and is thus widely scattered and inaccessible to the general reader or new student of the subject. I have tried to bring together in a coherent framework much of this material, to which reference is made at the end of each chapter, together with some ideas of my own. Much of the material in Chapters 4 and 8, for example, contains little of significant originality, but some of the theoretical concepts intro-duced, are, I believe, original, such as the inherent advantages of medium-sized urban areas (Chapter 2) and a simple model for optimization of stop spacing (Chapter 5). Parts of the book are related to research work carried out within the Transport Studies Group of the Polytechnic of Central London, either by myself (notably much of Chapter 2, based on a paper published in the

Journal of Transport Economics and Policy, January 1974) or other members, to whom specific reference is made in the text.

The resulting text will, I hope, fill the gap between basic works concerned with short-term planning and organization of public transport and textbooks concerned with long-term transportation planning and economic evaluation. The latter, in particular, often discuss means of assessing schemes but contain few practical ideas on the types of scheme that might be worth considering in a particular situation. Is an interurban demand best served by rail, limited-stop bus or coach? In what circumstances would a light rapid transit system be appropriate? Exact answers to such questions must depend on local circumstances, but I have put forward guidelines on which proposals can be based.

Since the growth of transport studies in the 1960s a change in external conditions has taken place. Long-term forecasts have become less certain in their application, and investment funds – for both roads and public transport – more restricted. It is acknowledged that the development of transport systems themselves will markedly affect demand, and that the form of development is not only a question of meeting forecast individual users' demand but also public opinions of environmental acceptability and mobility levels. I have therefore said little about long-term forecasting and deliberately ignored cost-benefit analysis. I have concentrated on assessment of short-term demand changes, cost structures, pricing policy and operating techniques. In doing so I am not denying the validity of attempts to take a long-term view, but am trying to complement texts already available.

In aiming to provide a fairly comprehensive text at a price which will make it available to a wide range of readers I have had to adopt a compressed style of presentation. Some readers may find the style rather concise, and those with wider knowledge of the subject may find some comments which appear wide-sweeping due to lack of qualifying statements. Despite such limitations I believe it is more valuable to produce a book of this type in order to extend much vital information about public transport than an 'academic' work littered with footnotes and hypotheses.

I am particularly concerned to put across ideas on how the existing public transport network can be improved by the more efficient use of existing resources. The favourable viewpoint towards public transport adopted in recent years by public, and some professional, opinion is in danger of reversal. Traffic levels were stabilized against a long-term downward trend from 1972 to 1975, but largely as a result of failing to increase fares at the same rate as inflation. In effect, a low-quality product was sold at a reduced price. The resulting deficits, combined with other economic pressures, have caused the Government to reverse previous subsidy trends in the bus industry, and to limit further growth in the massive rail deficit. It is vital that means of improving service quality be sought at minimum cost, wasteful overlap reduced and more secure financing obtained. For the present, the British public transport system is the most intensive and heavily used in Western Europe. It is to be hoped that it will remain so.

The 'Consultation Document' on transport policy

As this book went to press, the much-delayed Department of Environment 'Consultation Document' was published on 13 April 1976. Some amendments have been made to chapter ten in consequence, but it has not been possible to make any detailed response. Broadly speaking, I accept the suggested subsidy and investment limits, albeit with reluctance. However, far from being 'comprehensive', the Document merely treats transport on a mode-by-mode basis. This book looks at transport by function – urban, rural and inter-city – and also at related aspects of land-use planning and local authority finances. As such, it will hopefully complement the narrower analysis in the Document. The lack of positive thinking in it about means by which operations can be improved – other than some crude productivity measures and traffic restraint in urban areas – is alarming, and here also, this present volume will help to fill some gaps.

P.R.W. *26 April 1976*

Acknowledgements

Material in this book has been derived both from specific inquiries, and from a general interest in the transport field over several years. Among those providing specific material are P. B. Goodwin (formerly with University College, London), T. M. Glass (National Bus Company), R. Cox, and B. King (Tillingbourne Bus Company). Comments on earlier drafts were made by I. Yearsley and P. C. Stonham of *Motor Transport*, and Professor R. S. Doganis (Director), A. Jessop (Senior Lecturer) and S. R. Lowe (Research Associate) of the Transport Studies Group, Polytechnic of Central London. Work undertaken by students within the Transport Studies Group under my supervision has also formed the base for some material in the book, including that by D. M. Calver, P. Stanley, R. Burton and M. Donnellan. For assistance in providing diagrams and photographs I am grateful to Messers P. C. Stonham, J. Glover, A. Dare, S. R. Williams and J. Harbridge.

Among the many individuals and members of organizations with whom I have had useful discussions over the last four years I would like to acknowledge the stimulation provided by A. Moran and W. H. Jones (formerly on the research staff of the University of Liverpool School of Business Studies), A. P. Young (Greater Manchester PTE), D. Field (Department of Civic Design, University of Liverpool), W. J. Tyson (University of Manchester), S. Joy and K. Westoby (former chief, and, senior economists respectively, British Railways Board), A. Beetham, J. S. Madgett, I. Mitchell and P. Lutman (involved, at various levels, in traffic planning within the National Bus Company), G. I. Millar (Ulsterbus Ltd), D. McCracken (Scottish Bus Group), R. Slevin (Cranfield Institute of Technology), D. Hollings (AMV Ltd), K. W. Swallow (Merseyside PTE), T. McLachlan (Grey-Green Coaches), W. Lambden (Isle of Man Road Services Ltd), J. Parke (Editor of *Buses*), and J. Hibbs (City of Birmingham Polytechnic). Organizations whose meetings and individual members have proved helpful include the Transport Economists Group, Omnibus Society and Chartered Institute of Transport.

In following an academic career within transport studies, I have received much help and guidance from H. P. White (Reader in Geography, University of Salford – and, as *Private Eye* would put it, 'no relation'), Professor J. A. Proudlove (University of Liverpool), and, as a colleague, Professor R. S. Doganis of the Polytechnic of Central London.

All responsibility for the accuracy of statements and views expressed in this book is, of course, my own.

P.R.W. 24.9.75

1 Organization and control

Major Acts of Parliament

Before discussing the internal organization of transport industries in Britain, it is necessary to review the context in which they exist and were created. Acts of Parliament form the major external influence.

The Road Traffic Acts

The Road Traffic Act of 1930, enforced in 1931, introduced a national system of regulation for the bus and coach industry. Public Service Vehicles (PSVs) – buses and coaches carrying passengers at separate fares – were subject to annual inspection by a Ministry examiner. In order to be licensed as a PSV, each vehicle was also required to carry a valid 'Certificate of Fitness' (CoF). This document, relating to the condition and dimensions of the vehicle's structure, was issued by a Ministry examiner, and valid for up to seven years (and is now being replaced by an annual 'freedom from defect' notice). Annual licences were required also for drivers and conductors of PSVs.

Each separate service required a road service licence issued by regional Traffic Commissioners. Applications for such licences generally require details of route, fares, timetable (frequency and running times, often each specific journey) to be given. In addition to considering factors such as the safety of each route on highway grounds, the Commissioners were also required to have regard to the provision of 'unremunerative services', and co-ordination of services. In practice, objections to a new road service licence may be made by any affected party. Other bus and coach operators, the railways and local authorities account for most objections made. In the event of a licence application being rejected or modified the applicant may appeal. In such cases a hearing is held before an Inspector appointed by the Minister (now, the Secretary of State for the Environment), whose report and recommendations are considered by the Minister, but not binding on him in making a decision.

The Road Traffic Act of 1960 re-enacted the above provisions of the 1930 Act. The Road Traffic Bill of 1973 proposed substantial changes, particularly in rural areas, but following a change in government during its progress through Parliament in 1974, it emerged with proposals regarding road passenger transport largely deleted.

The Traffic Commissioners are organized on a regional basis: at present Scottish, Northern, Yorkshire, North Western, East Midland, West Midland, Eastern, Metropolitan, South Eastern, Western, and South Wales. London Transport is both operator and in effect licensing authority within the GLC area. A different form of regulation applies in Northern Ireland, whose relevance to the rest of Britain is considered in Chapter 9. The chairman of each Traffic Area is a full-time civil servant, usually with a legal or administrative background, appointed by the Secretary of State. Proposals for new or modified licences are published in the Notices and Proceedings of the Commissioners for each area. Objections may be placed within a given period, and a public hearing may be held by the Commissioners to consider them. Parties concerned may appear in person, or be represented by lawyers. The procedure is, however, less formal than a court of law.

The effect of the 1930 Act on the structure of the bus and coach industry was to enable large semi-monopolistic organizations to be built up by acquisition of smaller concerns. The major territorial companies made numerous takeovers to establish comprehensive networks, within which the principle of profitable services cross-subsidizing unremunerative ones applied.

Four major types of service were defined in the 1930 Act which remain applicable today:

1 *Stage carriage service:* A service operated on specified timetable, on which separate fares are payable (i.e. the great majority of bus services). Note that it is not necessarily open to all members of the public: a 'works bus' on which employees are charged fares in cash, or by deduction from wages, is a stage carriage service, the licence of which may indicate that it is restricted to specified employees.

2 *Excursions and tours:* Services operating over a specified route at predetermined fares, according to demand. The number of occasions per annum upon which the service may run, or number of vehicles that may be used, can be restricted.

3 *Express services:* Not defined by length or speed, but timetabled services on which separate fares are charged, and the minimum fare is 11p or more (5p or more until 1971).

4 *Hire or contract:* These are operations in which separate payments are not made by passengers. Vehicle and crew are required to carry PSV licences, but a road service licence is not usually required. Private coach hire, school contract services, etc., come into this category. However, there is a fine distinction between certain types of contract/hire and stage services, and disputes frequently arise.

The Transport Act 1968

Among the changes introduced by this Act in finance and control of transport were many affecting directly the structure of organization. Existing territorial bus operators fell into two groups, those owned by the Transport Holding Company (THC, a nationalized body), and the private sector. Most of the latter were under a holding company, British Electric Traction (BET). The Act created the National Bus Company (NBC), which controls both the former THC operators and those acquired voluntarily from the private sector shortly after introduction of the Act (the BET group, and the West Riding Automobile Company). Two large territorial operators remain in the private sector, Lancashire United Transport and Barton Transport. Some further takeovers have been made by NBC since its formation, especially within the coach industry, but there are no powers of compulsory acquisition.

In the major conurbations, proponents of the Act felt that more drastic change was required. Three major factors were:

1 the desire to plan conurbation networks as a whole, to improve co-ordination between existing operators, and to plan for rail and rapid transit networks with integrated bus services. Existing local authority operators did not cover sufficiently wide areas.

2 a belief that economies of scale exist in the bus industry, to be gained by mergers. All subsequent evidence points to the opposite and it is noteworthy that the most successful conurbation operator (Tyne and Wear) has the smallest operating units.

3 the need to update the traditional pattern of management within municipal bus undertakings, to incorporate long-term planning, industrial relations and marketing. Under the Act the Minister of Transport was given powers to designate Passenger Transport

Authorities (PTAs) comprising elected members of local authorities in a defined area, plus some members appointed directly by him. The PTAs were policy-making bodies, concerned with questions such as pricing and investment. Day-to-day operation of services and ownership of assets were vested in the Passenger Transport Executives (PTEs), who are also the employers of the staff.

Four PTAs were initially designated in 1969: Merseyside, SELNEC (South East Lancashire North East Cheshire, now Greater Manchester), West Midlands and Tyneside; a fifth, Greater Glasgow, was added in 1973. At the time of their formation the future pattern of local government was still undecided. Following the 1972 Local Government Act (see below) the PTAs were replaced by Metropolitan County Councils. This involved some change in the areas of the original four PTAs – for example, Tyneside lost some parts of Northumberland but gained the area around Sunderland to become Tyne and Wear Metropolitan County – and creation of two new Metropolitan Counties with a similar role, West Yorkshire and South Yorkshire.

Other sections of the 1968 Act related to the bus and coach industry as a whole. New buses 'primarily for stage service' (later defined as working on stage service for at least 50 per cent of mileage run during the first six years of their life) and meeting certain design standards (see Chapter 3) qualified for a 25 per cent government grant towards capital cost. This share was increased to 50 per cent in 1971. Local authorities were given powers to subsidize rural bus services, under section 34, although not until 1971 were substantial demands made by operators. The rebate on fuel tax on fuel used on stage carriage services was increased to 12·50p of the then 22·50p per gallon. Early in 1974, to offset the effect of further increases in fuel cost, the rebate was increased to the full 22·50p. The rural subsidy provisions have been incorporated in the Transport Supplementary Grant system with effect from 1975–6 (see below), but fuel-tax rebate and new bus grant continue to be paid by central government.

Under the 1968 Act, the British Railways Board (BRB) was relieved of a substantial capital debt, although the rate of interest payable on the remaining debt was increased substantially, so that annual payments of interest by the Board became about £40 million. Specific grants, estimated under the so-called 'Cooper formula' (see

Chapter 6), were introduced for 'socially necessary' but loss-making services. Virtually all services other than the heavier intercity flows fell into this category. The former regional boards were abolished, and the railway system as such placed under the BRB in London. Certain types of activity were, however, placed in the hands of new organizations, generally with commercial objectives. The Shipping Division operates as a separate entity under the 'Sealink' fleetname.

It forms the largest operator in the short-sea passenger and car ferry trade, being matched in Scotland by McBraynes and the Caledonian Steam Packet Co., which form part of the Scottish Transport Group. BR's 'Seaspeed' subsidiary is similarly the major hovercraft operator, paralleled by private operators on its Isle of Wight and cross-Channel routes. National Carriers Limited were set up under the 1968 Act, as part of the National Freight Corporation, to operate sundries and less-than-wagon load traffic, including most road delivery vehicles (although 'Rail Express Parcels' remain with BR as part of their passenger operations). British Rail Engineering Limited (BREL) controls the major rail workshops, building both for BR and for other customers where capacity permits.

The Local Government Act 1972

From 1 April 1974 local government in England and Wales was reorganized under this Act, counties becoming the major authorities in respect of planning and transport. Six Metropolitan Counties (see above) control the major conurbations within England, their boundaries including much of the prosperous commuter hinterland formerly within adjacent rural counties. The remaining forty-seven 'shire' counties are mostly rural in character, although some – South Glamorgan, Cleveland and Avon – are dominated by urban settlement. Counties are thus responsible authorities for structure planning, and highways. Each county is required to prepare an annual 'Transport Policies and Programme' document (TPP), indicating existing policies and progress made towards objectives, attached to which is a financial statement in respect of desired expenditure. The related system of grants (see below) has superseded specific grants for road schemes, rural bus subsidies and transportation studies.

Within counties, highway powers may be delegated to district councils, and in practice a number of former highway authorities (often large county boroughs such as Southampton) have retained significant powers. Municipal bus undertakings have been transferred to appropriate district councils, but in both these respects districts are required to co-ordinate their policies with those of the county in which they fall.

Involvement in public transport by counties is at present highly variable. The metropolitan counties, as bodies controlling PTEs, are concerned with financing new rail schemes, part of local rail deficits and other public transport schemes. The 'shire' counties, apart from a few schemes to renovate or reopen rail or bus stations, have virtually no concern with public transport capital expenditure, but are responsible for the majority of rural bus subsidies. Under section 203 of the 1972 Act counties are required to 'co-ordinate' provision of public passenger transport, that is, they have a *mandatory* responsibility in contrast to the *permissive* powers of the 1968 Transport Act. However, the requirement is vague and a county which shows little interest in public transport is under no specific legal obligation to take action.

Powers of district councils relevant to transport include operation of existing municipal bus services and control of car parking. They can influence pricing of their own parks, and are the second-tier authorities in planning, with powers to grant, refuse or modify development permission for private parking.

As local education authorities, county councils form an important sector of demand for bus services (public and contract) in rural areas, typically spending £1 million per annum per county. Some, such as Lincolnshire, operate their own school buses as non-PSVs, but counties do not have powers to operate public transport services.

Internal organization of major transport operators

British Railways Board

At present there are five regions: Eastern, Midland, Southern, Scottish and Western. These form the first tier below national level, and are responsible for much passenger and freight operations planning. Each region, apart from the Scottish, is split into several divisions, most of which are centred on major industrial cities such as Cardiff or Nottingham. Within each division, area managers (superseding former goods agents and most functions of station masters) are responsible for day-to-day running. Several attempts have been made to reduce the number of levels in this bureaucratic structure, and some years ago the divisions within the Scottish Region were abolished, area managers reporting direct to regional management. Under a scheme proposed by McKinsey & Co. a similar structure for the whole of BR was to be introduced in 1974, in which existing regions would be slightly reduced in size and increased in number, and renamed 'territories', to which area managers would report directly. After considerable opposition, such proposals were dropped early in 1975.

The railways have been the scene of a continued dispute between the merits of 'functional' (or 'centralized') management and decentralized management. Some activities in which specialist skill is required and in which economies of scale are seen, are best dealt with nationally, as a function of the BRB itself. Research and development work in new forms of rolling stock is an obvious example. Other activities, such as short-term planning of passenger and freight services, are better dealt with at a more local level, at which management will be familiar with both the market and operating constraints. During the 1950s and early 1960s there was a marked swing towards a decentralized pattern. After a swing back during the late 1960s, the position appears to have stabilized, with centralization of activities varying according to the function concerned.

The National Bus Company (NBC)

As indicated above, NBC came into being in 1969 to control regional bus and coach operators owned by the Government. Despite its title, its area of control does not include Scotland or Northern Ireland. A total of thirty regional bus companies are controlled by the board of NBC Federation Ltd. A small headquarters section deals with long-term planning, finance, and negotiations with unions and major suppliers. The bus companies are grouped into three regions – Eastern, Southern, and Western – each with a director. Within each region are three or four chief general managers (CGMs), each controlling about three companies. These intermediate levels involve little bureaucracy, being mainly a means of co-ordination between companies, often with interlocking directorships. Each CGM is usually based with one of the companies which he controls.

Within each regional company, such as Crosville or East Kent, management is divided into traffic and engineering sections, with a small legal/financial group attached directly to central management. The company engineer is responsible for providing vehicles in serviceable condition to the traffic department, controlling workshops, maintenance staff and purchase of spares, and has some influence on vehicle purchasing policy. The traffic manager is responsible both for day-to-day operation, including allocation of crews to vehicles and collection of revenue, and long-term planning of fares and services. The latter function may often receive little systematic attention in companies where little imagination is displayed by traffic management or much time occupied with industrial disputes or traffic cases. A recent innovation has been the introduction of marketing and planning posts within more progressive companies' traffic departments. The regional company is the owner of vehicles and premises, holder of road service licences, and employer of staff, not NBC as such.

The formation of NBC created an obvious opportunity to bring together the extensive network of express coach services and extended tours operated by constituent companies into a national system, which could be marketed and planned more effectively. From October 1973 'National Travel' was established, as part of the Central Activities Group of NBC. It operates many, but not all, of NBC's coaches, and plans the national network and timetable. On the formation of NBC a number of concerns working purely in the coaching field were acquired, such as Standerwick of Blackpool. These formed the nuclei for five regional companies – National Travel (South East) Ltd (and similarly 'South West', 'Midland', 'North West' and 'North East') – which operate tours and certain parts of the express network. They have taken over vehicles and licences for trunk routes from regional companies, but the latter continue to operate many coaches themselves – albeit in the National white livery – especially on seasonal services.

Municipal and PTE bus operators

The majority of municipal bus operators were set up as tramway operators at the turn of the century. At this time local authorities used statutory powers to acquire existing horse or steam tramways which they electrified and extended. In contrast to the uninspiring image of most local authority activities, here we see an example of local authorities being in the forefront of transport progress, applying a new form of traction with radical results in productivity and patronage. In many cases electricity undertakings were also controlled by local authorities, for which the tramway was often the biggest customer. In a sense local authority transport activities reached the height of their power around 1912, before motor transport offered competition. Some local authorities, such as Eastbourne, adopted motor buses from the start but others were slow to switch over, or transferred to trolley-buses as an alternative which would utilize existing investment in power supply (local authority electricity undertakings were nationalized in 1949). Some smaller undertakings, such as Norwich, were sold to regional bus companies during the interwar period, and as late as 1968–9 the Exeter and Luton undertakings were sold to the National Bus Company.

Within the municipal undertakings a rigid management structure was formed, characteristic of the period. Engineering received prime importance, as the area of decision in which most skill was required, and even today many municipal managers retain the title of 'General Manager and Engineer', themselves qualified primarily in engineering. The problems thus created have been mentioned above in respect of PTEs.

The PTEs established under the 1968 Act continue in the original four PTA areas, and two new PTEs have been set up matching the Metropolitan Counties in Yorkshire. A PTE is empowered to make agreements with bus operators (usually subsidiaries of the National Bus Company) and British Rail for the provision of services. It may specify fares and levels of services, subject to provision of subsidy. West Midlands and Greater Manchester acquired most NBC services in their areas by direct purchase of vehicles and depots. In the other four PTEs joint agreements exist with NBC companies, mainly in respect of fares. Under section 20 of the 1968 Act, the PTEs pay part or all of the grant aid to local rail services in their areas. British Rail supply services according to levels and fares stipulated by PTEs. Integrated planning of rail and bus services is thus made easier, and given a financial incentive. PTEs are responsible for long-term rail/rapid transit planning in their areas, including schemes such as the Tyneside light rapid transit system and Glasgow 'Clyderail'.

Following formation of the PTEs about sixty municipal bus undertakings remained in England and Wales. Their internal structure has changed little. As within NBC companies, traffic and engineering form the main diversions, with little separation of long-term traffic planning from day-to-day management. Despite the rigidity of structure, many small municipal undertakings have fared better than NBC or PTE operators in retaining traffic. As discussed in Chapter 2, this is partly because local management is more sensitive to both internal operating problems and external market opportunities. In some cases useful cross-fertilization has taken place with planning or finance departments of the parent local authority. In others, survival of a relatively stable traffic level may be fortuitous, and an expansion of certain management functions is required urgently.

Internal organization of PTEs at operating level largely resembles that of municipal operators which they absorbed, but with the addition of geographical divisions, to form manageable units for day-to-day control.

Independent bus and coach operators

Apart from Barton Transport and Lancashire United Transport, who resemble NBC regional companies in structure, most independents are fairly small, operating between one and fifty vehicles. Many of the companies in stage carriage operation, generally found in rural areas, date from sole proprietors setting up business during the 1920s. Today they continue under their descendants, as partnerships or limited companies. Even where stage carriage working is important, however, it rarely accounts for more than half of total mileage or revenue. Newer concerns are based almost entirely in the contract and private hire field, apart from some set up specifically to take over rural services abandoned recently by NBC. They range from one-man concerns working minibuses to limited companies with fleets of frequently renewed coaches, specializing in high-quality markets. Most school contract work for local authorities is handled by independents.

Internal organization is often informal, with the owner or managing director as operating manager. As Turns (1974) has shown, this policy may often limit the size of business as much as restrictions due to inability to obtain licences, or market opportunities. Operation of private party coach hire or excursions may require frequent decisions on pricing and scheduling, and hence a small span of control for each manager is desirable. Maintenance facilities may be very limited, problems of major overhaul and recertification being handled by sale of a vehicle to a dealer who provides a re-conditioned vehicle in part exchange. Capital requirements may also be eased by using low-cost second-hand vehicles on contract work, or buying new vehicles on hire purchase.

Many small independents lack expertise in costing and matters such as reclaiming fuel-tax rebate. As part of their responsibilities for public transport, most 'shire' counties have appointed public transport co-ordinating officers, whose duties include assessment of subsidy requests, co-ordinating timetables of different operators, etc. Such officers may also serve to advise smaller independents on procedure.

Some coaching groups exceed the fifty-vehicle range mentioned above, notably the publicly quoted Wallace Arnold combine, whose fleets total about 300 vehicles. Such operators are concerned primarily with coach hire and extended tours, and are part of the travel industry rather than the basic public transport system.

Another form of organization to be found in the bus industry of other countries is the co-operative, of which Israel offers the best examples. Some cases exist in Britain of small independents working as co-operatives or on joint services with pooled revenue, notably the 'AA' and 'A1' groups in south-west Scotland.

Passenger transport organization in Northern Ireland, Scotland and London

From its inception in 1933 London Transport has been unique. Pressures from both trade unions and private capital supported the establishment of a nationalized public corporation with extensive monopoly powers. Within its area, LT did not require road service licences, and any other operator providing the equivalent of a stage carriage service did so only with LT's consent. However, the heavily used network of the main line railways within London was not absorbed, apart from some extensions of the LT underground system over former main line branches, and some pooling of revenue.

The area designated for LT included not only London as such but much of the adjoining counties. This situation continued with little change until 1969 when the Transport (London) Act reformed the system so that the greater part came under control of the Greater London Council, instead of a nationalized body with members appointed by the Minister of Transport. In many ways a PTA/PTE form of organization was established, except that only one authority, the Greater London Council (GLC) was involved. The London Transport Board was retitled the London Transport Executive (LTE), and continues to operate all underground railways and the central (red) bus fleet. The country (green) bus fleet and Green Line coach network was handed over to a new operator, London Country Bus Services (LCBS), part of the National Bus Company, and subject to normal licensing provisions. LT retains its monopoly powers within the GLC area. The GLC controls long-term policy on matters such as fares and major investment.

In many ways the London situation is less satisfactory than that in other PTEs. There is little integration with BR passenger services, and subsidies towards them are paid entirely by central government, in contrast to the share contributed in other PTE areas. In effect, the prosperous London and South East Region receives a double subsidy. The GLC boundary does not include the prosperous outer suburban areas. Potential rate revenue is thus reduced, but facilities used by peak period commuters from the outer areas are nonetheless provided (such as distributor services within central London) at the expense of less wealthy GLC residents. From the viewpoint of the home counties, the situation also has drawbacks: the country buses were formerly cross-subsidized by central buses, and sharp cutbacks have been necessary in order to achieve viability. The doughnut-shaped operating area of LCBS is also very inconvenient to manage. There is substantial interpenetration of LTE and LCBS bus services in the boundary areas, creating difficulty in co-ordination of fares policies. (For example, as a result of a GLC decision to keep down fare levels from 1972 to 1975, high subsidy demands were made in respect of LT services outside the boundary. The counties affected would probably have favoured a different policy if in control.)

In Scotland the Scottish Transport Group (STG) took over interests of the nationalized Transport Holding Company following the Transport Act 1968. Buses comprise the majority of the Group's activities. Six regional companies, similar in structure to those of NBC, form the Scottish Bus Group. They are smaller on average than NBC companies, and also engage directly in express coach operation, there being no equivalent of 'National Travel'. Some routes are worked jointly with English operators, but trunk routes to London entirely by the Scottish companies.

Local government structure in Scotland also differs from that in England and Wales. Under the 1973 Local Government (Scotland) Act the Scottish authorities were re-formed from May 1975 into regional authorities, below which are districts. The regional authorities are generally based on major cities such as Edinburgh and Aberdeen. Glasgow falls within the exceptionally large Strathclyde region, extending as far as the outer isles, but it is not yet clear whether the boundaries of the Greater Glasgow PTE will be correspondingly enlarged.

Control of transport in Northern Ireland has (apart from the present powers of the Northern Ireland Office) been exercised by the assembly at Stormont. Legislation followed a similar pattern to that in the rest of the UK, except that more rigid and monopolistic nationalized systems were formed, in which both road and rail services were controlled by the Ulster Transport Authority (UTA). The Transport Act of 1967 split up the UTA, forming a separate body to operate the remaining rail services, ·Northern Ireland Railways (NIR), and Ulsterbus Ltd, a company similar in size and structure to an NBC subsidiary. Although Ulsterbus controls the majority of bus and coach services, especially since its takeover of the Belfast Corporation fleet (renamed 'Citybus'), it is not a statutory monopoly. A road service licensing system similar in some respects to that in the rest of the UK applies, but without the detailed control of fares and timetables. A greater degree of competition is possible, and less freedom given to existing operators, such as the railways, to make objections.

Other organizations concerned with public passenger transport

Regulatory bodies

Reference has been made already to the role of the Traffic Commissioners in the bus and coach industry. Under the Transport Act 1968 regulatory powers were to be given to PTEs in a similar fashion to the powers enjoyed by London Transport (see above), but the relevant sections of the Act never became law. Under European Economic Community (EEC) regulations, the Department of the Environment is responsible for processing applications for international coach services to other EEC countries.

British Rail and the small number of private railways (mostly preserved lines) are not subject to detailed control of timings or fares. However, the Government does exercise strong direct control on overall price levels and investment policy. Any new section of track or signalling installation is subject to close inspection and approval by the Railway Inspectorate, a government department staffed largely by former military officers of an engineering background. They are responsible also for reporting on railway accidents. While their technical competence is not in question, the far more stringent investigation and control, often without economic assessment, imposed on railways places rail operations at a disadvantage to those of road transport. A much higher accident rate is accepted implicitly in present policies towards the road system.

Trade unions

In view of the complex situation in manufacturing and maintenance work, only those unions concerned directly with passenger transport operation are described.

The majority of bus drivers and conductors are members of the Transport and General Workers Union (TGWU), whose head-quarters organization includes a national secretary responsible for this sector of membership. Stemming from the period when major railway companies operated buses, or held interests in regional bus companies, some NBC staff are members of the National Union of Railwaymen (NUR). Supervisory and clerical staff belong to different unions, membership of the National Association of Local Government Officers (NALGO) being common in municipal undertakings.

In the railways there is a sharp demarcation between manual, 'skilled', and clerical staff. The majority of railwaymen, including guards, maintenance staff, station staff and signalmen, are represented by the NUR. Drivers and second men are represented by the Associated Society of Locomotive Engineers and Firemen (ASLEF). Frequent clashes have arisen in recent years on the demarcation of status and earnings between ASLEF members and other railwaymen. Clerical and supervisory staff are represented by the Transport Salaried Staffs Association (TSSA).

User groups and other pressure groups

In principle, passengers' interests *vis-à-vis* nationalized concerns are represented via the regional Transport Users' Consultative Committees (TUCCs) which were set up following major nationalization in the late 1940s. An annual report is submitted to the Minister by the Central Transport Users' Consultative Committee (CTCC). In practice these bodies are largely ineffective and have been primarily concerned with procedure for railway closures.

As already mentioned, the regional Traffic Commissioners are responsible for regulating bus and coach traffic, and any interested party may object to a licence application. The Commissioners are also responsible for ensuring that conditions of a licence already awarded are adhered to, including timetable and display of destinations. Such matters are often the cause of passengers' complaints, and a complaint on these scores directed to the Commissioners can often be effective in stirring an operator into action.

In London the London Passenger Transport Committee (LPTC), is equivalent to a TUCC but more active. A wide membership is drawn from nominations by many organizations, individual complaints are examined and an annual report published.

In many cases a local authority may act as a users' group, for example in dealing with major bus and rail operators in its area. It may also be an important customer in its own right, by allocating subsidies, and contracts for school bus services.

Less formal users' groups also exist. Some are shortlived, and devoted to specific action such as retention of a branch line. Others, notably associations of season ticket holders in the south-east of England, are better organized, although ironically, they are among the more privileged passengers. The most poorly served users, those in rural areas, find it difficult to organize, in part because transport facilities are so poor already. More enlightened operators have sought to consult the public on matters such as extensive service revisions, sometimes by calling public meetings.

External effects of transport modes have received increasing attention, together with concern about the need to encourage ecologically efficient modes. 'Environmentalist' action may often comprise local pressure groups defending more affluent areas against incursions of heavy traffic or road schemes. However, the nationally organized pressure groups do represent a broader interest, which is generally favourable to public transport. They include groups concerned with environment and ecology as a whole, such as Friends of the Earth (FoE), and the Conservation Society. Other groups such as the Council for the Protection of Rural England (CPRE) and the Ramblers Association, are concerned both with these issues and with maintaining the social structure of, and access to, rural areas. A confederation of such groups, together with the three major rail unions have formed a national pressure group under the title 'Transport 2000'.

Role of the Department of the Environment (DoE)

This Department was established in 1970, incorporating the existing Ministries of Transport, Public Building and Works, and Housing and Local Government. The principal government Minister responsible for the Department is the Secretary of State for the Environment. The Minister for Transport (from 1970 to 1973 known as the Minister for Transport Industries) occupies a subsidiary position and does not hold Cabinet rank. Major decisions such as appeal cases on road service licensing, or planning inquiries into road schemes, are determined by, or in the name of, the Secretary of State.

The internal structure of the Department is headed by a Permanent Secretary. Certain 'staff' functions are placed with directors responsible directly to the Permanent Secretary. The Director General (Economic and Resources) controls sections with responsibility for local government finance, and economics of transport. Major divisions of the DoE are controlled each by a 'Second Permanent Secretary'. One such is responsible for much of the former Ministry of Housing and Local Government, but some strategic transport planning also falls within this division, including urban and passenger transport, local transport and roads. This division also maintains co-ordination with regional offices of the DoE (see below), and has responsibility for major planning issues relevant to transport such as new towns, and the London and South East Region. Another 'Second Permanent Secretary' is responsible for much of the activities of the former Ministry of Transport, including ports, railways, freight, the highway programme, and research activities such as the Transport and Road Research Laboratory (TRRL).

Bodies related to the DoE include the regional economic planning boards, the Countryside Commission and the Development Commission. Within Scotland, Wales and Northern Ireland functions of the DoE are handled via the Scottish Development Department, or appropriate 'Office'. Within England there are eight regional offices. These have superseded the Divisional Road Engineers (DREs), and now take an active role in assessing public transport proposals and general transport strategies of local authorities. In connection with TPPs (above), it is intended to devolve some of the appraisal of schemes to the regional offices.

Two other government departments also have substantial influence on transport policy. The Department of Trade is concerned with aviation policy. The Department of Industry provides extensive support for motor vehicle manufacture by Leyland and Chrysler. The Treasury is responsible for overall allocation of government revenues and expenditures between departments, and may thus establish limits which appear to contradict other stated government policies (for example, the current pressure to reduce bus operating subsidies). Changes in duties and taxes, notably on petrol, may also be made for fiscal reasons rather than transport considerations.

The Government, through the DoE, is responsible for all expenditure – construction, improvement and maintenance – on motorways and trunk roads, although in many cases county councils may act as agents in carrying out the work. A total of about £300 million was thus allocated in 1971. The greater part of the road network is the responsibility of local authorities, but financed largely via central government. From the financial year 1975–6 previous separate grants have been replaced by 'threshold' payments via the rate support grant (RSG) and Transport Supplementary Grant (TSG). All public transport expenditure, save for new bus grants, bus fuel-tax rebate, and national railway subsidies, is now derived from these sources, and local authorities have the opportunity to split their total grants between capital and operating or maintenance expenditure, in public and private modes. Major public transport and road investment schemes can thus be examined on a comparable basis.

Each county or metropolitan county in England and Wales submits to the DoE an annual Transport Policies and Programme (TPP). This specifies the transport planning objectives of the county, its current proposals for expenditure, progress to date in reaching these objectives and priorities within the desired programme. As yet the system is rudimentary. Many authorities have faced for the first time the need to state explicit objectives and compare public and private transport schemes on a like basis. Since most counties in their present form were created only one year before the new system came into effect, little time was available for making the first TPP submission. In the short run, much expenditure is committed to road maintenance (especially in rural counties) and road construction schemes for which contracts have been signed. In the metropolitan counties, a higher share is devoted to public transport – about 30 per cent in contrast to less than 10 per cent in 'shire' counties – including major schemes such as the Tyneside rapid transit system initially approved under the previous grants structure.

The procedure is that, following receipt of each TPP, the DoE assesses its contents. A total level of expenditure is approved (an action which in some ways limits the freedom of local authorities in contrast to previous systems). A 'threshold' figure is determined for each county, at present related largely to grants previously received in respect of roads, and is paid to the county via the rate support grant (RSG). The remaining government money available is then paid to each authority as a fixed proportion of the difference between the threshold figure and approved expenditure; this is known as the Transport Supplementary Grant (TSG). Eventually, this separate grant may be absorbed in the rate support grant. In 1975–6 counties in England asked for an approved expenditure of £593 million at 1974 prices. The total approved by the DoE was £388 million (in real terms, a drop of 11 per cent on the previous year's total). The threshold total amounted to £289 million. Of the remaining £99 million approved expenditure, £70 million was paid via TSG, the remainder to be found directly by the counties.

The benefits to public transport from the new system have been small outside the metropolitan counties, in part due to much of the available expenditure being fully committed, in part to an uncertain attitude towards public transport by the 'shire' counties.

The role of the DoE *vis-à-vis* the railways has been strengthened by the Railways Act 1974. The Minister of Transport is empowered to require the Railways Board to continue specified services, and shortly after the passage of the Act a number of borderline cases already proposed for closure were saved in this manner. The separate grants for each service provided under the 1968 Transport Act have been abolished and replaced by an overall grant. This could resolve some of the problems of marginal costing (see Chapter 6), but also creates a largely open-ended subsidy, careful control of which will be necessary to ensure that public benefits equal the growing cost.

References and further reading

Bonavia, M. R. (1971) *The Organization of British Railways,* Ian Allan.
Hibbs, J. (1975) *The Bus and Coach Industry: its economics and organization,* Dent.
Smith, L. H. (1975) 'Public transport and local government reorganization', *Chartered Institute of Transport Journal,* **36**, no. 8, 185–90.
Thomson, A. J. and Hunter, L. C. (1973) *The Nationalized Transport Industries,* Heinemann.
Turns, K. L. (1974) *The Independent Bus,* David & Charles.

The annual reports of the following bodies indicate current trends in major sectors of the transport industry:

National Bus Company, London
Scottish Transport Group, Edinburgh

British Railways Board, London
Traffic Commissioners (summary of reports from each area Commissioner), Department of the Environment, London

Government publications of relevance include the Acts of Parliament and subsequent orders mentioned in this chapter, and circulars issued by departments giving guidance on implementation of new policy. Of particular importance are those relating to the TPP system, including DoE circulars 104/73, 27/74 and 43/75, the last-named indicating the information on public transport to be presented in future TPPs.

Directories of relevance include the *Little Red Book*, published approximately annually by Ian Allan, which includes details of all major and most independent bus operators in Britain, other organizations related to the bus and coach industry, major operators in West European countries, etc.

Note

From 1 January 1976 Lancashire United Transport became a wholly-owned subsidiary company of Greater Manchester PTE. However, it continues to operate under its existing title as a self-contained fleet.

2 The role of public transport

Mileage and trip frequencies

The latest available estimate of passenger-miles and trips completed by all modes of motorized transport within Britain for 1973 is as in Table 2.1:

Table 2.1 *Motorized transport : passenger mileage and trips*

Mode	Mileage (thousand million)	Trips (million)	Percentage of total mileage	Miles per person (approx.)
Private road vehicle	223·5	NA	79·6	4000
Bus and coach	33·8	8455	12·0	610
Rail	21·9	1388	7·8	400
Air and sea	1·5	6·5*	0·5	30

* Domestic air services only

Such estimates may be misleading in two respects. First, much of the data is obtained from transport operators who are themselves uncertain of their passenger trip totals, let alone passenger-miles. Car passenger mileage is obtained by even less direct means. Secondly, by their presentation as components of a total, each share appears as an allocation from the total. In practice, few public transport trips are the result of voluntary choice between modes by those with cars available: most are made by so-called 'captive' users. Many trips by car have been generated as a result of ownership. As an example one may consider trends from 1973 to 1974. Passenger-miles by car fell to 79·1 per cent of the total, and those by bus rose to 12·2 per cent despite car ownership continuing to rise slowly. Much of the car mileage curtailment was a result of optional off-peak trips being cancelled in order to economize on fuel. The smaller population that remained captive to public transport, however, saw extension of its mobility in some areas stemming from free travel for pensioners, and retention of unchanged fare scales during a period of rapid inflation (effectively, a decrease in fares). The modal split is largely a result of decisions by separate groups of people, rather than transfer of the same trips from one mode to another (although there are some examples, such as 'park and ride' traffic).

Since we are concerned with public transport (which is taken to mean modes available for public use rather than any distinction based on ownership) it will be appropriate to use measures specific to those modes.

Passenger trips per head per annum

This *absolute* measure can be estimated each year by dividing adjusted ticket sales by population served. Land-use transportation studies and similar surveys give indications of demand only at long and irregular intervals. If data from ticket sales can be split by time of day, then an indication of peak and off-peak trends can be obtained, of significance both to operating economics and possible transfer from private car (the latter opportunity being confined largely to the work trip).

Bias due to form of ticket issue is considered in an appendix (p. 53), together with means of estimating passenger-miles. Any annual trend estimate for passenger trips per head is subject to the accuracy of population estimates. Censuses may be used to interpolate a trend. Due to high rates of migration between local authority areas updating local birth and death records would not be meaningful in most cases. The annually updated register of electors now contains almost all persons aged over eighteen, and if trips by schoolchildren can be estimated separately, a trend can be estimated for trips by adults. Bias due to non-educational trips by those under eighteen would be small. Annual passenger totals are of course relevant to the operator in planning service levels, but to understand passenger behaviour knowledge of the trip *rate* is required.

Modal split

Land-use transport studies and estimates of mileage by all modes in a defined area are none the less useful to operators in indicating their share of markets for different types of trip (i.e. a *relative* measure). By collection of data from households, such studies can also establish relationships between household character-istics such as size, number of employed members, income, car ownership and trip rates by different modes. These may be useful in long-term planning, although their uncritical use in many cases may have done more harm than good (see appendix). Unfortunately, most land-use transport studies have been 'one off' jobs or, at best, repeated after about ten years. Time-lags in release of survey data may also be critical, especially if this remains unpublished until a final report is issued. Similarly, workplace/mode of travel data from the cenuses of 1966 and 1971 were not available until over three years after collection.

Both modal split and 'trips per head' measures will now be used to illustrate the existing role of public transport.

National relationships between public transport use and other factors

Analysis of the 1965 and 1966 National Travel Surveys by Goodwin indicated several important relationships, confirmation of which is given by the 1973 Survey. Taking household income per head as the base for comparison, it can be seen from Figure 2.1 that mileage by all modes increases steadily with income. Travel time does so at a lower rate, and appears to approach a limit of about nine hours per person per week in the middle and upper income ranges. Expenditure in money terms increases more rapidly than mileage. As a crude simplification we can say that middle and upper income groups obtain a higher mileage by using faster and more expensive modes. The private car replaces walking, cycling and bus travel over short distances. Rail and air rather than coach are used for public trans-port intercity journeys.

The relationship between rail travel and income is surprising, rising as income increases to an even greater extent than in the case of private car. The national picture could be biased, however, by very high mileages on rail by high income commuters in the South East Region, and intercity rail travel by high income groups through-out the country. Rural services probably display much lower trip rates within high income groups.

On weekdays (Mondays to Fridays), to which many urban surveys are confined, many trips are made within a confined time budget. Time spent in sleeping, eating, working, etc., occupies much of the day. Since travel itself is rarely a leisure activity, it is unlikely

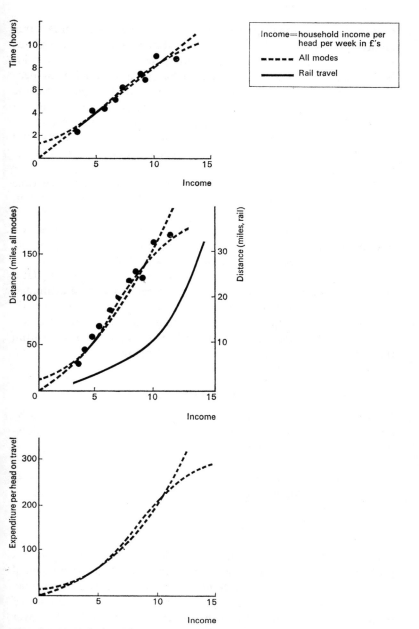

Figure 2.1 Relationships between travel time, cost and distance, and household income (1966)

B

that more than a small period would be allocated to travel if a free choice were available. From Goodwin's data we can infer that about fifty minutes per person is typical. Since his figures are household-based, and the average thus affected by the low mobility of pensioners, young children, days not working by adults, etc., a realistic figure per working day for adults would be sixty to ninety minutes in travel. The low travel time per head by lower income groups in Goodwin's data is accounted for partly by households containing many economically non-active people such as children and old-age pensioners.

For the majority of trips made on weekdays, it is likely that time is the most important single factor for all modes, often predominant. This is not true for some weekend trips which are less constrained (especially of interurban travel), or trips made by groups who are not economically active and have low mobility at present (notably pensioners), but even in these cases time is probably important.

Work by Zahavi, published in 1973, on car use has shown that a similar figure for hours in motion per car per day can be estimated from studies in North American and European cities of greatly differing characteristics. To a large extent car use in this case is a proxy for individual travel. Relationships of a similar form within the public transport market are discussed below.

Public transport in urban areas

It is well known that there has been an overall decline in trips by public transport. Municipal operators in Britain carried the following numbers of passengers:

1937–8	4700 million
1950–1	7000 million
1959–60	5700 million
1968–9	4200 million

Data on trip lengths is not available, but average length has probably increased. Some successive annual returns for municipal operators have shown a decline in trips, but an increase in revenue, despite fare scales being unchanged. London Transport's estimate of passenger-miles by bus has shown a much lower rate of decline over the last ten years than that of passenger trips. Work by Tyson (1973) on Manchester has shown that during the 1960s increases in average trip length largely offset the decline in number of trips in estimating annual passenger mileage. Very short trips have been discouraged by lower service levels, irregular running and relatively high fares. In many towns, new housing areas on the fringe produce a substantial demand for longer-than-average trips, even if frequency of trip-making declines. The major decline is known to be in evening and weekend travel.

Factors affecting demand

Work by several writers has established three major relationships, affecting *number* of trips made:

1 *Change in the real level of fares:* An elasticity of about -0.3 has been suggested by Mullen (1974), and by McIntosh (1974). Fare elasticities are discussed in more detail in Chapter 6.

2 *Change in vehicle mileage:* Unless significant change also occurs in network structure, this is a fair proxy for change in service frequency. The elasticity is about $+0.7$, i.e. substantially greater than that of the level of fares.

3 *Increase in car ownership:* Estimates by McIntosh suggest a reduction in trips of about 1·6 per cent per annum due to this and other causes external to bus service quality. A similar calculation by Wabe and Coles (1975) places the reductions in several large cities at several hundred trips per annum per car purchased.

Time-series regression equations using two or all three of these variables have indicated relationships significant at the 95 per cent confidence level, with multiple correlation coefficients of about 0·95. Cross-sectional modelling tends to confirm the importance of service frequency (in that it affects waiting time and hence total travel time) and car ownership.

It is noteworthy that similar high correlations can be obtained for foreign cities with pro-public transport policies (such as Göteborg, Sweden) in which public transport has retained a strong role despite high car ownership. We can identify not only a correlation between factors such as trips, car ownership and service levels, but of different degrees of response (i.e. in similar equations, different coefficients) to changes in these factors, according to managerial and planning policies.

Trends and levels of use

Attitudes towards public transport in urban areas have changed markedly over the past few years. From its role as a residual mode for those unable to use cars, it has come to be accepted as essential if present patterns of city life, especially journeys to work in city centres, are to be maintained. The work of Buchanan and Smeed in the early 1960s established that space available in existing centres simply did not permit the full use of private cars which might be owned in future by those now working there.

Congestion is most acute in the largest cities, where public transport networks remain intensive. The essential role of public transport for the work journey is accepted even in the USA, but, stemming from this approach, there has been a tendency to understate implicitly its role both for non-work journeys and in smaller urban areas. Since most trips which contribute to net revenue are in the off-peak period, this approach could be detrimental to the viability of public transport (and hence its ability to meet without high subsidy the peak demands implicit in many urban plans). It would also be unfortunate if the role of public transport in smaller towns and cities were to be ignored simply because it carries a smaller share of work trips than it does in larger centres, and because in other countries (particularly the USA) it is known to have a smaller share of total traffic than it does in the conurbations.

It would be reasonable to deduce from the dependence of large city centres on public transport, and the limited parking space available, that total public transport trips should decline more slowly in larger cities. However, this did not occur during the 1950s, as Sleeman has shown. Trends in the 1960s are shown in Table 2.2.

Table 2.2 *Public transport trips per head 1960–1 and 1970–1*

Size group (by 1961 population)	Number of areas/operators	Passenger trips per head*		
		1960–1	1970–1	% decline
Over 500000	2†	446	306	31
300000 to 499000	5	341	233	32
150000 to 299000	12	317	216	32
100000 to 149000	9	270	228	16
Under 100000	32	322	225	30

* Bus only. Local rail trips are insignificant in all cities in the above sample, except Glasgow.
† Glasgow and Leeds.

There is very little evidence of variation by size of urban area, save for the distinctly lower rate of decline for operators in the 100 000 to 149 000 group. Operators in the Isle of Man, Northern Ireland, those taken over by PTEs, and those whose catchment areas did not match local authority boundaries were excluded. All data refer to municipal operators.

Trends from 1972 to 1975 indicated some reduction in the overall rate of decline, to less than 2 per cent per annum among municipal and PTE operators. This was offset by an increase in bus travel in London, such that total stage carriage passenger carryings remained virtually constant. This was not related to any general improvement in service quality, but rather to decisions to hold down fare levels, in effect causing the real price level to fall in a period of rapid inflation. Those operators with the smallest passenger loss, or with gains in traffic, were those that permitted deficits to rise to high levels before imposing fare increases, notably London Transport.

Apart from Tyne and Wear, PTEs have lost passengers more rapidly than remaining municipal operators. A sample of municipal operators serving towns of below 100 000 population displays a decline of 16 per cent in passenger trips between 1967 and 1974, but Greater Manchester, Merseyside, and Tyne and Wear PTEs show an aggregate decline of 23 per cent over the same period. Reasons for this disparity are examined below.

Another feature of the general downward trend in bus traffic is that a few operators, notably those with better marketing policies and planning measures which favour public transport, have succeeded in holding patronage virtually constant since around 1970. They include Reading, Leeds, Southampton and Leicester.

Very little is known of trends for rail usage within British cities other than the fact that the London underground system has maintained a steady demand of about 650 million trips per year over the last twenty years. Railways in Merseyside and Glasgow account for about one-fifth of peak period work trips to the city centre, and between 5 and 10 per cent of all public transport trips. Even a substantial rise in their loadings, however, would do little to offset the decline in bus trips within those cities in recent years (although, since rail trips are substantially longer than bus trips on average, the effect on passenger-miles may be greater).

The lowest trip rates among municipal operators are generally found in small isolated centres such as Lincoln, at about 130 per head. The highest trip rates are to be found in Newcastle, Edinburgh, Leeds and Glasgow at around 330 trips per head per annum, including an estimate for local rail travel. If BR trips are included, then public transport trips per head in London were about 350 in 1971. This rate is slightly higher, but probably due to numerous 'linked' trips made by bus and rail, on which a passenger has to purchase separate tickets. In a provincial city most passengers use a single bus to reach the centre. Within the limits of accuracy of the data it is reasonable to suggest that the trip rate for London is no higher than for Edinburgh, Leeds or Glasgow. However, London *is* exceptional in that the average public transport trip is longer than the average car trip (this is due to the rail feeder and intrasuburb role of the car); the reverse applies in other cities. In terms of passenger-miles, public transport accounts for a higher share of trips in London than in any other British city.

The trip rate for entire PTE areas (as distinct from major cities served by their own fleets) is difficult to determine, due to the large role of NBC. The present annual rate in Tyne and Wear is probably about 250, that in Merseyside, Greater Manchester and West Midlands between 200 and 250 per annum (these estimates allow for trips on NBC services within the PTE areas). It should be noted that areas of low density suburban and rural population are included, whereas in the South East Region such areas fall outside the GLC/London Transport area into the home counties, where the trip rate by bus is less than 100 per head per annum.

These absolute levels of public transport use found in Britain are the highest in Western Europe and North America. Eastern Europe (an extreme case, with very low car ownership and intensive public transport) displays rates of up to 900 trips per head in cities such as Warsaw and Bucharest. A level of seventy is typical for bus travel in major US and French cities, and even those cities which are well known for public transport, such as Toronto, display trip rates below those in Britain.

Differences by size of urban area

The absolute trip rate is higher in larger towns and cities within Britain, although the variation – from an average of about 200 in towns of about 100000 population to 300 in the largest – is not as great as one might expect. When one recalls that a higher proportion of total trips in smaller towns is made by cycle and on foot, it is reasonable to suggest that the public transport share of *motorized* trips may be just as high in smaller towns and cities. The availability of studies of land-use in relation to transport and similar surveys from the 1960s permits examination of this hypotheses.

Table 2.3 indicates the share of motorized trips held by public transport, according to trip purpose. Areas are ranked in approximate size order, with the 1971 Department of the Environment's rural Devon study for comparison.

Table 2.3 *Public transport's share of motorized trips, by purpose* (percentages)

Area	*Trip purposes*					
	All	*Work*	*Shop*	*Business*	*Social rec'n*	*Education*
Devon	23	16	15	6	9	79
Worcester	32	31	46*	—	25	—
Cambridge	23	16	36	—	—	—
Exeter	47	—	67	—	—	—
Norwich	29	35	65	—	36	65
Northampton	57	48	82	52	61	80
Plymouth	53	58	75	37†	—	82
Coventry	39	44	70	19	33	77
Brighton	49	51	70	25	56	79
Merseyside	54	59	62	47	46	76
Glasgow	72	73	87	57	67	91
London	60	65	62	25	42	74

* Including education.
† Including social and recreational.

Most surveys were carried out in the period 1964–7 (Northampton 1962), and are broadly comparable. The proportion of all motorized trips accounted for by public transport was standardized to 1966, permitting comparison with census results, by assuming a 5 per cent decline in public transport trips per annum, and constant number of car trips. Thus for a town with a 50:50 public:private modal split in 1964 a figure of 45 per cent by public transport is shown.

Figure 2.2 shows the proportion of urban motorized trips made by public transport (largely bus, except in conurbations). A broad trend, of a greater public transport share as size of urban area increases, is apparent. But such an interpretation would be superficial. The observations can be split into three bands: the lowest comprises small towns in rural areas with company rather than municipal services, the middle band includes the majority of municipal services and PTEs, the highest includes two cities (Dublin and

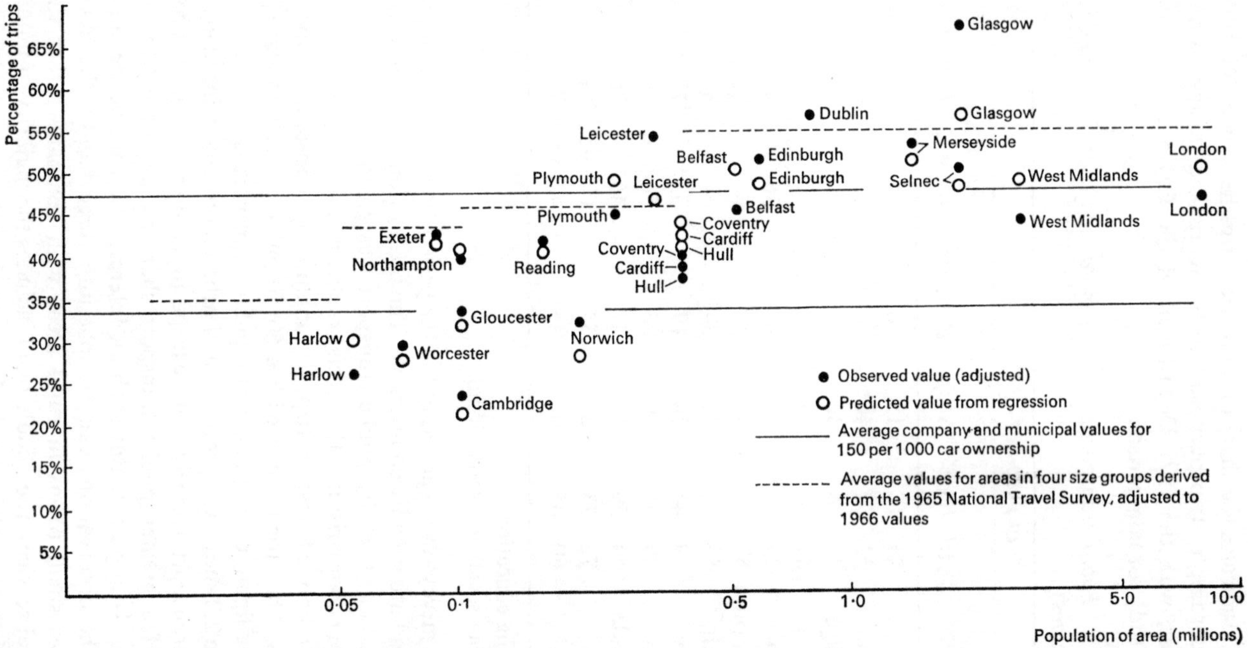
Percentage of trips
65%
60%
55%
50%
45%
40%
35%
30%
25%
20%
15%
10%
5%
Glasgow
Dublin
Glasgow
Leicester
Merseyside
Belfast
Edinburgh
London
Plymouth
Leicester
Edinburgh
Selnec
West Midlands
Belfast
Plymouth
West Midlands
London
Coventry
Cardiff
Hull
Exeter
Coventry
Northampton
Reading
Cardiff
Hull
Gloucester
Norwich
Harlow
Worcester
Harlow
Cambridge
Observed value (adjusted)
Predicted value from regression
Average company and municipal values for 150 per 1000 car ownership
Average values for areas in four size groups derived from the 1965 National Travel Survey, adjusted to 1966 values
0·05
0·1
0·5
1·0
5·0
10·0
Population of area (millions)

Figure 2.2 British Isles urban areas: share of motorized trips held by public transport

Glasgow) of exceptionally high public transport use. Within the centre band, there is little evidence of a trend by size of urban areas.

The apparent low share of public transport in smaller towns is biased, in that the sample of towns subjected to detailed studies of land-use and transportation tends to feature above-average car ownership. This is not surprising, as large cities carried out extensive studies to allocate the high investment involved in new road systems. In the lower range, only towns with high car ownership would feel the need for major road planning at that time.

Company bus services in towns have often been used to cross-subsidize rural bus services. They have therefore developed lower quality and higher fares than municipal transport which is normally operated on a breakeven basis within each town. The comparative remoteness of company management from the needs of a small town within a large operating area may also have an effect. As smaller towns are less likely to control their own municipal undertakings, the modal share of public transport may be smaller, but this is not due to size *per se*. The sample of towns subjected to detailed studies unfortunately does not yet include in published form small industrial towns with municipal services and those provincial cities (Bristol, Stoke, Swansea) with company services. Passenger trips per head in Bristol in 1971 were about 145, a figure which compares unfavourably with municipal data, and probably implies a low share of total trips by public transport. Its car ownership level in 1966 was quite high, but lower than that in Coventry or Leicester, comparable cities with municipal services and over 200 trips per head per annum by bus.

A regression analysis calculation gives:

$$P = 50 \cdot 6 + 14 \cdot 4D - 0 \cdot 12T \qquad (R^2 = 0 \cdot 80)$$
$$(9 \cdot 6) \qquad (5 \cdot 32) \qquad (4 \cdot 1) \qquad (T\text{-ratio values})$$

in which

P = percentage of motorized trips by public transport
D = dummy variable, taking value 0 if company service, 1 if municipal
T = cars owned per 1000 population (1966)

All terms are significant at the 95 per cent level. A population variable was tested in the model but was not significant.

It can be seen from Figure 2.2 that the estimates from this equation were in most cases very close to values actually observed, the only major exceptions being Leicester (observed 54 per cent, estimated

45 per cent) and Glasgow (observed 67 per cent, estimated 56 per cent respectively). Low fares and high service quality probably account for the first difference, and high population density for the second.

Many transport models are tested only with reference to the data from which they were calibrated. A more stringent test is to take further examples from the same population, and compare actual with estimated values. Subsequent to calibration of the model data from three further studies became available:

	Observed	*Estimated*
	%	%
Greater Manchester	48·0	45·5
Edinburgh	51·0	48·5
Torbay (company)	27·5	25·5

All the above estimates and observations are standardized to 1966. Using the same independent variables, an equation for trips per head per annum (H) was formulated:

$$H = 402 + 0.000024C - 1.5T$$
$$\quad (5.3) \quad (3.4) \qquad\qquad (2.6) \qquad (T\text{-}ratio\ values)$$

C denotes population

This was based on a sample of eighteen municipal operators, data for trips per head by company services in specific towns being very difficult to obtain. As expected, population in this case was significant. After calibration another operator reported 160 trips per annum; the value estimated by the model was 162.

I would stress that the above models are not forecasting devices. They do not take account of variables changing over time, such as the real level of fares or car running costs, service frequency, etc. What they do provide is an interpretation of relationships in the mid-1960s from which present trends have developed. Overall modal split was not determined by population. The absolute level of public transport use (trips per head) in smaller towns was certainly lower, but this was because the overall need for motorized transport was less. Many trips were, and still are, within walking or cycling distance even in towns of over 100000 people.

Differences related to time of day

Another means by which urban public transport demand can be analysed is by time of day. Evening and weekend trips, mostly for social and recreational purposes, have fallen steadily. A survey carried out by Manchester City Transport (and now the PTE) at regular intervals since 1959 has shown that the percentage of evening travellers within the weekday bus trip total has fallen. However, the

Table 2.4 *Total daily bus trips in Manchester, by time period*

Hours commencing	Oct 1959 %	Oct 1969 %
0500 to 0700 (inclusive)	12·9	11·0
0800	15·2	13·2
0900 to 1600 (inclusive)	32·5	40·5
1700	14·0	13·8
1800 to 2300 (inclusive)	25·5	19·5
Total passengers	1 157 000	746 500

share of trips during 'shopping' hours (i.e. between the two journey-to-work peaks) rose substantially.

A survey on city services in Oxford in 1971 indicated that, compared with 1970, traffic in the morning peak was down by 3 per cent,

Table 2.5 *Purposes of public transport trips* (percentages)

Area	Work	Shop	Social	Business	Other	Education
Devon	15	9	9	3	—	64
Exeter	28	35	21	14	2	*
Worcester	37	46†	8	—	8	—
Cambridge	24	24	17	16	—	19
Norwich	40	23	6	20	—	10
Northampton	34	38	26‡	—	—	2
Brighton	38	18	14	8	8	14
Coventry	42	16	10	8	—	17
Plymouth	40	20	27‡	—	—	13
Leicester	38	25§	—	—	37	—
Belfast	45	10	20	6	12	7
London:						
underground	72	3	8	6	7	4
bus	53	14	13	8	5	9

* Very small proportion. Data refer to central area only.
† Including education.
‡ Including business.
§ Including personal business.

in the evening peak by 1 per cent, but the 'between peaks' period showed an increase. This may have been due in part to shorter working hours, but also an increase in shopping trips.

Some studies also provide sufficient data to estimate the composition of public transport demand during the mid-1960s.

The importance of shopping trips is again noteworthy, especially in the smaller urban areas for which it can be as important a category as work trips. In towns of about 100000 shopping is often concentrated into a single centre, whereas walking and cyling trips may serve dispersed workplaces. In Figure 2.3 the ratio of work to shop trips within the public transport total is shown against population. A similar trend can be discerned for the ratio between 'work + education' and 'shopping + business' trips – a value of about 1·0 for smaller towns, rising to 4·0 for conurbations, and 7·5 for rail trips in London.

The vehicle utilization ratio (vehicles in service at morning peak: late morning off-peak) is similar, although less marked, as peak traffic is accommodated at higher load factors. This peaking has an effect on operating costs, as outlined in Chapter 6. Staff for 'split shift' duties receive extra payment, or spend only a small part of their guaranteed shift in driving. Vehicle utilization is poor, and much bus mileage operated under congested traffic conditions. A study by Tyson of an operator near Manchester suggested that neither weekday peak traffic nor Sunday traffic was profitable, but a surplus was shown for weekday off-peak and Saturday operation, in which shopping trips predominate. A study by Lee and Stedman (1970) established that economies of scale in British municipal undertakings are not significant.

Peaking ratios and size of urban area

The relationship between size and profitability may thus be examined, on the hypothesis that smaller operators, with less of a peak effect, are more profitable. It is difficult to discern significant relationships, as variations in fare policy, delay in obtaining increases to match rising costs, etc., can affect net revenues irrespective of size of operator or urban area. Nevertheless it is notable that in the past five years the smaller municipal operators have lost a smaller proportion of their traffic than larger operators, and have done so with relatively small subsidies (very rarely more than £1 per head of population per annum) whereas those large operators which have succeeded in stabilizing public transport use have done so either with substantial

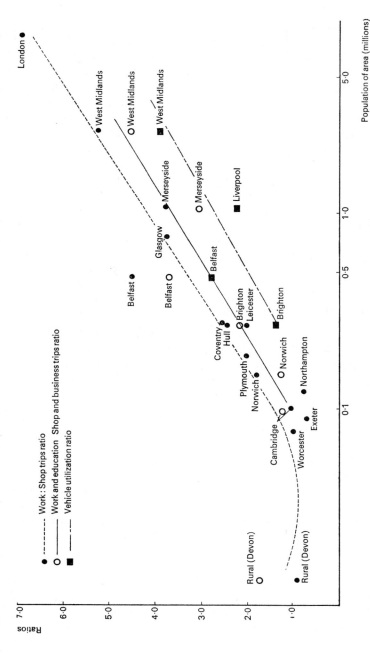

Figure 2.3 UK urban areas: 'peaking' ratios in public transport demand

subsidies to keep down faies (as in London and the West Midlands) and/or increased use of reliable but heavily subsidized urban rail services. Total subsidies in London in early 1975 amounted to over £10 per head.

From Figure 2.3 evidence can be adduced supporting the fixed time-budget concept. The ratio of work to shop trips increases so rapidly with urban size that not only does the absolute number of work trips increase, but the absolute number of shop trips falls. This does not necessarily imply that inhabitants of large urban areas do less shopping, but rather that shopping trips are made as part of journeys to work (e.g. people working in a town centre shop at midday near their places of work). Within a fixed time-budget, as work trips become longer, less time is available for shopping and recreational trips on weekdays. An increase in the peak load on public transport may thus, if implying that work trips take longer than they would otherwise, create diseconomies due to extra peak vehicles *and* and absolute reduction in off-peak demand.

The role of public transport in rural and intercity markets

This subject is best discussed in relation to each sector (see Chapters 7 and 8). Modelling work on intercity demand has established the importance of travel time, frequency and various household characteristics. The overall share of intercity travel accounted for by public transport is about 30 per cent, in contrast to the 20 per cent share of the total market. Higher service quality is largely responsible, and substantial use is made of air and rail services by travellers with cars available.

In rural transport little work has been done on existing relationships affecting trip levels. Little data is available for a long time period, save for operators whose areas also include substantial towns. Very few public transport trips are made by those with a car available, and in many cases the existence of a public transport service determines whether or not a substantial part of the population travel with any regularity. About 15 per cent of rural trips are by public transport.

It is important not to write off all areas outside nucleated urban centres as 'rural'. There is a settlement pattern, half urban, half rural, rarely considered in transport policy, but which is of growing importance. This includes areas such as coal-mining regions in which large villages of several thousand people justify frequent bus services, which are well loaded throughout the day. Little analysis of the relative role of each mode has been completed. Within the bus industry trip rates of about 100 to 150 per head per annum (compared with 40 to 50 in agricultural areas) have been found. Further reference to this type of settlement is made in Chapter 7. Coupled with the importance of smaller towns within the urban sector outlined above, this intermediate population category has major implications for public transport policy, outlined in Chapter 10.

External factors affecting public transport use

The importance of rising car ownership is clear. Until recently, however, two assumptions were made that were only partially true:

1 That household car ownership was the major variable, and that most trips in car-owning households could be made by car. Subsequent work by Hillman (1973) and others has indicated that not all members of car-owning households have use of a car. Some of these, such as elderly people or very young children, make few trips in any case, but others, such as housewives and teenage children may not be able to use a car (not qualified to drive, for example) and thus require alternative transport. The family will probably travel together at weekends, but greatly differing demands for each member can be identified during the working week. The importance of this is already evident from the fairly stable demand for shopping trips by bus in urban areas. Housewives rarely have use of the family car during weekday shopping hours. Many surveys have included questions such as 'Is there a car in your household?'. While of some relevance, a positive answer does not indicate that it was available for all trips. A more relevant question is, 'Can you drive a car and was one available for you to use on this trip?' In this chapter, car ownership rates per 1000 people have been used as a variable rather than household ownership rates.

2 That the proportion of households containing a car was rising rapidly. Between 1969 and 1973 the proportion of households with one or more cars rose by only 2 per cent, from 51 to 53 per cent. Effects of fuel prices could retard this trend even further. The *number* of households with a car has risen, from 9·3 million in 1969 to 9·9 million in 1973, in part due to population increase, in part to a reduction in household size. The latter may

reflect a marginally greater increase in car availability to individuals, since as members of a larger household (albeit car-owning),
they may not have had use of a car.

Public transport demand has also been affected by decline in
demand for certain types of trip. At the height of demand around
1950 many people worked a $5\frac{1}{2}$-day week, that is, making an extra
return trip on Saturday morning. Survival of this pattern can be
seen in some rail services to the City of London. The average length
of the work trip has increased due to lower housing densities,
increased size of some businesses, and deliberate decisions by heads
of commuting households to locate in areas of more pleasant environment and/or lower cost by living farther from their place of
work. Such is the rationale of residential location models of the
form

$$C = CT + CH$$

in which C represents a constant term for a given income level, CT
the fares paid plus value of travel time, and CH the cost of rates,
mortgage repayments or rent. Underpricing of rail season tickets
and lower rate payments in suburban and rural districts has tended
to encourage this pattern well beyond that which a realistic charging
policy would have done. However, despite the obvious importance
of this phenomenon in regions such as the south-east, there is
reason to believe that other factors may also be important:

1 Demands made by other members of the household. Wives and
   older children may be in employment, or making costly trips to
   higher education. The household location may be a compromise
   rather than a trade-off related solely to a place of employment in
   the central area. An opportunity is thus created for public transport in that few households possess more than one car, and if
   trips above walking or cycling distance are being made in different
   directions at the same time, some of these will be captive to
   public transport.
2 The growth of 'intertia' commuting, in which the location of
   work changes but not that of the household. Owner-occupation
   creates inertia, as financial and perceived costs of relocation
   become very high. Even such moves as are made are often to a
   higher quality house within the same area, in order not to disrupt
   friendships, children's education, etc. This pattern also creates a
   demand for long-distance trips, including some intercity com-

muting (Birmingham to London, for example). However, the demand for intersuburban trips is met poorly by public transport (see Chapter 5).

Decline in cinema attendance, now at about one-tenth of its peak, has had a marked effect on evening demand. Similar factors, conveniently summarized in a London Transport Planning Note (1972), include decline in attendances for greyhound racing, football and other mass audience sports. Activities which have replaced them, such as sailing and golf, are individual pastimes, highly dispersed and often wholly dependent on use of the private car.

Shopping trips are tending to fall as the traditional pattern of convenience shopping (for food, etc.) almost every weekday is replaced by occasional visits to supermarkets. This pattern applies particularly to households in which both husband and wife work, with little spare time for shopping, often using a car to carry loads of frozen foods and packaged goods. As yet its effect on public transport does not seem too serious. Many of the 'convenience' trips are, or were, made largely on foot, and an increasing proportion of the national population consist of groups such as old-age pensioners who may find a regular shopping trip a social activity as much as a necessity.

Visits to friends and relatives (VFR trips) have become more dispersed due to lower housing densities, and migration between local authority areas. A potential market for motorized travel has thus been set up, where walking trips were previously typical. This market has been more clearly defined in the intercity sector (see Chapter 8). Urban land-use transport studies do not distinguish clearly VFR demand from other recreation and leisure trips, which, as have been argued, have become less favourable to public transport.

Normative approach to public transport's role

Recent discussion on transport policy, notably that by Hillman (1973), and the Independent Commission on Transport (1974), has tended to concentrate on what the role of public transport *ought* to be, and many readers may have read such an implication into the title of this chapter. As far as possible I have tried to confine this discussion to an objective analysis, reserving policy matters for later chapters. None the less it is clear that in many areas public transport is catering for a specific sector of the population, which has little alternative choice of mode, and is thus dependent on continued public transport provision. The provision of a minimum level of service is already urgent in many rural areas.

Appendix: Demand forecasting

Public transport demand may be predicted in two ways. First, as a byproduct of forecasts for all modes of transport produced within an urban land-use/transportation study (LUTS). Such forecasts usually relate to a specific design date about fifteen years hence, and are based on population, car ownership and income forecasts for zones within the area concerned. Existing relationships between these variables and trip generation derived from recent survey data are applied to predict total trips, and their geographical distribution, which are then assigned to proposed networks. The public transport forecasts thus produced take account of the likely reduction in households without any car owner and public transport trips which are made by members of car-owning households. Diversion from cars to public transport can also be estimated, usually in respect of city centre journeys to work for which penalties placed on car use (congestion, parking charges, etc.) and the relatively high quality of reserved track public transport systems can result in substantial public transport use by those with cars available. The modal split models used in this process incorporate factors such as ratio or difference measures of private and public foot-to-door trip times, perceived costs, etc.

Such forecasts are subject to numerous criticisms, as expressed by Plowden (1972). Not only are population, car ownership and income forecasts themselves uncertain, but the assumption that the same *relationships* as now will apply is also doubtful (for example, that a household of given income and size will make a certain number of trips per day, irrespective of transport service quality, changes in life-style, etc.). Some of the trip-generation techniques do take account of service quality indirectly (for example, regression equations which include variables reflecting average accessibility of public transport services in an area). But the most popular method, category analysis, is applied in a fashion which is based almost exclusively on household characteristics.

Apart from contradicting commonsense knowledge that the quality of transport services, both public and private, will affect use made of them, LUTS forecasts are also limited in that they deal only with urban traffic, and average weekday patterns. Apart from a crude split between work and non-work trips there is little that might indicate off-peak usage or variations through the week. However, the LUTS method remains of value for major journey-to-work flows. Analysis of surveys from such studies has greatly extended our knowledge of public transport demand.

A second approach to forecasting is that of *mode specific estimates*. In the long run these also relate to variables such as population size, income and (usually indirectly) car ownership. But they place much greater emphasis on aspects of service quality such as frequency, speed and price, which can be influenced markedly by the operator in the short run. They have been developed most fully in the intercity rail and air sectors, in which quality factors such as speed and frequency exhibit much greater short-run variation than the external factors of population or income. A common feature of such models is the lack of importance of variables reflecting characteristics of competing modes. In forecasting air travel for example, inclusion of competing rail service characteristics adds very little to the explanatory power of the model. The impact of car ownership on rail travel is similarly marginal: in the intercity sector each mode tends to generate its own demand.

In the bus and coach industry, long-term forecasting work has received little attention to date. This is in part for good reasons: whereas large, fixed investments are made in road systems, new aircraft or intercity railways in anticipation of growing demand, investment in the bus industry is related to a static or declining demand, and almost entirely to the vehicles themselves. Should a particular service be poorly used, they can be diverted to other areas, or sold to other operators. The element of risk is thus lower. Certain types of demand, notably for express coach travel and rural bus services, are highly dispersed and can be predicted more accurately from good local knowledge: the averaging and aggregation of data implicit in most modelling processes is inappropriate. There is, however, a greater need for better forecasting for trunk inter-urban routes and services in urban areas; changes in service patterns involve considerable managerial effort, and may confuse existing passengers. Frequent experimentation 'on the ground' is an expensive and time-consuming means of reaching a correct solution. Flows are sufficiently large to permit use of aggregated modelling techniques, which can suggest, prior to implementation, which of several plans will produce the best outcome. Bus priority measures,

new control systems, and busways all involve heavier fixed investment than previously, and hence long-term forecasts of their use. At
regional or national level, predictions of demand for manpower and
new vehicles could enable long-term planning to be introduced, in
the hope of ensuring a more stable supply of these factors of production than is now the case.

Of specific forecasting methods, *extrapolation* forms the easiest
method, often used implicitly. Its limitations are obvious: assumptions that the same trends will continue in those external variables
affecting demand (population, income, etc.), and that the same relationships will apply between them and transport demand. A practical difficulty lies in selecting the past period from which a trend is to
be drawn for projection: some periods are obviously untypical. For
example, urban bus trips fell by about 3 per cent per annum from the
1950s to 1973, then held steady for two years. Extrapolation from the
last period would produce a virtually constant prediction, that of the
previous trend a continued decline.

Before dismissing extrapolation too readily one should remember
that it may be useful in the short run, particularly if broken down
into meaningful categories (different trends exist, for example, for
weekday/shopping trips and evening/weekend demand). Many
apparently sophisticated models are in reality based on little more
than glorified extrapolation. A regression equation calibrated from
annual data over the last fifteen years may produce a statistically
significant relationship between trips made and average income.
When one comes to use this in forecasting one finds that there is
very little income data available, and that most studies simply
extrapolate the 1960s trend (a real increase of about 3 per cent per
annum). The extrapolation has been removed from one level of
calculation to another, not eliminated.

The most useful forecasting models for urban bus demand appear
to be those based on time-series regression in which elasticities of
demand of major quality variables such as frequency and fares are
incorporated. Reference has been made in Chapter 2 to such elasticities derived by Black (1974). The forecasting equation of Hill
incorporates these together with a trend variable reflecting annual
decline due to rising car ownership, etc:

$$PC = -1{\cdot}6 - 0{\cdot}3 \text{ (percentage change in revenue per mile in real terms)}$$
$$+ 0{\cdot}7 \text{ (percentage change in vehicle mileage)}$$

In which *PC* denotes percentage change in total trips per annum. The variables incorporated are proxies for real fare levels and service quality. It can be seen that the general declining trend could be offset by reducing fares in real terms and/or increasing vehicle mileage. Analysis of urban bus demand from 1971 to 1974 shows that the relationship suggested by Hill remains valid, stabilization of traffic during that period being due to reductions in real fare levels sufficient to offset effects of the trend variable and cuts in off-peak mileage. In long-run calculations care should be taken if possible to measure the trip *rate*, rather than total trips per annum, since population changes may also affect demand significantly. In some cases, a separate model of similar structure may be calibrated from historic data for the specific operator(s) being examined.

A general limitation on any public transport forecasting models at present is the poor accuracy of initial data, especially on trips made. Operators frequently quote figures which, when analysed, contain a wide margin of error. For example, bus operators know how many tickets they have sold, but for an urban operator this is a poor indication of trips made. Ticket systems such as the 'Ultimate' in which a machine can issue only a limited range of denominations, frequently require several tickets to be issued to make up a single fare. Unless the operator adjusts his ticket sale total by an appropriate factor to allow for this, substantial overstatement of trips made may result. On the other hand, the increasing use of pensioners' free passes, or monthly tickets, may result in understatement of trips made. The use of separately printed tickets for most categories and routes on the railway system reduces this danger somewhat. However, the four-weekly computations of ticket sales (National Passenger Analysis and Accounting System; NPAAS) do suffer some bias; tickets sold through travel agents may not be included, handwritten tickets are not recorded in full (from smaller stations these can account for half of total revenue), use of seasons has to be estimated, and little detail is recorded of trip patterns on 'paytrain' services.

Before further modelling work is undertaken it would be desirable to improve the accuracy of these basic measures which do, after all, serve as the criteria for judging the 'success' of many policies.

References and further reading

Black, I. (1974) *See* McIntosh and Smith.

Goodwin, P. B. (1974) 'General cost time and the problem of equity in transport studies', *Transportation*, **3**, pp. 1–21.

Hill, G. J. (1973) 'A Procedure for Determining Economic Base Levels for Public Transport Services for Transportation Study Design Years', PTRC Summer Meeting, June 1973.

Hillman, M. (1973) *Personal Mobility and Transport Policy*, PEP, London.

Lee, N. and Stedman, I. (1970) 'Economies of scale in bus transport: some British municipal results', *Journal of Transport Economics and Policy*, **4**, no. 1, January 1970.

London Transport (1972) *Economic Indicators*, Planning Note no. 40, April 1972, and subsequent editions.

McIntosh, P. and Smith, M. G. (1974) 'Fares elasticity: interpretation and estimation', in *TRRL Report* 37*UC* (incorporates work by I. Black).

Mullen, P. and Lewis, K. (1974) 'The demand for urban bus travel', Research Paper, Buchanan and Partners, London (and in *Transportation*, **3** (1974), no. 1).

National Travel Survey 1972/3 (1975) HMSO.

Plowden, S. P. C. (1972) *Towns Against Traffic*, Deutsch.

Independent Commission on Transport Report (1974) *Changing Directions*, London, Coronet.

Sleeman, J. (1962) 'The rise and decline of municipal transport', *Jnl of the Municipal Passenger Transport Assn* (reprinted separately by the Omnibus Society).

Tyson, W. J. (1970) 'A study of peak cost and pricing in road passenger transport', *Inst. of Transport Jnl*, November.

Tyson, W. J. (1974) 'Trends in bus passenger miles', *J. Tpt Econ. Pol.*, **8**, pp. 40–7.

Wabe, J. S. and Coles, O. B. (1975) 'Short and long run costs of urban buses', *J. Tpt Econ. Pol.*, **9**, no. 2, pp. 127–40.

Zahavi, Y. (1973) 'The TT-relationship: a unified approach to transportation planning', *Traffic Engineering and Control*, **15**, no. 4/5, 205–12.

Annual estimates for all passenger transport are published in *Passenger Transport in Great Britain*, HMSO. Data for British Rail, the National Bus Co. and the Scottish Transport Group appear in their annual reports, for municipal and PTE bus operators in *Motor Transport* (1973/4 figures in issues dated 23 May and 18 July 1975).

3 Bus and coach systems

Design of the vehicle

Stage service buses

The designer has to produce a compromise between many conflicting requirements: to minimize fuel consumption and maintenance costs; to maximize passenger capacity with certain comfort limits; to minimize capital cost; to permit one-man operation. In addition, most countries specify safety standards and maximum dimensions. In Britain the Certificate of Fitness (CoF) requirement (see Chapter 1) imposes maximum dimensions which have acted as a severe restraint. The present limits of 12 metres length and 2·5 metres width are generous, and operators are often compelled to select shorter or narrower designs to suit roads over which they operate. But until 1956, for example, the maximum permitted length for a double-decker was less than 30 ft (9·5 metres).

Until around 1950 (in the case of single-deckers) or the 1960s (double-deckers) the typical layout in Britain consisted of an engine mounted vertically over the front axle, on the offside of which sat the driver, still seen in types such as the London 'Routemaster'. A transmission shaft ran to the rear axle, located centrally below the gangway, or in some later models, on the offside to enable a sunken gangway and hence lower overall height. Double-decker bodywork usually incorporated an open rear platform, with staircase adjacent, and seated fifty-six passengers. This figure was raised to over seventy by adoption of the 30 ft length and closer seating pitch. Despite its antiquated appearance, the design remained very popular and might still be produced for the home market but for its exclusion from the government grant scheme. The relatively short wheelbase produced a manoeuvrable vehicle with well-balanced axle load. The driver became rapidly aware of any overstraining of the engine adjacent to him, which was accessible and easily cooled. Coupled with the avoidance of such frills as automatic transmission, the production of such vehicles over many years created a high level of reliability. Models such as the Leyland PD2 and Guy Arab offered a combination of low maintenance costs and high availability that many fleet engineers wish to see return.

Since 1950 most single-deckers have been built with underfloor, horizontally mounted engines. Within a 30 ft length, forty-two passengers can be seated, and fifty-six within the 36 ft (11 metre) limit introduced in 1962. The positioning of the entrance forward of the front axle, opposite the driver, enables easy conversion to one-man operation.

Just as the single-deck layout was changed to reduce the length of vehicle taken up by the engine, double-deckers were changed radically by the introduction of the Leyland Atlantean in 1957. This chassis featured a vertically mounted rear engine, its crankshaft transverse to the main chassis members. Low floor height and an entrance ahead of the front axle, opposite the driver, could be provided. Total seating capacity within the 30 ft length increased to eighty. Unlike the single-deck market, that for double-deckers remained split between new and traditional designs. The rear-engine layout created a more complex transmission layout in a confined space. This created a tendency for driving to be less sensitive, with risk of overstraining both engine and transmission. A cooling flow of air over the engine could not be obtained as easily as in the front-engine layout. Intrusion of wheel arches resulted in cumbersome layouts on the lower deck.

Not until one-man operation of double-deckers became legal in 1966 did this type attain a clear popularity. Not until the conditions for government grant introduced in 1969 excluded it did domestic demand for the older type cease. The higher maintenance costs and poorer availability of the rear-engined models (about 80 per cent, compared with 90 per cent for front-engine types) would probably have led to continued demand for front-engine models had the grant been applicable.

The rear-engine layout was also adopted for single-deckers, especially those of 36 ft length. It permitted a low-height front entrance, with gradually sloping or stepped floor to the rear of the vehicle. In practice, the poor weight distribution of this type led to its virtual demise from production lines except in integral form. Conventional, centre-mounted underfloor engine types continue to hold a remarkably large share of the market.

The 1960s saw an interest in integral construction, coupled with a

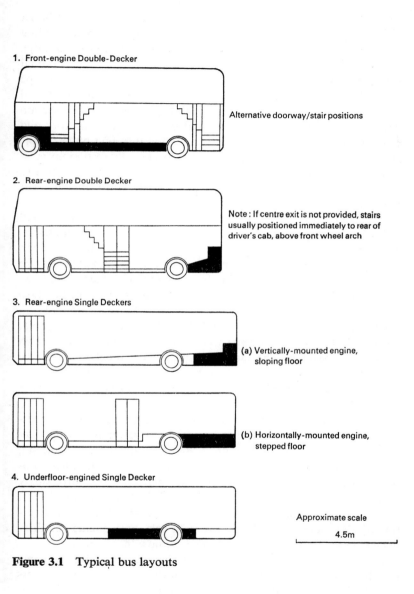

1. Front-engine Double-Decker

Alternative doorway/stair positions

2. Rear-engine Double Decker

Note : If centre exit is not provided, stairs usually positioned immediately to rear of driver's cab, above front wheel arch

3. Rear-engine Single Deckers

(a) Vertically-mounted engine, sloping floor

(b) Horizontally-mounted engine, stepped floor

4. Underfloor-engined Single Decker

Approximate scale

4.5m

Figure 3.1 Typical bus layouts

desire to improve passenger comfort (bus manufacturing resembles a craft industry in many respects, in which separate bodybuilding firms complete small batches on chassis manufactured separately). The main outcome of this was the establishment by the National Bus Company and British Leyland of a company to build a new type of single-decker, the Leyland National. This vehicle has an integral modular structure, to which strength is given by a single-section double-skin roof. Air suspension and comprehensive heating and ventilation (equipment for which is mounted in a pod on the roof) also distinguish this vehicle from earlier models. By setting up mass production in the style of private car manufacture, it was hoped to offer a sophisticated vehicle at a lower cost. Unfortunately, the Leyland National, although offering marked advantages in safety, heating and suspension, has not sustained earlier hopes. The small turbocharged engine is noisy, and many early batches were unreliable. Mass production has led to very limited flexibility in operator's choice of colour scheme or internal layout, and has not achieved the hoped-for cost saving. The swing back to double-deckers, following evolution of satisfactory methods of one-man operation, has also hindered its sales.

A parallel development to the National was the Metro-Scania, a single-decker of similar appearance but heavier construction, also with air suspension. The larger engine gives a quiet performance albeit at the cost of relatively high fuel consumption. However, this design has been adapted very easily to double-deck layout (under the name 'Metropolitan') and is now in series production.

An attempt to combine the mechanical advantages of the front-engine layout with an entrance opposite the driver to permit one-man working is found in the Ailsa-Volvo, manufactured in Scotland, using some Swedish components, notably the engine, which protrudes into the driver's cab and entrance platform to a surprisingly small extent. A total seating capacity of about seventy-five is obtained. The major limitation in such a design is the high proportion of total weight placed over the front axle, both engine and driving cab being forward of it. Deliveries are now in progress.

The recent history of double-deck design has been given at some length, as it offers a valuable example of the way in which attempts to optimize a design on one set of criteria (capacity, suitability for one-man operation) result in a poorer performance in others (reliability, cost).

Coaches and minibuses

Despite their apparent sophistication, most luxury coaches are mechanically simpler than urban buses. A synchromesh or semi-automatic transmission is quite adequate, as steady running replaces the frequent stopping and starting of urban operation. Coaches are produced to a seasonal pattern, including a limited number 'on spec' for sale through dealers. Maximum dimensions are limited as for buses to 12 by 2·5 m. Seating capacities for any given length tend to be lower, due to wider seat pitch, typically forty-five to fifty-two within 11 metre length. Additional features such as toilets are confined to vehicles in regular long-distance operation, such as the Alexander M-type on trunk London-Scottish services.

The major types fall into 'heavyweight' and 'lightweight' categories. The former are literally heavier, around 7 to 8 tonnes unladen weight, and are used on trunk motorway and limited stop services. Engines are mounted at the rear (Bristol RE) or underfloor amidships (Leyland Leopard, Volvo B58). The lightweight chassis are typified by Bedford (YMT, YRT) and Ford (R1014, R1114) types, featuring smaller engines, sometimes mounted at the front. They are popular with smaller independent operators active in the private hire and excursion market. They have also formed the basis for lightweight buses or dual-purpose coaches for rural services. The bus grant scheme introduced in 1969 applies to vehicles of coach design provided they are fitted with driver-controlled doors and a front layout suited to one-man stage operation. This has encouraged the introduction of new and attractively designed vehicles into rural independent service, often the first vehicles purchased new for many years. In rural areas low service frequencies are inevitable, and offering a good quality of vehicle is one of the few ways of improving quality of service.

Most rural services are operated by conventional single- and double-deck designs, despite the naïve enthusiasm of the layman for minibuses. Such a size is inadequate for peak loads of shoppers and schoolchildren, and as most operating costs are labour, permits a saving of only about 15 per cent of total cost per mile. Much more common is the use of lightweight coaches, or short versions of standard single-deck models (such as the Bristol LHS, a 35-seat version of the 45-seat LH underfloor-engine type). Minibuses in rural service are confined largely to post office services and a few specialized services (see Chapter 7).

Minibuses are more often found in private hire work and 'dial a ride' services. The diesel-engined Ford Transit with 16-seat bodywork is popular. The most recent development is the 'midibus', a 20- to 25-seater, usually based on conventional underfloor single-deck chassis, with a very short wheelbase (or on goods chassis such as the Ford A-series). The manoeuvrability thus offered is useful in operation of city centre circular services, and in housing estates not designed for bus penetration. An early model, the Seddon, is used in both roles by Greater Manchester PTE.

Despite the interest in non-conventional bus and coach designs, they account for only a small share of total PSVs licensed in 1973 – 74402, comprising 29146 double-deckers, 45160 single-deckers and 96 trams.

Other aspects of PSV design

A ratio of 10 bhp/tonne (11 bhp/tonne for single-deckers) power to laden weight is specified for buses receiving grant. A typical diesel engine generates about 150 bhp, consuming 8 to 10 mpg in urban areas (6 to 8 mpg for rear-engine models), 12 to 15 mpg in rural and express work. Low-cost insulation around the rear engine has enabled production of 'quiet' versions of the Metro-Scania and Leyland National, reaching maximum noise levels of 77 dBa, well below the proposed limits for private cars, and little more than the noise made by tyres alone. Noise levels can thus be acceptable within pedestrian or housing areas. Transmission is the aspect of design for which satisfactory systems have yet to be produced. The need to serve closely spaced passenger stops combined with other intermediate delays, imposes frequent retardation and acceleration not experienced in any other type of vehicle. The traditional 'crash' or 'synchromesh' gearboxes were reliable and cheap, but gave a rough ride for the passenger and required considerable physical effort from the driver. Fully automatic systems have now become fashionable, but their capital and maintenance costs have deterred wide use, as has their tendency to increase fuel consumption. The most recent attempts consist of simpler systems such as Leyland G2, designed to offer some of the advantages without high costs.

The increasing proportion of elderly passengers makes safety on stairs and at doorways important. A layout of broad steps forming short flights with right-angled turns is preferable. Stairs ascending towards the front of the vehicle are safer, since passengers standing on them are not thrown downwards should the driver brake sharply.

Open rear platforms of conventional double-deckers permitted rapid loading and unloading, but could be dangerous, as passengers were tempted to board or alight between stops. Driver-controlled doors are now normal, usually comprising leaf sections which fold back to offer a clear loading area.

Control and supervision of bus services

Until recently supervision was confined to inspectors at termini and major intersections checking running numbers of buses (numbers assigned in a roster, not route number) against scheduled timings. This method is labour-intensive, especially if observation at frequent intervals is desired, and may lack co-ordination between inspectors. For example, in Dublin it was found that inspectors at either end of a heavy cross-city route might issue contradictory instructions to drivers running out of schedule. A central control point may be able to detect overall patterns of delay and their causes better than can inspectors sited at limited points with only local knowledge available.

Systems now in use or being tested include:

1 Closed-circuit television (CCTV) – Cameras mounted at strategic points in the central area scan intersections and stopping points, usually with variable focus and direction. General traffic conditions, abnormally long queues, etc., are thus detected at central control room and instructions then issued to drivers via street inspectors and/or radio. Major UK examples are Leicester and Leeds.

2 Radio telephone – Often used to combat vandalism, etc., as much as for operational efficiency. Driver reports position at frequent intervals, and receives instructions. Inspectors may use walkie-talkie equipment. In theory, use of a limited number of available radio frequencies for voice communication is less efficient than coded signals (Bristol, below), but industrial relations may be much better, and drivers may respond spontaneously with information on traffic conditions.

3 Bus Electronic Scanning Indicator (BESI) – London Transport system using fixed scanners mounted on posts, emitting horizontal beam at about three metres above ground. This intercepts indicator strips on nearside of double-deckers, each with slots to unique binary code corresponding to running number. The reflected signal is received by a scanner and transmitted to controller, being

decoded to appear as a number on a screen. The detection rate is low, there being only one opportunity to scan each bus, with effect of parked vehicles. The high cost of fixed scanners limits frequency of observations.

4 Marconi–Bristol – In effect, reverse of BESI principle. High frequency beam emitted from bus in vertical plane on circular arc many times per second. Etched metal plates to unique binary code fixed at 70-metre intervals on lamp posts or other street furniture are scanned several times by each bus as it passes. Low cost of scanning points, but high for equipment on bus. The signal received by the bus is transformed into a radio code, transmitted to controller. Similar codes to indicate 'bus full', 'breakdown', etc., can be sent by the driver by pressing appropriate buttons, eliminating use of microphone and obtaining better use of available radio frequencies.

5 Marconi–London route 11 – Each bus is fitted with an odometer (accurate mileage indicator), connected to a coding device and radio transmitter. Mileage covered from start of each trip is signalled at frequent intervals. Fixed scanning points are not required, but accuracy may be affected by variations in loading, and driving of each bus.

All the above systems are only of value if they can be supported by a control strategy. This could include drafting in extra vehicles (if crews are available) to fill gaps in service, or reallocating vehicles between timings and routes at termini, turning vehicles short in one direction to fill a gap in the other (already practised, and unpopular with passengers forced to transfer to the following vehicle). In many respects good results can only be achieved if accurate running times are scheduled, buses given priority so as to reduce variations in running time, and sufficient crews are available. Technology is no substitute for poor management.

Buses on road networks

In very broad terms, measures which benefit all road vehicles also benefit buses. Traffic lights reduce accidents and delay at busy intersections, new roads improve peak traffic flow, and one-way schemes prevent increased traffic entering a system from overloading it. In many respects, however, the opposite is true. One-way schemes usually increase route mileage between certain points. For the car user this is offset by higher speeds, but buses may often be taken away from major traffic attractors, their network becomes more confusing to passengers, and mileage is increased. At traffic lights a relatively long cycle time maximizes total flow but as shown below leads to significant and variable delays for buses. A case for bus priority can therefore be made, firstly, on grounds that buses should not suffer adverse effects from management schemes. As a wider policy, buses can be made more attractive, for example, by permitting them to use a direct route via a contra-flow lane when other traffic is rerouted around a one-way system. In this fashion they can retain more passengers and reduce the need for expenditure on new roads. In conditions of scarce road space, giving priority to the most efficient users of that space (buses) may reduce total travelling time within the system.

At intersections and traffic lights

About half of the stationary time between termini is at bus stops, and determined mainly by boarding time per passenger, the other half at intersections or queues approaching them. Other factors, such as pedestrian crossings, road works, etc., are of only marginal importance. In urban areas nearly all junctions at which significant delay occurs are controlled by traffic lights.

Traffic light timings comprise three elements:

1 Phases – A phase is that length of time for which a single aspect (e.g. red) is displayed to an approach lane.
2 Cycles – A cycle is the period of time in which a sequence of phases is performed, returning to the start of the original phase.
3 Intergreen time – The time between one phase and another, usually denoted to an approach lane by showing amber. This exists purely as a safety margin, and for purposes of calculating potential flow through a junction it is assumed that no flow takes place during this time. Hence the more phases per cycle, and/or shorter each cycle, the higher the proportion of time per hour in which no flow is assumed, and the lower total capacity per hour.

For the majority of road users, average time taken to pass through a junction is the only relevant criterion. For the traffic engineer, this together with maximizing the flow of pcu (passenger car units) per hour, was the major criterion. A bus carrying fifty passengers thus received little more weighting than a single car driver. In addition, buses form a time-linked system, so that delays to one affect others. *Variation* in delay may be more important than average delay. Consider Figure 3.2. Buses are scheduled to depart from A at three-minute intervals. Passengers accumulate at each stop at the rate of two per minute. Each takes 5 seconds to board the vehicle, and hence average scheduled time at each stop is 30 seconds. Scheduled running times between stops and across intersections (20 seconds) are shown. Assume that the first bus just misses a green phase at the

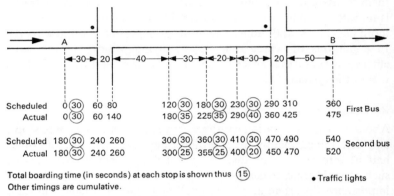

Total boarding time (in seconds) at each stop is shown thus (15)   • Traffic lights
Other timings are cumulative.

Figure 3.2   Effect of traffic lights on bus service regularity

traffic lights (or joins a queue of vehicles which does not discharge entirely during the first available green phase). It is delayed for 80 seconds instead of the scheduled 20. When it arrives at the next stop, more passengers have arrived and hence stop time is extended. This process is repeated at each stop, the bus running further and further behind schedule. The following bus has fewer passengers to pick up, and hence gains on schedule. If the first bus suffers a similar delay at the second traffic-light junction, and the second only the scheduled delay at each junction, the two buses will be only 45 seconds instead of three minutes apart at B. Delay to passengers waiting at stops may be greater in total than that to those already on the buses, and particularly inconvenient and irritating.

A simple solution to this problem is to reduce cycle time and hence intervals between each green phase. This, however, would reduce total junction capacity by increasing the proportion of intergreen time per hour and if the junction were already running near saturation would merely create worse congestion, in which buses would be delayed. But if, as part of a comprehensive traffic restraint scheme, traffic volumes over a wide area were reduced, this solution could apply.

At the least, one can ensure that each bus reaches the junction so that the next available green phase is used by it. By making the nearside lane 'bus only' buses can overtake queues of other traffic and be sure of reaching the stop line without delay. Most bus priorities to date have been of this type. Their success depends on adequate enforcement (often lacking), and queues into which all other traffic is placed not being so long as to obstruct other junctions which are also used by buses. Few bus priority evaluations have allowed for enforcement costs, and in view of current pressures on police time, extra traffic wardens are probably required for whom costs should be allocated. Variations in hours of operation of lanes, and lack of physical separation of with-flow lanes from other parts of the road surface add to the problems. Attempts are now being made to standardize on twelve- or twenty-four-hour periods of operation.

If bus flows are relatively small, motorists may be tempted to turn into the lane to overtake others. At junctions, discharge rates from the remaining lane(s) for other traffic may not permit full use of potential capacity. Following studies by the Transport and Road Research Laboratory (TRRL), it is now official policy to stop bus lanes about 60 metres short of a junction. Buses can thus get close enough to the junction to be sure of using the first available green phase, but other traffic, especially left-turning traffic, can make full use of the junction capacity.

In one-way systems and traffic management

In order to avoid losses to buses when one-way schemes are introduced, they may be allowed to continue to use a road in both directions, that against the (new) one-way flow in a *contra-flow lane*. Whereas with-flow lanes are separated only by a solid white line (above), physical barriers are required for contra-flow lanes in order to prevent head-on collisions. As a byproduct, enforcement is made easy. The first major contra-flow scheme was that along Tottenham High Road, North London, in 1968. Almost a mile long, it enables buses to continue along a major route and avoid a devious south-bound one-way routing.

Bus speeds may be increased substantially, although variations in running between buses may be greater. (Differences in driver performance partly account for this. Also, buses are unable to overtake

C

one another at stops.) Since the road surface in the lane is used only by buses, rutting may develop along paths followed by the wheels. Costly resurfacing has already been necessary in Tottenham. Pedestrians may become familiar with most traffic proceeding in one direction, and forget that buses still run in both directions. This problem has been particularly serious in the Piccadilly bus lane, London, which was introduced after several years of one-way operation.

Another common means of ensuring bus priority is to exempt buses from right-hand-turn bans, causing little inconvenience to other traffic if the bus service is not frequent. Where traffic lights exist, buses making right-hand turns can be given priority by selective detection in the approach lane. At experiments in Derby and Leicester, buses approaching the junction as a green phase was about to finish have had the phase extended in their favour, or if approaching during a red phase, had an additional green phase provided. Losses to other traffic flows were compensated by extending green times on their next phase. Variation in delay to buses was markedly reduced, with little effect on other traffic.

Area traffic control schemes are now being introduced in major cities in which successive signals are linked so that cars can pass through a series of green phases. The start of each green phase is offset according to the average time required for a 'platoon' of cars to travel between junctions. Such systems give substantial time savings and some improvement in system capacity. However, running times of buses between junctions may be longer due to presence of intermediate stops and low acceleration. Buses thus fail to benefit, or may even hit more red phases than before. A revised version of the standard fixed-time linking system called 'Transyt' has been tested in Glasgow in which the offsets between green phases were timed to suit buses, and duration of each green phase timed for buses to pass through after allowing for delay due to intermediate stops. Bus speeds increased by about 9 per cent, with no significant worsening for cars.

Bus station design

The great majority of bus passengers continue to be picked up and set down at kerbside stops. This is not merely a measure enforced by low investment in public transport but is often desirable. Stops are placed close to main traffic attractors, and buses not diverted from their routes. Only recently has the importance of improving conditions at conventional bus stops been realized. 'Bus stop clearways' limit parking by other vehicles which obstruct bus movement. Better shelters and timetable information reduce unpleasantness of waiting. Many shelters are now being built free of charge by companies which cover costs by revenue from posters. Bus stations have often been built at the insistence of local authorities, often to 'tidy up' town centres rather than to aid bus passengers. Many of those in market towns have been quite unnecessary from the passengers' viewpoint and by taking passengers from points such as market places have reduced the use of subsidized services.

Nevertheless many bus stations are required in busier urban areas, especially at interchanges. For frequent services, a parallel platform design is best (see Figure 3.3). Buses load alongside a platform at kerb height. Space between platforms is sufficient for buses to overtake one another. A good example is that at Sheffield. Major snags with

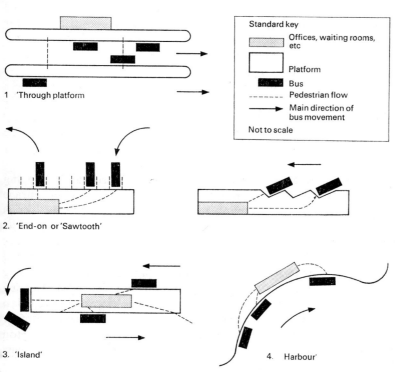

Figure 3.3 Bus station layouts

this type are the space requirements and extensive pedestrian/bus conflict. The end-on or 'sawtooth' layout remedies this by providing only one platform area, on which all facilities such as waiting rooms and enquiry offices are concentrated. Buses park end-on, or at an angle, so that their front entrances adjoin the platform. This pattern is favoured for many NBC or rural stations, but is limited by the need for buses to reverse on departing, with associated accident risk. Service frequencies of half-hourly or above are difficult to handle. Other layouts offering minimal pedestrian/bus conflict and concentration of facilities are the 'island' and 'harbour' types. The island type, as at Newark, can handle high frequency services, with some pedestrian conflict. The harbour type, as at King's Lynn, minimizes this conflict but involves awkward manoeuvring of buses unless designed to a wide radius. The 'island' type can be expanded by adopting end-on loading along each of its sides, as at Preston where the main platform area is entirely enclosed, and access to buses gained through sliding doors. Many bus stations in medium-sized towns combine both through-platform and sawtooth layouts for different types of service.

Busways and bus links

The concept of providing bus priorities on existing roads, and building separate stations, may be extended to that of building entirely separate busways, usually conventional road structures of single lane width about 3·5 metres. They may provide direct routings, or routes parallel to congested roads.

Many cases exist of adjacent housing, industrial and shopping areas between and within which it is not desired to encourage heavy traffic flows. Enabling buses to link areas directly avoids costly and indirect routing over conventional roads, and permits them to offer substantial time savings over comparable car trips. A recent example of such a link is that in Portsmouth between the former airport (now an industrial estate) and an adjoining housing area. An existing bus service to the housing area has been extended via the busway to the industrial area and back via existing roads to form a loop working convenient for one-man operation. Similar links have been created between neighbourhood units in Washington New Town. (The question of public transport access within new towns is discussed in Chapter 5.)

Within a number of town centre pedestrian/bus priority schemes short links have been restricted to buses only: usually short, narrow streets with a very low capacity. Examples can be found in Redcar and Rugby. In some cases principal shopping streets have been confined to buses and/or delivery vehicles and taxis. Such schemes, as in Cornmarket, Oxford, are intended primarily to give better conditions for shoppers and buses, and advantage over cars in accessibility. Apart from removing excessive delays caused when too many vehicles attempted to make use of the streets, changes in average speed of buses are not usually substantial (or necessarily desirable; the higher speed of buses along Oxford Street since priority was introduced has prevented hoped-for reduction in pedestrian accidents).

The busway concept is now being extended to that of building substantial new links, parallel to existing congested radial roads, to form an alternative to rapid transit schemes. British advocates have taken their lead from American experience, notably that of a segregated bus lane over one mile long in Lincoln Tunnel, which links New Jersey with New York City. Flows of about 25 000 passengers per hour have been achieved, similar to the maximum capacity of heavy rapid transit lines. However, conditions are not comparable – being in tunnel, the busway includes no intermediate stops, sharp corners or terminal areas. At an average spacing of about 10 seconds, buses would have to pull into parallel lanes in order to slow down and call at intermediate stops, whereas rapid transit trains do so on a single running track in each direction, which platforms adjoin directly. At present buses also have a lower acceleration rate than modern rapid transit stock (although a very high rate would be possible due to friction between rubber tyre and concrete surface, a very high power:weight ratio would be needed, with marked increase in fuel consumption at normal running speeds. Highest acceleration rates on contemporary buses are about 0·7 M/S/S compared with over 1·0 M/S/S on rail stock).

The most likely role for busways is in extending the existing network of reserved track public transport in cities which have lost their local rail services (notably Edinburgh) or links to serve major new development within existing cities (New Addington to Croydon, south of London could be an excellent opportunity). As such, they offer very similar characteristics to light rapid transit (moderate capital cost, a fairly intensive network) and current studies in Edinburgh indicate that a clear-cut choice between the two can be very difficult. They share the advantage that they can be constructed in stages, to which access may be gained by diverting existing routes. Thus some return on capital invested can be gained at an early stage. Problems of alignment affecting all rapid transit systems, and further comment on busways, appear in the next chapter.

References and further reading

Bus and coach design

Apart from texts dealing with motor vehicle design in general little is available on bus and coach design in book form, but it forms a major part of the coverage of technical journals such as *Motor Transport* (weekly, with Bus and Coach supplement), *Commercial Motor* (weekly) and *Coaching Journal* (monthly).

Kerridge, M. S. P. (1974) 'The bus grant and urban transport', *J. Tpt Econ. Pol.*, **6**, no. 3, 237–43, discusses the bus grant scheme's effect in distorting operators' purchase patterns.

Rhys, D. G. (1972) 'Economics of change in road passenger transport', *J. Tpt Econ. Pol.*, **6**, no. 3, outlines the implications of recent changes.

Bus lanes and priority measures

This subject has been extensively documented. The most comprehensive single reference is the Proceedings of Bus Priorities Symposium held at the Transport and Road Research Laboratory (1972) recorded in *TRRL Report LR570*.

Department of the Environment, Bus Demonstration Project (1973) *Summary Report no. 1, Bus Detection at Traffic Signals*, describes priority measures at traffic lights, in particular experiments in Derby and Leicester, and Report no. 3 on bus priorities in Reading.

Ridley, G., Rushton, P. and Cracknell, J. A. (1973) 'Bus lanes in London', *The Highway Engineer* (Journal of the Institution of Highway Engineers), May.

Traffic Engineering and Control (1972/3) : a series of six papers under the general heading 'Bus priority in Greater London', **14**, 324–6, 382–6, 429–32, 482–5, 522–5, 592–4.

London's extensive priorities, are the subject of a critique by

Holmes, R. and White, P. R. 'A comparison of the effectiveness of separate bus priority schemes and those affecting entire networks' (In preparation).

See also:

Camden, London Borough of (1972) *Buses in Camden.*

Bus operating methods and control

Lambden, W. (1970) *Bus and Coach Operation*, Iliffe.

Particular attention has been paid by researchers to the effects of one-man operation (o.m.o.) and are discussed in the following sources:

Brown, R. H. and Nash, C. A. (1972) 'Savings from one-man buses', *J. Tpt Econ. Pol.*, **6**, no. 3.

Cundill, M. A. and Watts, P. F. (1973) *TRRL Report LR521*, on boarding and alighting times.

Department of the Environment, Working Group on One-man Operation of Buses (1971) *Report*.

Fairhurst, M. H. (1974) 'The impact on receipts of conversion to one-man bus operation', *J. Tpt Econ. Pol.*, **8**, no. 3, 223–36, on revenue losses.

4 Rail and rapid transit system design

Early developments

During the nineteenth century railways were called on to serve almost all demands for mechanized transport, including provision of little-used stations and lines within urban areas. Specialized urban railways developed in the larger centres, notably the London Underground system from the opening of the Metropolitan Line in 1863. A number of main line companies also developed a strong interest in suburban traffic, especially where long-distance demand held little potential. Thus the railways to the south and south-east of London displayed markedly greater interest than that of the companies operating over greater distances to west and north. In smaller cities frequent steam-hauled services played an important role towards the end of the century, as in the Potteries, Edinburgh and Birmingham.

The growth of electric tramway systems at the turn of the century, often under municipal ownership (see Chapter 1) caused a rapid transfer of short-distance trips to this new mode, which offered much better accessibility than railways whose routes had been located primarily from the viewpoint of long-distance traffic. It was the tramcar which gave the first opportunity to the majority of the population to make frequent use of mechanized transport to travel to work, at low fares. In the provincial centres mentioned above it was sufficiently competitive over the entire network to ensure that no further expansion of local rail services took place. As early as World War One some minor stations and routes were closed. This process continued – for example, the twenty-minute headway service in Aberdeen ceased in 1938 – and the 'Beeching era' of the 1960s saw the virtual elimination of local systems in Edinburgh, Bristol and much of the West Midlands conurbation. The electric tramway has likewise given way to the bus in all British industrial cities.

In some larger cities of Europe and North America railway companies responded to tramway competition by electrifying some of the better used suburban services. The first decade of this century saw conversion of routes from Liverpool to Southport, Ormskirk and Rock Ferry, Manchester to Bury, on Tyneside, and in south London. This trend continued into the 1930s, notably in the Southern Railway's electrification of all its inner commuter network. Other schemes were delayed until after nationalization – the 'Blue Train' network on Clydeside, and major projects in east London. Main line electrification has permitted local schemes as a byproduct, notably in south Manchester.

From the turn of the century a more dramatic development than that of electrification of existing routes was the growth of self-contained urban railway systems such as the Paris Metro, the elevated lines of North American cities, and the London Underground, which from 1890 included the first 'tube' lines. Other British development was confined to the Glasgow underground loop and the Liverpool Overhead Railway (closed 1956). From the 1920s little growth took place, save for suburban surface extensions of the London system, but in other countries a steadier growth was maintained, including new systems in Osaka, Moscow and Barcelona. Since World War Two many systems have been inaugurated, including Munich, Stockholm, Rome, Cleveland Ohio, San Francisco and Rotterdam. From the early 1960s a 'boom' has taken place, following the realization that only reserved track systems can offer an attractive alternative to the private car and buses or trams mixed with other traffic on heavily congested roads. In Britain the Victoria and Fleet lines have been constructed, and schemes for other major cities are either in progress (Tyneside, Glasgow, Liverpool) or planned (Manchester).

The electric tramcar remained in much more extensive use outside Britain after World War Two than is often realized. Small-town systems based almost entirely on street track have disappeared, but in cities of about 500 000 population or more many have remained, either as the major spine of the public transport network or a secondary system feeding an underground railway. New suburbs have been built around reserved track extensions, and older sections of the network placed on reserved track (often in tunnel) so that most of the network is thus aligned.

Types of transit

Following closure of the minor surface railway branches and smaller tramway systems, three types of urban railway and rapid transit may be distinguished, using German terminology:

U-bahn

As its title indicates, this form is based on full-size underground railways, although in practice over half the network may be on elevated or surface tracks outside the central area. As a rule, ownership and control is vested in municipal authorities, and the network largely self-contained. Close station spacing (about every 1000 metres) permits a high proportion of passengers to reach stations on foot, and all-stations operation of trains is normal. Simple fare systems, often flat fare, apply. Examples of such systems include, by definition, those in Hamburg, and Munich, together with the London Underground (apart from the Metropolitan Line), New York, Madrid and Chicago. Although often adopted as a generic term for such systems, the 'Metro' in Paris (whose title was in any case derived from that of the London Metropolitan Railway) is an extreme form of the type: very close station spacing coupled with short trains and high acceleration rates place it closer to the street tramways which it supplanted than a modern urban railway.

S-bahn

Again, an expression associated with West Germany which has become commonplace. It denotes those routes and branches of main line surface railways on which a frequent service (usually at regular intervals, at least half-hourly) is offered. Station spacing within the inner city may approximate to that of U-bahn but intervals of about two or three kilometres are more typical. Average speeds are thus somewhat higher, despite lower acceleration rates. Peak services levels may be limited by the sharing of track capacity with long-distance services. A recent trend in Germany, now being followed in Britain, is the creation of links across city centres, usually in tunnel, to enable S-bahn trains to offer better accessibility within the central area. Thus improved, they can offer an alternative to bus services, or the need to construct entirely new U-bahn systems at very high cost. Examples of such schemes include Hamburg, Liverpool and Manchester's 'Picc-Vic'.

Light rapid transit (LRT)

This term is applied to electrically operated systems with similar characteristics to U-bahn but generally without block signalling (see below), full-height station platforms or ticket issue at all stations. Trains of up to three or four cars, or articulated cars, are one-man operated. The advantages given by full-size railways are thus obtained for a much lower investment. Except in the largest cities such systems are adequate for peak flows. As yet, they are all derived from upgraded urban tramways, but the Tyneside Metro system in Britain will be a case of a new system based on this technology.

In some cases tramways have been upgraded to form an intermediate stage to full-scale urban railways, as in Brussels, by operating from full-height platforms and stations which will be served eventually by full-size trains (so-called 'pre-metro'). In other cases, a tramway may be upgraded by extensive construction of city centre tunnels, with a limited amount of pre-sale of tickets, and some platforms to full height ('semi-metro'). A financial advantage of such systems is that trams can be diverted into relatively short sections of tunnels as they are built. There is no need to wait for completion of a whole route before gaining a return on infrastructure capital costs.

Basic system characteristics

Capacity

This is a function of three variables:

1 Seating capacity of each car, and proportion of standing passengers. Typically 100 to 150 in total, of which about 50 may be seated. A distinction may also be drawn between 'tolerable' loads, including some standing, and 'maximum crush loads', in the case of London Transport 1938 tube stock, 810 and 1158 per train respectively. The smaller loading gauge of LRT reduces this figure to about 110, but articulated LRT cars can accommodate up to 200 or 250.
2 Average length of train: up to ten or twelve cars may be possible in the case of S-bahn, seven or eight typical of U-bahn (most London 'tube' lines operate seven-car trains). For LRT, up to three or four single cars.
3 Spacing between trains. This is determined by the block signalling system, down to a minimum headway of about 75 to 90 seconds.

In practice, in order to give some margin for minor operating delays, two minutes may be taken as a practical minimum, as on London Transport.

LRT cars may operate at intervals of down to about 45 seconds based on control by drivers at sight distance, combined with high acceleration and retardation rates.

Combining these elements, we can say that a maximum peak hour passenger flow per single track in one direction is about 25 000 for U-bahn and S-bahn systems, about 15 000 for LRT.

Flow

In addition to factors affecting capacity, this is also subject to:

1 Rate of acceleration – A maximum of about 1·2 metres/second/ second (M/S/S), or about 3 mph/second, may be derived from dangers of slipping between wheel and rail, and of discomfort to passengers. Most newly built U-bahn and LRT stock achieves this performance, but much older stock (for example, London Transport 1938 tube stock, still in general use) is limited to about 0·5 to 0·7 M/S/S.
2 Station spacing and stop time – On single track with one-way flow, a train in a station obstructs the route until it departs. Hence, time taken to clear a block section can be reduced firstly by minimizing the duration of stops. High boarding and alighting flows are achieved with stock fitted with sliding doors, the floor of which matches platform height. Operational or historic considerations frequently require lower platforms. Trams designed for operation both on street and in tunnel often have steps adjustable for loading at various platform heights.
   Flow can also be increased by offering a high rate of acceleration. For example, in Stockholm, two stations within the central area (Slussen and Gamla Stan) are located only 440 metres apart. In order to maximize peak flow, trains accelerate more quickly so as to clear the section in 50 seconds instead of the off-peak level of 58 seconds, but at the expense of a 40 per cent increase in power requirements.

An alternative means of maximizing station throughput is to build a station in which a single track carrying a one-way flow bifurcates to form a loop around an island platform (see Figure 4.1). A French study predicts that by permitting a second train to enter one side of the platform as the first was departing from the other side, a flow of

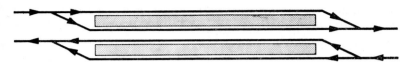

Figure 4.1 Island platform loop layout for an urban railway operating at headways of under two minutes

up to sixty trains per track per hour could be achieved, or forty-five to fifty as a practical figure.

It will be evident from the above that one means of avoiding the need to build new tracks to meet higher peak flows is to improve train performance. This will itself increase energy consumption and capital cost of rolling stock, but in many cases be much less costly than new construction.

The above statements assume implicitly that trains are of identical performance. Where there is a variation in speeds and acceleration, peak flows may be much lower. In the case of the link between Brussels Nord and Midi stations, for example, on which local and main line trains are mixed and maximum acceleration available is only 0·46 M/S/S, a maximum of only eighteen trains per track per hour is attained.

Power supply and control

Direct current (dc) power supply is typical, usually at 600 to 750 volts, via a third rail. This form of current and voltage is suitable for use on trains without rectifiers or transformers, but requires the provision of substations at frequent intervals, about every 3 to 5 kilometres. Where dense traffic is found, the cost of such substations is lower than that of mounting extra equipment on trains, but this is not the case on intercity routes, many of which have been electrified at 25 000 volts (25 KV) alternating current (ac). Where S-bahn services share tracks with such routes, a penalty is incurred in extra train weight, sometimes affecting performance. This is the case in Manchester, for example. British Rail also standardizes on 6·25 KV or 25 KV even for systems created largely to handle suburban traffic, such as those in east London or Glasgow. (A description of intercity electrification appears in Chapter 8.)

Tramway systems and LRT lines are supplied at about 750 volts dc by overhead wire. A number of older S-bahn lines (in Britain, the Manchester–Glossop route) operate at 1500 volts dc overhead supply typical of prewar main line schemes. This voltage has been selected also for the Tyneside LRT system, enabling a reduction in the number of substations required from thirteen for a 750-volts system, to only seven.

On trains, supply of electrical power to motors, usually mounted on bogie frames, is through 'series-resistor' or through 'chopper' control. Direct supply of full traction current to motors in a train about to accelerate would cause components for burn out. The traditional series-resistor system consists of banks of resistances connected in series, through which current is passed to the motors. These are successively switched out, enabling higher levels of current to reach the motors. Modern equipment offers about fifteen such 'steps' in switching-out before full speed is reached. A further sequence may be inserted by connecting motors in series during the first stage of acceleration, and then in parallel.

The series-resistor system dates back to the 1890s, and has thus acquired a high degree of reliability and familiarity from long use. However, it involves waste of energy as the resistances are heated (warming the passenger saloon is one use for this byproduct, at least in cold weather). An alternative, thyristor (or 'chopper') control, is now passing from the experimental stage into series production. A thyristor is a solid-state switching device, originally applied to ac equipment, in which a 'gating' pulse of a few milliseconds duration breaks the main current flow at intervals which are varied in relation to desired current flow to the motors. Waste of energy is avoided, and a smoother acceleration sequence obtained, of particular value when high acceleration rates are required. Major limitations to date have been the cost of partially experimental equipment, and interference between the high-frequency gating pulses and similar frequencies in communication cables. None the less, energy savings of up to 35 or 40 per cent in urban use give the thyristor an assured future.

Early electric trains picked up current via the control car, which was then passed through one set of series-resistor equipment to other traction motors along the train. (Locomotives were tried, for example, on the Central London Line in 1903, but created heavy noise and vibration on underground lines, and required extra turn-round time at termini.) This necessitated a high voltage cable along the train, creating fire dangers. An American engineer, F. J. Sprague, therefore designed the multiple-unit control system in 1897. In this system, the series-resistor (or now, thyristor) equipment is repeated on each power car, and operated by relays connected to the driving car by a low voltage cable. A spin-off from this layout is that a high proportion of train axles can be motored, and adhesion increased in line with peak passenger loads, so that high acceleration can be maintained without risk of wheel-slip.

Energy consumption

Two main requirements of rolling stock are:

1 Energy for acceleration, proportional to the weight of the stock multiplied by the square of the speed attained.
2 Energy to overcome rolling resistance while the train is accelerating and maintaining a steady speed.

The need for frequent bursts of high acceleration imposes a much higher energy consumption per tonne–km on urban stock than for intercity stock: a French analysis suggests that 25 per cent of urban train direct movement costs is accounted for by energy costs, but only 14 per cent of those for intercity trains. The need for high acceleration imposes a weight penalty, due to the higher proportion of motored axles (up to 100 per cent for rates of 1 M/S/S and above) on the train.

The best known means of reducing consumption is that employed on some London tube lines: a downward gradient of not more than 1 in 20 on leaving a station aids acceleration, and an upward gradient of not more than 1 in 30 aids retardation. However, for subway or surface lines such frequent variation in level is less easy to incorporate. The use of stainless steel instead of conventional construction saves about 3 tonnes per car on an average total weight of about 25 tonnes. A further 3 tonnes may be saved by use of light alloy. The French study mentioned above suggests that an extra cost per car of up to about £1200 may be justified by such energy savings. Weight may also be reduced by mounting adjoining cars on common bogies, usually in sets of two or three cars, eliminating one or two bogies. Recent Hamburg stock follows this pattern.

For a mean acceleration of 0·9 M/S/S to be achieved in the range 0 to 100 km/h a power:weight ratio of about 10 to 12 kilowatts per tonne is required.

Energy consumption between stations may be derived from a speed/time curve, as shown in Figure 4.2. In simplified form, a trapezoidal curve may be used, assuming constant acceleration and deceleration rates and steady running speed. The area under this curve is proportional to distance (i.e. speed × time). A second curve

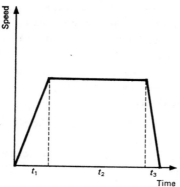

(a) Simplified trapezoidal form, train running at steady speed after acceleration period

(b) Form in which a higher rate of acceleration is followed by a 'coasting' period

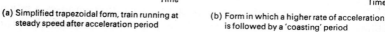

t_1 – time during which train accelerates
t_2 – time during which train runs at steady speed or 'coasts'
t_3 – time during which train decelerates

Figure 4.2   Energy consumption curves for urban rail services

is shown in which a slightly higher rate of acceleration is used to reach a higher speed, from which point power is cut off, followed by a period of coasting. In this second form, which follows the same constraints of time and distance, less energy is needed. No energy is used to overcome rolling resistance after acceleration has ended. Braking takes place from a lower speed, reducing waste energy in the form of noise and heat, and wear and tear on equipment.

Internal layout of rolling stock

From the 1920s or even earlier, the pattern of three or four sets of sliding doors per car, usually worked by compressed air, has been characteristic of U-bahn stock. This is related to an interior layout of limited seating capacity, often arranged longitudinally, and a high proportion of standee space. A greater density of standing passengers is usually achieved in the areas between doorways on either side of the car than between rows of seats. High rates of acceleration necessitate a large number of grab rails.

For S-bahn services, a higher proportion of seats, usually arranged in 'four across' layout, is normal, with fewer doorways. This difference can be observed in London by comparing the C69 Circle Line stock, built with four double sets of doors per car to permit rapid loading and unloading, with the stock operated on the Metropolitan Line to Amersham and Watford, built with 'five across' seating and three sets of doors. On much of the British Rail system, the antiquated layout of slam doors and compartment seating continues, notably in new Southern Region stock (the VEP type). This is associated with extended station stop times, numerous minor accidents, and irritating noise. It also works against one-man operation of trains without a guard. The new standard BR suburban stock, the PEP type, incorporates sliding doors, and is suitable for one-man operation.

Another problem associated with S-bahn services, or outer, surface sections of U-bahn lines is that the opening of all sliding doors at each station is unnecessary outside peak periods, and admits cold air and rain into the train. Selective opening by passengers with overriding control by the driver to close all doors, can alleviate this problem, and is being provided on PEP stock. In continental cities, Hamburg for example, this principle also applies to U-bahn stock. By permitting passengers to open doors as a train enters a station, shorter station stops can be achieved. Few accidents seem to occur as a result.

In some cities, notably Sydney and Chicago, double-deck stock is provided for outer suburban trips, extending the principle of high-seating: low-doorway ratios to its limit. Passengers enter a vestibule located above the end bogie, then into lower or upper passenger compartments, the former within a well section of the conventional chassis frame. British loading gauge does not permit such forms – the 'double-decker' trains operated on the Southern Region from 1949 to 1971 were of a cumbersome 'half-decker' type – but many outer suburban services in Paris are to be thus opera ed.

Signalling and control

A simpler system than that found on main line railways can be used, due to regular timetable patterns, and lack of variation in speeds, braking distances, etc., of different types of train such as intercity passenger, local and freight. The network of most U-bahn systems is very simple, with few passing loops or crossovers save at terminals. S-bahn may be somewhat more complex, due to mixing with other rail traffic, but even here tracks are often largely segregated from parallel main line tracks (for example, the Euston to Watford local service not only has its own tracks, but a different electrical system to that of the adjacent intercity line).

A semi-automatic sequence of trains can be signalled, with manual control as an override to handle only exceptions and emergencies. On London Transport 'programme machines' have been in use for many years, in which a perforated roll is moved on by a clock mechanism, controlling the sequence of pointwork settings, signals and platform route indications.

As on main line railways, the basic signalling system is that of block working (Figure 4.3, below). A train may not enter a block

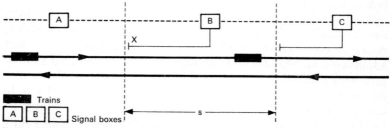

X: denotes the home signal protecting section B
S: denotes safe backing distance

Figure 4.3   Block section signalling

section until the previous train has cleared it. The length of the block section is normally at least equal to the minimum safe braking distance from the maximum speed permitted. On surface railways, presence of a train in section was observed by signalmen in signal boxes adjacent to each block section. On the tube lines in London such a method was clearly impracticable and at an early date a system of semi-automatic block working was devised. By providing the traction current from an outer rail, and its return via a central rail, the two running rails could be fed independently by a low-voltage ac current. When a train enters a section of track it completes the circuit set up by this current in the running rails (the 'track circuit'). The completed circuit can light an indicator switch in a control cabin, and set to red a signal protecting the block section from following trains. Together with a trip-cock which ensures that any train passing the red signal will cut off power, the system makes collision between following trains on a single track almost impossible. Later versions of the track circuit principle on surface railways no longer require complete independence of circuit and traction currents, and are thus compatible with the third rail or overhead wire supply systems as well as the London Transport four-rail system.

In theory, complete automation of urban railways is possible, and it has been partially achieved on London's Victoria Line. High frequency pulses, at about 35 cycles per second, vary in frequency to indicate, through the traction supply, rates of acceleration, maximum speed and retardation. The function of the driver is confined to that of supervising passenger loadings at station platforms (with the aid of closed-circuit TV) and overriding the automatic equipment in cases of emergency. In the long run, complete automation may be possible.

Stations

Much of the labour efficiency inherent in the high passenger:train-crew ratios of urban railways is offset by high labour costs of station staff. The first stage in reducing these costs normally comprises the adoption of a simple fares structure, either flat rate or coarsely graded (such as London's 10p, 15p, etc). Service times per passenger, either from staffed office or machine, are thus reduced. Depending on the complexity of the network, an almost complete elimination of station staff to sell tickets can be achieved.

A more critical cost, especially at evenings and weekends, when working hours are inconvenient, is that of staff to check tickets at barriers. On a flat-fare system a simple turnstile may be adequate. For multi-fare systems, barriers can be evolved to 'read' the tickets to ensure validity, which then admit passengers to the platform. London Transport has been involved heavily in such work, using magnetically coded tickets sold from modified conventional coin slot machines with, in latest work, open gate barriers which remain open to the passenger unless an invalid ticket is presented.

A major limitation of the LT system is its inability to deal with season tickets and passes, creating delays or the need for numerous extra ticket staff during the peak period. British Rail have partly overcome this problem by use of multi-journey magnetically coded tickets on the Glasgow to Gourock and Wemyss Bay lines, using ticket barriers similar to those on the LT system.

Multi-journey and graduated-fare tickets can also be issued from multi-ticket machines, in which the passengers press buttons to indicate ticket fare, type and/or destination, and insert required money. Such machines may be found in London at Broad Street, and in Paris. Their use is limited mainly by cost, passenger familiarity and service times.

Where all passengers can use automatic machines, or have unlimited travel monthly cards (see Chapter 6), inspection at barriers can be eliminated altogether. Ticket inspection then takes place on trains, with on-the-spot fines for passengers without tickets. Such a system requires reliable issuing machines, so that passengers can be certain of obtaining a ticket, and intensive inspection, usually by squads of inspectors on a single train. In Britain, parliamentary approval has not been given to requests for such powers, but in many continental cities, Hamburg and Rotterdam for example, such powers do exist. Provided the system is accepted by the public, very large manpower savings, and reductions in delay in boarding at stations, can be obtained.

In designing stations it is desirable to minimize the number of changes of level, make such changes as are necessary easier by use of escalators and lifts, and prevent conflicting pedestrian flows in passageways. In order to supervise lightly manned or unmanned stations effectively, short passageways, preferably straight, well lit and without 'blind spots' are desirable, in order to deter vandalism and attack.

Escalator width required for a single person is about 60 cm, 80 cm with luggage, or 1 metre to allow overtaking. In order to reduce energy consumption created by continuous operation, escalators may be activated by a passenger breaking a photo-electric beam.

Passages and other entrances leading directly on to a platform should be located at different points on successive stations so as to distribute passenger loadings throughout a train. If only one entry can be provided, then the midpoint is best, if two (or separate entry and exit), then one at quarter length from each end of the platform. The situation to be avoided if possible is the repetition of the same entry/exit positions at successive stations, which result in parts of the train being overcrowded, others almost empty. The terminal station layout is particularly ill-suited to suburban operation, as boarding passengers may concentrate at only one end of the train, while seats at the other end remain empty. Further arguments for through running in place of terminal working may be found in Chapter 5.

At interchanges, differences in level between routes may be inevitable, but where different routes run parallel, cross-platform interchange may be possible, or interchange through short horizontal passageways between adjoining tunnels containing platforms. Many recent London underground stations, such as those at Oxford Circus and Stockwell, incorporate such features.

Track and structures

The cross-sectional size of urban rolling stock is determined primarily by the height of standing passengers, use of standard rail gauge, and the clearance required for motors and equipment below the train floor. A box section of 3·5 metres square is typical. Where electric power is supplied from overhead wires, a vertical clearance of about 4·5 metres may be required. More limited clearances may apply to LRT systems based on upgraded tramways. Swept area on curves is a function of radius, lateral overhang and length. On LRT systems, relatively short or articulated cars may be used to permit continued operation over street tracks, as in Amsterdam. Ends of cars may be tapered to reduce overhang on curves.

Surface tracks may be relatively simple, although welding of rail joints is now common as a means of ensuring a smoother ride. At merging junctions on LRT systems, pointwork may be set to admit trains from either direction at low speeds. LRT systems may also be operated within pedestrianized areas, especially where tramways have been established for many years. Bremen was one of the first major European cities to pedestrianize its centre in the early 1960s. The trams, now being upgraded to LRT, remain the only vehicles in major shopping streets. The swept area of the cars is indicated by distinctively coloured paving.

Where land is not available, the cheapest alternative alignment is an elevated structure. Such an alignment may also be a means of avoiding conflict on the same level between rapid transit and other vehicles. (Close headway operation makes any interruption undesirable, and breaks are required in conductor rails.) This solution was common on early systems, and substantial sections may still be seen in American cities, and Paris. However 'environmentalist' demands are nothing new, and on recent lines this system is confined mostly to sections where topography dictates its use, it remains cheap – axle weights rarely exceed 10 or 12 tonnes – and may be acceptable in industrial areas or those of low density population.

An underground alignment became necessary in the largest cities in the nineteenth century because of high land costs and environmental demands. Most systems are subways, aligned not more than about 10 metres below the surface and usually built by 'cut-and-cover' methods, often along existing major roads. The first London lines, such as the Metropolitan, were of this pattern, but at a very early stage clearances at this level were already restricted by existing railways, sewers and the Thames. The deep-level tubes were therefore built, such as the Bakerloo and Piccadilly, in which train and track were constrained within a tube built by shield tunnelling, of about 3·5 metres diameter. Such an alignment should be regarded solely as one imposed by necessity. Although tunnelling costs per mile in the central area may be no higher than for 'cut and cover', and the need for compensation to adjoining property for nuisance during construction be less, station construction is much more costly. The driving of short tunnels for station platforms, and inclined ones for escalators cannot easily be mechanized. Operating costs, notably those of escalators, are higher than for subway stations. The passenger access time from surface deters use of tube lines for short trips. Whereas a subway line can cater both for suburban trips and trips within the central area, tube lines require costly duplication by bus. The Londoner's habit of referring to all underground railways as 'tubes' is inaccurate in his own city and even more so in respect of other cities. Only Moscow offers another major example of this type.

Sharp curves are undesirable, creating passenger discomfort, and dangerous alignment for station platforms. Older London tubes followed surface roads in order to avoid legal complications from 'mining' below private property. The Victoria Line is more directly aligned, so that all station platforms are straight, enabling supervision of passenger loading by the driver/operator.

An American study suggests the following approximate costs for a two-track route, here converted to £ per kilometre:

	£ *million*
On surface	2·0
Elevated	4·0
Bored tunnel/tube	11·0
Cut and cover:	
CBD	12·0
suburb	6·0
Per station:	
subway	3·0
surface/elevated	1·0
tube	5·0

In aligning a route it is obviously desirable to avoid waterlogged or unstable ground if possible, though the engineer may have little choice when following major passenger desire lines. Contrary to common opinion, London clay does not offer marked advantages. Although its softness makes driving a shield relatively easy, continuous support from steel or concrete rings is necessary. The Stockholm 'Tunnelbana', constructed through granite and including sections of bored tunnel, was completed at much lower cost per track-kilometre. Once the tunnel has been driven by blasting, the adjacent rock is often self-supporting and tunnel lining not required.

New rapid transit modes

The revival of interest in public transport of the 1960s saw many new schemes, many of which have now been rightfully discarded as irrelevant. Inventors took little account of the basic system characteristics defined above. Maximum acceleration rates, for example, are defined not by rail technology, but by passenger tolerance. Overall speeds can be improved by wider station spacing, but this again is dependent on passengers' willingness to walk further or use other feeder modes. Alignment is often dictated by social factors. If an elevated railway – or as the 'Westway' case showed, motorway – is unacceptable due to effects of noise and visual intrusion, why should a monorail or hovercraft vehicle be able to follow such a practice? Many monorail schemes in particular displayed a remarkable ignorance of these facts, happily proposing support columns along dual carriageway reservations, and structures up to 7 metres high or more outside houses. Unrealistic average speeds (given proposed station spacing and passenger tolerance of acceleration) were suggested.

For the record, two monorail systems remain of importance, and some examples of both are operated, mostly in Japan. The Alweg system comprises a beam track which is straddled by the vehicle. The Safège system comprises an inverted U cross-section track, from which the vehicle is suspended; total height of structures is thus greater than that of the Alweg for a given clearance above the ground. In both systems, pointwork is complex and formation of long trains difficult to achieve. A variant of Safege, the URBA, utilizes a reverse hovercraft principle, in which air is sucked in around the bogies within the U-shaped track to support the vehicle while minimizing physical contact with the track. An appreciably smoother ride may thus be possible. Monorails offer no advantages over existing modes in reducing staffing or energy costs.

Variants of existing modes include the Bay Area system (BART) around San Francisco, and the pneumatic system evolved in Paris. The latter – *le métro sur pneumatiques* – offers very high acceleration rates without wheel-slip (due to greater friction between concrete and rubber), and some reduction in noise. After initial general use, and export to Montreal and Mexico City, the system is being confined within Paris mostly to conversions of older elevated lines, where noise reduction is of particular importance. The BART system uses conventional steel wheel/rail technology, but with futuristic rolling stock design and control systems. The latter in particular have proved an expensive failure, and BART as a whole has been an extravagant project, in many ways deterring interest in rapid transit. The new Lindenwold line, in Philadelphia, though less well known, is an excellent example of using existing technology but maximizing performance by high acceleration trains, wide station spacing (with many park-and-ride feeder trips) and unstaffed stations.

Air cushion or magnetic levitation is likewise a gimmick in the urban context. Toronto's magnetically supported test route is now to be built as conventional LRT, following withdrawal of the West German government's support for Krauss-Maffei, which had tendered successfully for construction.

Such comments are not intended to dismiss the case for improvements in rapid transit technology. Noise levels are often too high, and if tunnelling costs were reduced many more schemes would become viable. The latter, however, are often due as much to social constraints, such as limits on 'cut-and-cover' work, as geological ones.

Major contenders for new rapid transit schemes are the busway and 'Minitram'. Fully segregated busways would be subject to most of the alignment constraints that affect rail rapid transit, but might offer lower signalling and station costs. Intermediate stations and terminals would require more space than comparable rail facilities, due to longer boarding times per vehicle. The system would also require more skilled driving staff than rail, but a major advantage would be the ability to run 'through' services beyond the segregated route into medium-density housing areas. It is unfortunate that supporters of busways have concentrated largely on their alleged savings in replacing existing railways (often failing to compare like with like) instead of their role for extending the existing network of reserved track public transport through conversion of existing bus routes. Minitram offers the advantage of small unmanned vehicles which can offer high-frequency services throughout the day without high labour costs. However, unmanned operation is already possible within existing rail technology, and limited mainly by social acceptability. Passenger, rather than technical constraints, are almost always the most critical.

References and further reading

The February and April 1973 issues of *Rail International* contain many useful papers on existing rapid transit systems, which have formed a base for parts of this chapter. They include:

Charles, J. and Meyer, M. (1973) 'Capacity of suburban lines', February.
Heise, H. and Weiner, L. (1973) 'Planning and development of S-Bahn networks . . . in the German Federal Republic', April.
Lefebvre, M. and Depaemelaere, D. (1973) 'Brussels: twenty years' operation with urban rail connection', February.
Portefaix, A. and Boileau, R. (1973) 'Rolling stock for suburban services', February.

Examples of recent conventional systems may be found in:
Hellewell, D. S. (1974) 'S-Bahn in Hamburg', *Modern Railways*, January, pp. 24–8.
Manchester Corporation (1967) *Manchester Rapid Transit Study*, vol. **2**. Evaluates new modes.
Relton, E. and Walker, P. J. (1970) *Modern Tramway*, July, pp. 228–36, on the Lindenwold line.
Tyne & Wear Passenger Transport Executive (1973) *A Plan for the People*.
Urban Railways and Rapid Transit (1971) IPC Business Press. A study manual.

Light rapid transit systems have been advocated for many years by the Light Railway Transport League (LRTL), some of whose publications are to professional standard.
Walker, P. J. (1973) *Light Rapid Transit*, rev. edn, LRTL. A basic account.
The LRTL monthly journal, *Modern Tramway*, gives extensive foreign news and other features.

Automatic ticket systems
Modern Railways (1972) on the Glasgow system, May.
Sharp, B. F. (1973) 'Automatic fare collection on LT Executive', *Railway Engineering Journal*, May.

Energy consumption on urban railways

Dover, A. T. (1965) *Electric Traction*, 4th edn, Pitman. (Somewhat dated.)

Scott, M. (1973) 'Energy consumption on urban railways', *Modern Railways*, December, pp. 482–5.

Rolling stock

Jowett, W. G. (1973) in *Open University Technology Course, File T100*: discusses rolling stock design. This source contains also papers on personal rapid transit and busways.

5 Urban network planning

The demand

The task of a traffic manager or transport planner is to effect the best compromise between the desired trips of separate users and the characteristics, particularly speed and cost, of the modes available.

An inevitable result is that very low, or widely dispersed, traffic flows are not catered for by public transport. The minimum viable average load for a bus service at typical fare levels is about ten to fifteen passengers throughout the day. As yet, few come below this level, save for certain weekend and evening services.

Within towns of less than about 200 000 population, there is rarely sufficient demand to justify regular public transport services over circumferential routes between suburbs, except where convenient ring roads exist, or where development has taken place on a multi-centred pattern from previously separate settlements.

In the population range of about 200 000 to one million the great majority of regular services are also radial, but substantial circumferential flows exist, often justifying circular or semicircular bus routes within the inner residential areas. Such services are not well known, and rarely feature in major plans. However, they may be operated at very close headways (three minutes in the case of Manchester's route 53) and also be among the most profitable, as their traffic includes a high proportion of non-work trips and tends to flow in both directions during the peak period.

In cities of one million or above, the structure consists of a conurbation developed from previously separate settlements, each of which often remains an urban centre in its own right, and may until recently have controlled its own bus fleet. Separate networks have coalesced to create interurban links, and are overlaid by heavier long-distance commuting flows to the conurbation centre. Such a pattern is particularly noticeable in Greater Manchester, in which Bolton, Stockport and other towns are to a large extent separate centres with their own networks. Large city centres generate substantial internal demand, for which circular or shuttle bus services are now becoming common to serve commuters and shoppers, as in Manchester. They are rarely profitable, but encourage use of the network as a whole.

Rail rapid transit is common on major routes within cities of one million or above, but is rarely justified for non-radial flows, save for some light rapid transit feeder lines and, in the very largest cities (London, Moscow), some routes in the inner suburbs.

A noteworthy exception to the above comments are school or work journeys provided by special services to trading estates, large factories or educational institutions not in the central or inner areas. The probability of such attractor being able to justify a network of bus services is largely related to its size and concentration of the workforce. A small factory may operate a few minibuses driven by its own employees to meet demands of those without cars. A large trading estate, such as Trafford Park in Manchester, can justify its own peak-period bus networks which cover virtually every major radial corridor within the city.

Evolution of urban form in Britain

Until the late nineteenth century urban growth was virtually uncontrolled, save for a few attempts at comprehensive development, such as Saltaire near Bradford, or by the Great Western Railway at Swindon. Housing conditions were insanitary, often with very little open space, and frequent multi-occupation. Industry and housing were intermixed. Partly as a result of this, average length of the journey to work was very low, and walking or cycling sufficed in most cases.

Early attempts at planning

The first national attempts to control this pattern came in the Public Health Acts of the 1870s, in which minimum standards of housing design were specified. This so-called 'bye-law housing' soon became commonplace and can still be seen in many urban areas – lines of two-storey terraced housing spaced at minimum authorized distances. When occupied by single families such housing accounts for an average density of about 150 persons per acre (or 340 per hectare).

The reaction against the living conditions of Victorian cities continued, leading to the 'New Town' or 'Garden Suburb' move-ment. Writers such as Ebenezer Howard in 1898 proclaimed the advantages of life surrounded by green open space, in which housing and industry were separated. Rapid transit links between the areas of housing and industry thus separated were implicit in the concept.

Although private consortia began building Garden Cities (notably Welwyn), the major impact was on suburban development from 1919 onwards, a period characterized both by the first large-scale municipal schemes in Britain, and the 'semi-detached' boom of the 1930s. The low density concept remained, but without the related planning of local facilities. This development – infilling areas between tramway routes and covering points beyond them – was made possible by the growth of bus services and private-car ownership.

The growth of motor traffic also demanded better roads, first in surfacing of existing roads, then widening, followed by construction of entirely new roads. In the Victorian period some cities completed major schemes in central areas, such as New Street in Birmingham and the Embankment in London, but the major growth during the twentieth century was in improvement of principal radial roads beyond the limit of the then built-up areas, and construction of bypasses or ring roads. Dual carriageways were built where resources permitted, such as Queen's Drive in Liverpool, but often enlarged single carriageways were provided. The period up to 1939 saw the inception of many such schemes, some forming complete rings, some still unfinished, such as the North Circular in London.

Parallel to the 'Garden Suburb' of the interwar period was the 'neighbourhood unit' concept. Writings of Perry in the USA and Unwin in Britain, were based on the vision of a relatively small-scale community permitting face-to-face contact, yet of sufficient size to justify facilities such as primary schools and shops. Wythenshawe, Manchester, is probably the earliest example in Britain. Within the neighbourhood unit, most facilities would be within walking dist-ance, and through traffic would be routed around the area rather than through it. In the case of Wythenshawe, the design was based on major roads called 'Parkways'; these were surrounded by land-scaped strips, and, unlike most new major roads of this period, did not provide direct access from minor roads and houses. Similar developments occurred in other European cities, albeit at higher density, but with the noteworthy difference that municipal tramways were normally projected through the area, enabling public transport to offer good accessibility with little environmental disturbance. This was the case in the new suburbs of Stockholm, such as Nockeby. Some British cities also emphasized tramway development, notably Leeds, but in London large estates were built poorly located with respect to railways. Wythenshawe was served entirely by buses, which were compelled to use the roads designed for through traffic, with only limited penetration into the housing areas.

In 1942 there was published *Town Planning and Road Traffic* by H. Alker Tripp, an Assistant Commissioner of Police who had made a study of traffic accidents. He suggested that effective reduction could be obtained only by segregating various types of traffic, in particular pedestrians and cyclists, from through motor traffic. The latter would be confined to a network of purpose-built roads without direct access. The areas thus bounded by through, or arterial, roads were named 'precincts'.

New Towns and redevelopment

The postwar period in Britain saw some plans on the basis of segregating through road traffic, notably Abercrombie's Greater London Plan of 1944, but few were implemented in existing urban areas. The emphasis was on replacing housing stock lost during the war, and improving existing housing stock. Rapid growth of municipal housing took place, often with little regard for transport, and at significantly lower densities than earlier forms. Around London, the 'first generation' of New Towns were built, including Stevenage, Bracknell and Basildon. Here densities were in some cases very low, down to 30 persons per acre (30 ppa) net in the case of Crawley. The neighbourhood unit principle was applied, with typical unit sizes of 6000 to 10000 people. Major roads, often dual carriageways, were segregated from the neighbourhood units, forming a radial network with some cross-linking. Industrial areas were concentrated and separated from housing. This created sharp peaks in traffic, concentrated at a few intersections. Little account was taken of the need to provide direct bus routes penetrating the residential areas. Town centres were not located near railways, nor served by convenient stations until very recently (as in Stevenage and Basildon).

Rapid growth in car ownership was partly responsible for the change in New Town concepts during the 1950s. Towns of the 'second generation' such as Peterlee and Skelmersdale were built around high-capacity road networks, incorporating multi-level intersections, and defining more sharply than before boundaries of residential areas. The neighbourhood unit concept was watered down, and more housing concentrated at higher density within walking distance of the town centre. Within the residential areas the Radburn principle was adopted – a pattern introduced around 1930 in the USA, named after Radburn, New Jersey, where it was first applied. Within 'superblock' areas, low density housing was grouped around courtyards served by cul-de-sac roads for cars, facing outwards on to green open space. This made routeing of bus services through the areas almost impossible; they were thus confined to the peripheries of residential areas, and took indirect routes to the centre. Ironically, most of the second generation towns were built in regions of exceptionally low car-ownership and high bus use, and housed people displaced from inner areas of cities such as Liverpool who were accustomed to intensive services. Access to railways was also very bad: none of the second generation New Towns has a railway station adjacent to its main centre. The Radburn principle was also adopted to a limited extent in piecemeal developments around existing urban areas.

The 1950s also saw redevelopment of poor condition, high density housing in inner areas of cities. Partly in order to provide replacement housing at a similar net density, the building of blocks of flats of up to twenty storeys became popular, with results that are well known. The communal open space thus provided was not perceived in the same manner as gardens attached to individual houses, facilities for children were poor, and unreliability of lifts added to the unpleasantness of life. From the public transport viewpoint however, existing bus services at high frequencies were able to continue, and to benefit from a relatively high population density. Private car use was partially discouraged by the distance of garages and parking spaces from flats, coupled with dangers of vandalism.

The 1960s saw yet another series of changes in attitude. Towards the end of the decade, the concept of 'high rise' was condemned, to be replaced by 'slab' development of three or four storeys at similar net densities, and, under the 1969 Housing Act, grants to rehabilitate existing housing in good structural condition. At the same time, many private schemes on the fringe of urban areas, or 'adventitious' settlements in rural areas, were built at successively lower average densities, making provision of public transport services exceptionally difficult.

The third generation of New Towns, designed during the 1960s and now coming into existence, display a much greater emphasis on transport. Runcorn is laid out on a figure-of-eight pattern, which is followed by a high-capacity all-purpose expressway, and also, parallel to it and passing through the centres of neighbourhood units, a busway. By placing public transport on a segregated track, the advantages of good penetration of housing areas can be obtained together with a high average speed. Redditch incorporates busways, of which there are also short sections in Washington, Co. Durham. On the other hand Milton Keynes and to some extent Telford, are designed almost exclusively around the concept of the private car. A grid road structure based on American analysis of the 1950s permits a spread of traffic over the network such that few high-capacity/high-cost multi-level intersections are required.

Housing densities

Two measures must be distinguished: 'gross' residential density is that estimated from the area population divided by total land area, including major roads, schools, open space, etc. 'Net' density is that of the area actually occupied by houses, private gardens, access roads, etc., and thus somewhat higher than 'gross' density for the same area.

Table 5.1   *Typical levels of housing densities*

	Net density: Persons per	
Housing type	*acre (ppa)*	*hectare (ppha)*
High density Victorian housing, multi-occupation (e.g. inner London)	200	450
Inner city redevelopment, slab or tower blocks	100 to 150	230 to 280
Council estates and high density private estates, semi-detached	40 to 80	110 to 180
Private estates, some municipal housing in New Towns	20 to 40	50 to 90

In the above, a household size of about three persons is assumed: the average is tending to decline, as more old people live in households of one or two persons, and size of completed family falls. Typical semi-detached development comprises ten to fourteen houses per acre, the latter a maximum if each is to have a garage attached.

Much modern development is based on yet lower densities.

Although in line with personal wishes, this runs against the need to conserve scarce agricultural land and other resources. The fall in average household size is associated with an increasing proportion of households not including children, and unlikely to want extensive gardens. There is a case both for greater variety in the density of new housing and an increase in average density.

Costs are related to density. At the highest extreme, health may suffer, as in Victorian cities (for contrast with the above table, the Gorbals in Glasgow reputedly reached a density of 1000 ppa). In the case of blocks of flats above three or four storeys the cost per unit rises as greater structural strength, lift shafts, etc. are required. Stone's estimates of 1957 updated to 1967 suggest that construction costs excluding land costs, were minimized at about 70 ppa, with two- or three-storey dwellings.

Much development on agricultural land is at levels well below this, incurring the following resource costs:

1 Basic services such as gas, telephone, electricity and water require a greater length of pipe or cable to serve each residence, increasing capital and maintenance costs.
2 Other services such as postal deliveries and public transport provision require regular servicing of the household. A lower density increases the cost of maintaining a given level of service, which becomes increasingly severe as labour costs rise.
3 Opportunity cost of agricultural land in its original use.

Little incentive to higher densities is given by present rating and rent levels, and costs such as those of postal delivery are not perceived directly by the householder. From the public transport viewpoint the situation is worsened by the stimulus given to car ownership by low densities, both from the ability to garage a car at home, and the necessity to own cars to make trips that would normally be within walking distance (e.g. to a corner shop).

As an example, consider a square area of 100 hectares to be developed at 100 ppha average, housing 10000 people. Assuming only one bus route in the area (see Figure 5.1), the average walking distance to the bus route would be 250 metres. If densities were changed to encourage public transport, by developing the 20 hectares adjacent to the bus route at 200 ppha and the remainder at 75 ppha, the average walking distance would be cut to 200 metres. The higher density would be appropriate for old people and childless couples (who are also less likely to own cars), the lower for families. By

D

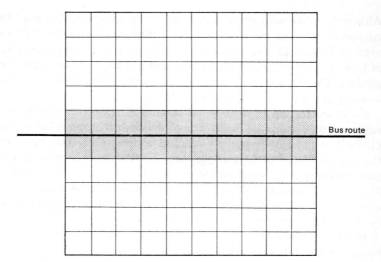

Bus route

Figure 5.1 Housing densities around a bus route

routeing reserved track public transport (a busway for example) through the centre of the area and locating major roads on the periphery, access to public transport could be almost as good as that to car parking areas.

Design of public transport networks

Stop spacing

The elements of total time in a single trip comprise:

Walk to public transport stop or station
Board vehicle
Vehicle accelerates to steady speed ⎫
Vehicle runs at steady speed ⎪ Cycle repeated for
Vehicle decelerates to stop ⎬ each intermediate
Intermediate stop time ⎪ stop
Alight from vehicle ⎭
Walk to destination *or* interchange point for further public transport journeys forming part of a linked trip.

Interchange could occur for several reasons: to save time by using a fast mode, to reduce cost by using a mode on which economies of scale are obtained from greater vehicle size, and/or to improve comfort. Transfer may often be enforced involuntarily by the lack of a through service (an aspect considered below). Walking and cycling may be affected by weather conditions so as to make short public transport trips attractive. In many cases interchange to a larger vehicle also coincides with the use of a faster mode, for example in transfer from bus to rapid transit route.

In the urban situation total travel time is usually the most important criterion in system design. As shown in an appendix to this chapter, an expression can be derived for the components of total trip time listed above, incorporating speed and average length of walking or other feeder trips, length of 'line haul' trip, vehicular speeds and acceleration rates. The 'line haul' sector of the trip is that which takes place on the major public transport mode in question. In conditions of a fairly uniform population density along the whole route, with some concentration around stops or stations, the feeder trip length is equal to about one-quarter of the average spacing between stops.

For a given set of speeds, acceleration rates and trip lengths, the expression thus derived can be simplified to incorporate only one unknown quantity, average spacing of stops or stations. If spacing were very close total trip time would be high, since each passenger's journey on the major mode would be interrupted by numerous intermediate stops. On the other hand, if average stop spacing were very wide, feeder trip times would lengthen, outweighing the benefits

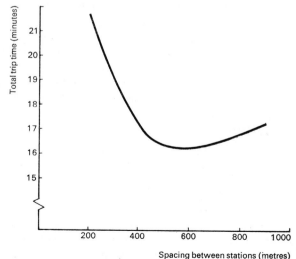

Figure 5.2 Optimal stop spacing to minimize total travel time

of a faster 'line haul' sector. A typical situation is shown in Figure 5.2. By differentiating the expression, as shown in the Appendix, the minimum point can be calculated. By substituting different values for acceleration, speed of the feeder mode, etc. 'trade-off' stituations between these variables can be illustrated. Four relationships can be derived:

1 If acceleration and/or retardation is increased, optimal spacing will narrow (i.e. an intermediate stop imposes a smaller time penalty).
2 If running speed attained after acceleration increases, optimal spacing will widen (i.e. an intermediate stop imposes a greater time penalty).
3 If the speed of the feeder mode is increased, optimal spacing will widen.
4 If stop time is reduced, optimal spacing will narrow (as for 1).

Many examples of these effects can be quoted. As Newell and Vuchic (1968) have argued, replacement of walking or feeder bus trips by park-and-ride substantially increases feeder trip speed, and hence optimal spacing becomes wider. Recent American systems, such as the Lindenwold line in Philadelphia, illustrate this trend. Many well-established systems in inner urban areas already incorporate features such as high acceleration rates and sliding doors (see Chapter 4) in order to minimize the penalty imposed by numerous intermediate stops. On intercity modes increased maximum speeds are associated with elimination of intermediate stops. This is even more marked in proposals for very high speed modes. The tracked hovertrain study suggested that insertion of three stops of two minutes each in a 100-mile trip would reduce average speed from a cruising rate of 250 mph to 168 mph (400 to 270 km/h).

Most urban flows are concentrated on the central area, hence loadings on vehicles or trains will be heaviest on the inner sections of radial routes. The penalty imposed by an intermediate stop is greater the closer towards the centre it is located. A poorly used intermediate stop thus sited may impose greater costs on passengers already on board than benefits to those boarding, who may often have the choice of local bus services. Estimates made in the Merseyside Area Land Use Transportation Study suggested that certain stations on the inner sections of the Southport/Ormskirk–Liverpool lines would not be justified, for this reason. In other cases, limited-stop bus operation in inner suburban areas may be justified where parallel services exist, as on the Wythenshawe–Manchester flows, served by all day limited-stop services.

A constraint on stop spacing exists in that if a comprehensive public transport network is to be provided an upper limit is imposed by walking distances. Experience of transport operators, together with some theoretical work in the Runcorn New Town Master Plan suggests that about 500 metres is the maximum distance over which most passengers are prepared to walk to a bus stop. This is equivalent to about five minutes' walk for the average adult, but can be up to twice as long for a woman with a pram, or an elderly person. If operators can minimize walking distances for these groups, off-peak traffic may be stimulated. In Oxford, buses but not cars run along and stop within major shopping streets, encouraging both extra off-peak traffic from 'captive' public transport users, and diversion from cars (using park-and-ride services described below).

Typical stop spacing on urban bus networks is about 400 to 500 metres, creating a series of overlapping catchment areas (Figure 5.3). Passengers tend to walk in the direction of their ultimate destination, especially if a fare stage is located at the next stop. This phenomenon may be much more acute in the case of park-and-ride traffic, in which 'railheading' occurs, that is the motorist drives as far as possible towards his ultimate destination before transferring to the public transport network.

From the calculations above one can suggest closer spacing in areas where, or at times when, many old people travel; their walking speed is lower, hence optimal spacing will be lower. Conversely, on routes dominated by commuter traffic, a wider spacing may be appropriate.

In the case of railways, capital and operating costs arising from provision of intermediate stations are much higher than for buses: minimum stop time is greater, as numerous doors have to be super-

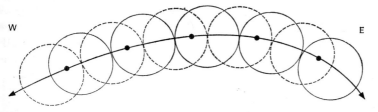

Figure 5.3 Bus route catchment areas eastbound (broken lines) and westbound (solid lines)

vised. Maximum speeds are higher, hence the penalty for an intermediate stop (given specified acceleration/deceleration rates) is also
greater. Due to the need to provide full-height station platforms and
more substantial station buildings, construction and maintenance of
stations is far more costly than for bus or light rapid transit modes.
In underground railways the cost of escalators, underground passageways, etc. incurs totals as high as £5 million for a station on a 'tube'
line. All these factors stimulate wider spacing than in the case of bus
operation.

To a large extent this spacing is accepted by passengers, who are
willing to walk greater distances to rail stations than bus stops, to
use a service of higher quality. German research suggests a gauss
distribution of probability of walking to a station (see Figure 5.4).

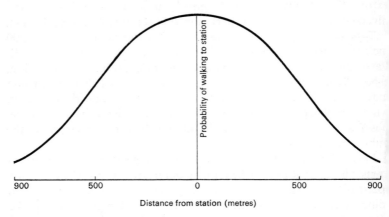

Figure 5.4 Probability of passengers walking to a station

The probability of walking falls gradually to a range of 500 metres
then rapidly down to about zero at 900 metres. Such estimates have
formed the basis for planning housing densities in Stockholm, in
which the innermost zone round a station is reserved for the highest
densities, the outermost for single-family dwellings. In London where
the exceptionally high level of rail use leads to a willingness to walk
even greater distances, a survey in 1969 was unable to detect signifi
cant differences in preparedness to walk within a half mile radius.

Route length and headway

This section is written largely in terms of bus operation, but simila
principles also apply to railways.

After selection of route and frequency for a proposed service – the latter probably a function of peak demand – a running time is derived either from existing experience over similar routes, or from trial runs under different conditions. Many operators set unrealistic conditions in that the same running time is applied both to peak and off-peak working. Research at the University of Newcastle has indicated that greater passenger boarding and alighting time alone may cause a service to run late during the peak, quite apart from effects of traffic congestion.

The number of vehicles and crews required to work a service is equal to the round trip running time (including an allowance for 'layover' time at each end), divided by the proposed headway. For example, if a single trip takes 30 minutes, and 5 minutes layover is allowed at each end, round trip running time will be 70 minutes. If a 10-minute headway is to be operated, 70/10 or 7 buses will be needed. If a 15-minute headway were intended, then the number of buses estimated would be 4·66 – in practice 5. This wastage becomes more serious the wider the headway, and the shorter the round trip time.

It may be possible to interwork two routes at a common terminus so that the combined round trip time is an integer multiple of headway. For example, if the 15-minute headway were desired on the above route, it could be matched with one having a round trip time of 35 minutes (itself using three buses inefficiently on a 15-minute headway). The combined round trip time of 105 minutes divides by 15 to give exactly 7 buses.

Crews are normally paid for a guaranteed day, thus the operator should aim to make maximum use of this period. Legal limits on bus-driving hours set a maximum period of five-and-a-half hours without a break of at least 30 minutes, a maximum per day and per week. Returning to the example above with 105 minutes round trip running time, it can be seen that a driver could not work more than two round trips in succession, although four round trips per day (seven hours) would represent a fairly efficient allocation of shift time. (The shift includes a 'signing on' period for checking the vehicle prior to service, 'paying in' if handling cash and, if taking a bus from a point not adjacent to a depot, travelling time to and from that point. The best proportion of driving time in an eight-hour shift that can be achieved is about 7 hours 20 minutes.)

The majority of crews work on early shifts (from about 0700 to 1600), or late shifts (covering the rest of the day). A substantial number of bus crews, the proportion often limited by union agreement, work 'split' or 'spreadover' shifts, covering both morning and evening peaks. These rarely account for as much as seven hours driving time, and in many cases an opportunity exists to schedule these crews for work between the peaks, increasing service frequencies at only the marginal mileage-based costs.

Interchange

In many cases, passengers have alternative mechanized modes available, either a through bus service in place of a bus/rail trip, a car, or for many optional trips the choice of not making the trip if it is too inconvenient. A significant time-saving is usually required before a passenger will divert voluntarily to a route involving interchange. Indeed, for many interurban passengers, a route involving interchange may not be perceived at all. Not only does interchange itself impose wasted time, especially if services do not connect, but it is also inconvenient. There may be uncertainty about catching a second bus or train, exposure to weather, handling of luggage and/or need to buy another ticket.

Evidence assembled by Wagon and Collins (1973) suggests that this penalty is in the order of two to nine minutes of generalized cost in time units. Estimates are derived from the calibration of modal split or trip distribution models; for example, a value of three minutes was obtained in the Coventry Bus Study. A limitation of such studies is that interchanges clearly vary greatly in quality, but most study areas rarely contain enough of each type (e.g. with and without through tickets) to permit calibration of separate models from statistically significant samples. The penalty is probably far less if through tickets are provided, timetable connections made, and adequate protection from the weather provided. Systems such as Stockholm and Hamburg have succeeded in stimulating substantial increases in public transport use despite numerous interchanges. A noteworthy result of the provision of unlimited monthly travel tickets has been the use by passengers holding them of many more multi-mode links, since the trouble and cost of buying separate tickets is avoided.

Interchanges themselves form another criterion for station location, especially when a new route is being devised in an established area. Between Finsbury Park and Brixton on London's Victoria Line all but one stations are at interchanges with other railways.

If interchange penalties can be minimized, then substitution of line-haul rapid transit for existing through bus services can be envisaged. Slow, unreliable and labour-intensive bus operation in the inner areas of cities can be replaced by reserved track rapid transit, less labour-intensive and of much higher quality. The 'tail ends' of bus services are converted to rail feeders. Such a process is illustrated by a breakeven chart, in Figure 5.5. So far as the operator is concerned, the 'fixed cost' element may be covered almost entirely

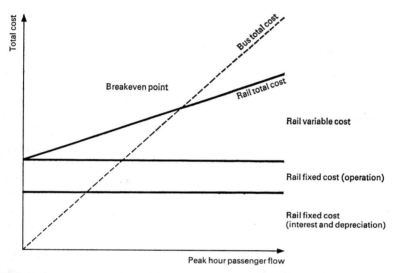

Figure 5.5 A breakeven chart for bus and rail services in an urban corridor

by central and local government grants. Bus total cost increases directly with peak flow (and at high flows buses delay one another, causing further rises in cost). Rail costs increase much more slowly once track maintenance and signalling costs have been incurred. If buses operate on a basis of fares covering total costs, the breakeven point becomes one between cost and revenue as well as one between bus and rail total costs.

Non-central area trips

An acute problem is faced by passengers wishing to travel between non-central points between which the total flow is very small. Unless their trip is coincident with a sector of a route, interchange will be necessary. Existing radial routes across the central area can be connected, cutting layover time in schedules and providing a wider range of through linkages. Problems arise, however, in matching frequencies and types of vehicle employed. In peak periods, congestion within the central area can make services unreliable, hence operation of separate routes may be desirable to reduce the effects of congestion at one point spreading through the network (some changes in the Bristol network early in 1975 were made for this reason).

As the distribution of both journeys to work and off-peak demand becomes more widespread, further measures should be taken to alleviate this problem, including:

1 Operate intersuburban services offering advertised connections and through tickets, with radial routes. This is possible on rail systems, but in bus operation requires very high reliability and simplified ticket issue.
2 Create limited-stop links between major suburban centres. Whereas most heavily loaded radial routes in large cities will justify both rail and bus routes, or at least limited-stop bus services, intersuburban travel is often not only indirect but also confined entirely to conventional bus services. It is noteworthy that some of the most heavily used Green Line limited-stop services in the London area link the major suburban centres with one another rather than with central London (notably the Gravesend–Croydon–Windsor route). Even on the radial Green Line services, the heaviest loads are often between inner and outer suburban centres. Within Greater Manchester a half-hourly limited-stop service, the Trans-Lancs Express, has attracted extra trips between Bolton, Bury, Rochdale, Oldham and Stockport.
3 When existing radial bus routes are converted to rail feeders, adjoining 'tail ends' can be linked (Figure 5.6). Trips to adjoining suburbs can be made without interchange, and longer trips via successive rail/bus interchange stations, which are more likely to provide facilities such as shelters and enquiry offices than at bus stops.

In the long run, a satisfactory solution to problems of intersuburban public transport services can be found only through changing land uses (see below).

Park-and-ride (P & R)

Despite wide interest, this feeder mode is confined to a relatively

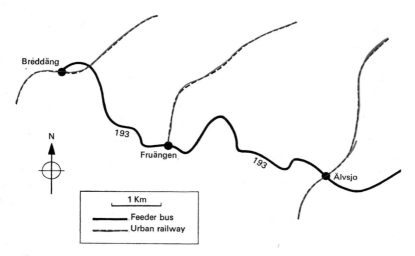

Figure 5.6 Use of rail feeder bus services as intersurburban facilities: an example in south-west Stockholm

small number of situations, mostly in outer suburban situations in which local bus services are thin on the ground, and housing densities such that a walk to the railway station is not feasible. Some spontaneous development has occurred, but to an increasing extent P & R is being deliberately encouraged by provision via transport operators or local authorities of car parks adjacent to stations. Many of these are on former railway goods yards, especially around London, not always ideally shaped or sited. Until recently site values in suburban areas and relatively low demand militated against plans for multi-storey car parks. However, the Greater London Council now consider demand sufficient to justify such a park at Boston Manor, where the A4 crosses the Piccadilly Line in west London.

Reference has been made above to 'railheading' by motorists. This tends to reduce public transport revenue without corresponding changes in cost. The innermost sections of peak hour services are still required, with associated track, station and operating costs. If the point of transfer can be placed as far as possible from the central area along the rail route, the position of the operator will be improved, since marginal costs of additional train mileage are relatively low, whereas fares increase substantially with distance. A recent example of an attempt to induce such diversion is the closure by London Transport of its car park in Finchley Road, located only three miles from the central area. Surveys established that users came from destinations well to the north, and could use other railway stations.

A certain amount of time is usually required as a net saving before a traveller will divert from through services to those involving interchange (see above). To a private car user, even a slow and congested trip over a major road may compare favourably with a rapid transit journey over a short distance, as no walking or waiting time is involved at the home end. Unless there are severe physical or price restraints, voluntary diversion is unlikely for trips of less than about 6 km (a figure suggested by Pampel (1971), based on extensive experience in Hamburg). Generally speaking, one would not expect significant P & R demand within cities of less than 500 000 population, as most cities below this size do not possess rapid transit systems or give rise to many long work trips.

There are, however, some exceptions. A growing number of cities are imposing parking restraint, and buses as well as railways are being used as a P & R mode. In Britain, until 1974, most bus park-and-ride trips were shopping trips, usually made in the weeks before Christmas during which town centre parking capacity was inadequate, special bus services operating from temporary car parks (as in Newcastle and Leicester). In that year, pro-public transport policies were adopted in Nottingham and Oxford (see Chapter 9). Conventional bus services have been improved, and direct diversion from car to bus encouraged by P & R facilities. Within a year, the first two Oxford services were carrying about 10 000 passengers per week, half of which were to or from work. It seems likely that most P & R trips originate in the scattered rural commuter hinterland beyond the city itself. By analogy with the railheading argument outlined above, one could argue that diversion to buses further out from the city should be encouraged. In rural areas, however, service frequencies are rarely better than half-hourly, and unlikely to attract the car user. Most of the P & R trips are probably net gains to public transport.

Some voluntary car feeder trips can be observed to rural and interurban bus services, particularly peak hour journeys into larger cities. A significant number of such trips was discovered in a survey of bus passengers between Morpeth and Newcastle, a trip of over fifteen miles. The high quality of a limited-stop bus service had attracted car users for a surprisingly long trip.

Park-and-ride is also of increasing importance for intercity travel especially rail (see Chapter 8).

The future of park-and-ride has four aspects:

1 A means of enabling existing car trips originating in diffuse, low density areas to transfer to public transport without the need to provide additional low density public transport services. This could be particularly important as fuel costs rise.

2 A means of permitting further dispersal of the population to such areas without the danger of high car mileages being generated. This is more likely to apply at regional level, as small and medium-sized towns increase in importance. Many are not sited on the intercity rail network, but are within a half-hour drive of a railhead. Thus Letchworth, Hitchin, Welwyn and Hertford are served by the railhead at Stevenage. On the local scale such further dispersal should not be encouraged, for reasons connected with costs of low density housing outlined above.

3 A means of enabling severe restriction of private cars in city centres to be implemented without the need to improve bus services over all routes in the network. Demand from fringe areas may be concentrated at certain points from which high-frequency services are offered.

4 On new suburban rail routes, the optimal spacing between stations could increase if a high proportion of feeder trips were by park-and-ride. Capital and operating costs of the railway could be reduced, although parking site availability near stations would be critical.

A variation on park-and-ride is 'kiss-and-ride', in which the passenger is driven to the stop or station – by his wife, for example – so that all-day parking at the station is not required. The car will then be available for use throughout the day, with harmful effects on public transport off-peak revenues. A one-way public transport demand could be created: for example, a lift to the station in the morning, but use of a feeder bus in the evening. This could accentuate peak problems. A good deal of this type of traffic probably exists already, in the form of 'a lift to the station' and car use within a family, but is not easy to detect in a survey.

Public transport networks in low density situations

To a large extent the problem of varying service levels to match low density of demand is met firstly by operating buses instead of railways, and secondly by varying service frequency. Most urban routes operate at regular intervals, the widest being forty or sixty minutes. A number of services can be found, particularly in smaller towns, operating either in peak periods only (as extensions of additional peak-hour short workings of all-day services), or off-peak only. The latter are often designed for shoppers, serving areas in which many elderly people reside, and interworked with a peak service using the same vehicle. The marginal cost of such services is low. In many market towns they may be interworked with peak period rural/ interurban services of the same operator.

Such services are often unsatisfactory, and offer little choice of trip timing. In many towns a moderate daytime service level can be provided, but evening frequencies may fall to levels as low as hourly. Consider Figure 5.7. Each route operates every twenty minutes,

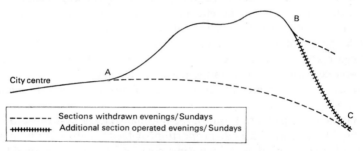

Figure 5.7   An example of evening/Sunday urban network rationalization

falling to hourly after 1800 hours. By combining both routes into a single, less direct, service a half-hourly evening frequency can be offered. Travel time from C to the town centre may be greater, but at such periods there is little traffic congestion, and fewer passengers boarding. It may be possible to operate the more devious route from C to the city centre in the same scheduled time that the direct route requires before 1800.

An example of such diversion comes from changes introduced in Oxford in 1971. On the west side of the city intensive daytime services are provided, including direct services from Headington to the centre. Much of the Headington Road has no housing adjacent, but runs in a cutting between playing fields and gardens. Its use during the day permits valuable time savings for a large number of passengers. In the evening, however, all services were diverted via estates to the north, in order to offer the best available frequency to areas of housing. Apart from the Polytechnic in Headington Road, no substantial traffic generators are deprived of a service. The Oxford policy extends to the entire city network. In some cases, rural/interurban services are merged with city services after 1830 hours, with the same intention. Travel times for passengers to and from the rural areas is extended, but relatively few people are affected. The major problem becomes one of information to passengers, who have to accustom themselves to two networks.

The principle of diverting services in order to combine all available traffic is seen most clearly in the rural situation, and is discussed in Chapter 7.

Another approach to low demand situations is the operation of demand-responsive services, such as 'dial-a-ride'. In view of extensive publicity given to this innovation, which has the effect of greatly overstating its importance, only a brief outline is given here. Two major types of service can be defined:

1 One-to-many – Operation from a fixed point, usually a rail or bus interchange, with variable routeing in low density suburban catchment areas. Fixed timings usually apply at the interchange point and some intermediate points. Most services operated in Britain to date fall into this category: Maidstone, Harrogate, Hampstead Garden Suburb, Abingdon, and Harlow.

2 Many-to-many – Unscheduled operation with a defined area. The route taken by each vehicle is a compromise between requirements of passengers already on board, and those to be picked up. In theory an optimal route could be devised by an on-line computer, and instructions transmitted to drivers from a control centre. In practice routeing is based on manual methods, and to a large extent on the drivers' discretion. Within their pick-up areas, some one-to-many services also fill this role (for example, trips within Hampstead Garden Suburb, although less than 10 per cent of trips this services handles fall into this category). Only one 'many-to-many' service as such is in operation, in Sale, Greater Manchester.

Cost per vehicle-mile of dial-a-ride is not greatly below that for conventional operation. Fuel and maintenance costs of minibuses are slightly less than for full-size vehicles (see Chapter 7) but the major element, drivers' wages, remains. Average speeds may be higher than of conventional bus, mostly because dial-a-ride services operate in suburbs with little traffic congestion. But added to direct operating costs are those of control facilities. A ratio of one controller to three or four vehicles is typical, although productivity may improve as existing schemes expand. At fares of 15p or 25p per passenger trip, about twenty calls per hour per bus are required to break even. The best of existing services – Milton Keynes, Harlow and Hampstead – generate about 600 trips per day, about ten to fifteen per vehicle per hour.

The primary advantage of dial-a-ride is that diversions within low density areas are made only on request, whereas a conventional operation would require far more vehicles, at very poor load factors, to give a similar level of service. They may also be better suited to the distribution of off-peak demand, which includes trips such as visits to friends and relatives, for which a door-to-door service is particularly appropriate. It is of interest that the Sale service, which started in November 1974, is based largely on this attribute, and is aimed at commercially viable operation. Criteria applied by American consultants in selecting suitable areas included customary factors such as high telephone ownership, but also 'a high density of population'. This should be qualified in that a 'high' density in American terms may be moderate or even low in British terms – about twenty to forty persons per acre. None the less, there is very little indication that dial-a-ride offers a profitable means of serving British 'low density' areas. It appears either as a subsidized means of serving such areas, and perhaps using a given subsidy to better effect than if paid to conventional services, or as an alternative means of serving moderate density areas commercially, which is better related to certain types of trip. In both cases connections to a trunk route leading to central areas are desirable.

The general image of dial-a-ride based on receipt of telephone calls and frequent radio messages from controller to driver also requires qualification. First, in a one-to-many situation, passengers joining at the fixed point(s) request the driver to serve a destination, and no radio contact is necessary. On the Hampstead service for example, most passengers in the evening join the vehicle at Golders Green station for a return trip to their homes. Other passengers may board by hailing the vehicle on service within the designated area. Another form of request is by standing order, usually a postcard to the control office, which generates significant demand on the Hampstead service. By this means those without telephones – including many in low-income groups dependent upon public transport – can

ny successful city public transport
ems, such as those of Hamburg
Stockholm, are based upon
rly delineated bus and rail
works. Good interchanges are
ential for such a policy. Seen
is Wansbeck-Markt, Hamburg,
sland' bus station, in the centre
which is located a radio control
ce, and below which is a station
ing two U-bahn lines. The
cle seen is built to the VöV
dard design, adopted by several
ufacturers to criteria laid out by
principal operators' association.
interchange between bus and
is made entirely under cover.
R. White)

ntrast in bus design. Two
cles of the West Riding company,
ographed at Wakefield, illustrate
ge over twenty years. On the
t is a double-decker of the
)s, with vertically-mounted front
ne, and rear entrance – in this
a Guy Arab. On the left is a
cal replacement, a Leyland National
e-decker. This offers a similar
passenger capacity – about sixty
it with a lower proportion
ed) – and is suitable for one-man
ation. The contrasting merits and
cts of these designs – geared
fferent criteria – are discussed on
s 55 to 58. *(J. G. Glover)*

cal of double-deck replacement
eries is this Leyland Atlantean,
mber of the Blackburn
fitted with locally-made East
s bodywork. The functional
ne with 'bustle' for the
mounted engine is typical. The
larity of layouts incorporating a
al staircase and exit has
ppeared in favour of the simpler
e-doorway form. *(P. C. Stonham)*

Contra-flow lanes are among the more effective forms of bus priority, enabling improved access to picking-up points as well as higher running speeds, with little enforcement work. A major problem in this case was that of pedestrian movements. For about ten years, all traffic in Piccadilly, London, flowed eastbound, and pedestrians failed to anticipate buses approaching in the other direction. Additional railings have been erected to channel pedestrian movement into signalled crossings.
(P. R. White)

Express coaches in Britain do not differ markedly from bus designs, save in wider seat pitch and external colour scheme. However, greater luxury is offered by the heavyweight vehicles operated by the Scottish Bus Group on overnight services to London. Seen here is a Bristol RELH of the Western SMT company, with Alexander 'M' bodywork reclining seats and toilet.
(P. R. White)

A minor but important example of railway modernization is the lapped rail joint. Tapered sections of rail overlap to permit some expansion without the discomfort imposed by end-on rail joints. The latter are also more expensive to maintain, and may develop fractures around bolt holes. In this example, photographed on the Southern Region third-rail electric network, the two adjoining rail sections are bonded to ensure current return (similar bonding may be found in sections fitted with track circuits). *(J. G. Glover)*

Among the modern features of heavy rapid transit stock displayed by the Hamburg U-bahn is the use of common bogies between cars as a means of reducing tare weight (P. R. White)

The C69 stock, in use on the Circle and Hammersmith lines of London Transport, is a design adapted to high-density, short-distance movement. Each car is fitted with four sets of double doors to permit rapid loading and unloading. This view, taken at Notting Hill Gate station, also illustrates the typical alingment of a subway line – a tunnel just below the surface, constructed by cut-and-cover methods (note the brick arch in the background). (J. G. Glover)

In contrast to the C69 stock, that built for the Metropolitan Line of London Transport in the early 1960s was designed for longer trips from the outer suburbs. Each car has only two sets of double doors, plus single end doors, and internal seating is arranged in 'five across' layout to maximize seating capacity. Loading, and acceleration, are much slower than in the C69 stock. (J. G. Glover)

To replace its outdated slam-door suburban stock, British Rail is adopting the 'PEP' design. Noteworthy features of the prototype train are the cleaner, more modern outline of bodywork and windows, and the sliding doors. Opening of the doors may be actuated by passengers on the platform by pushing vertical metal guides near the door edge. In experimental trials, it was found that only two sets of double doors were required (the centre set being closed). *(P. R. White)*

Light rapid transit offers a cheaper and more flexible form of rapid transit than full-scale underground railways, but retaining the advantages of electric traction and high peak capacity. The Göteborg system has expanded from a street tram-way into fully-reserved routes. Cars may be operated singly, or, as seen here on the recently-built Hjällbo line, in multiple. *(P. R. White)*

Where street tramway sections remain, other traffic may be excluded, both to remove conflict between trams and other vehicles, and to permit good public transport penetration into shopping precincts. The first such scheme was that in Bremen, adopted in 1964. Public transport only is allowed to penetrate major shopping streets within the central area. An advantage of trams in this situation is the predictability of their movement. Retention of cobblestones has permitted use of a different colour to denote their swept area. *(P. R. White)*

make use of the service. The task of the controller is also simplified, and some advance scheduling possible.

As yet, dial-a-ride services are confined to a limited number of areas, within which they aim to provide an all-day service. Another approach would be to use them at *times* of low demand, evenings and Sundays. Even in high-density urban areas bus loadings at such times may be very low. One solution is network adjustment as in Oxford (above), another, especially in smaller towns, to pull off conventional buses altogether at certain times and run demand-actuated facilities instead. Such an approach would be dependent upon suitable vehicles being available. Sources might include minibuses used in daytime by local coach operators or the post office, and midibuses used on city circle services. Another approach is the use of taxis in place of buses. At times of low demand, the city of Munich offers taxi services at public transport fares in place of some poorly utilized conventional services.

Shaping land-use to support public transport

Many criteria influence land-use plans – site availability, housing policy, industrial demand, etc. – but it is evident that in many plans a certain level of public transport use is implicit. If work trips are relatively centralized and restraint is applied to car trips within the central area, a substantial demand for public transport is produced. Recent planning has also moved towards 'social' objectives rather than simple architectural land-use concepts. A goal of providing a certain minimum level of mobility is now common, and for a significant sector of the population public transport is the only means of providing this. It is therefore incumbent on the planner to consider which patterns of land-use are most favourable to public transport operation, and to consider these in formulating an overall plan. They are not of course the only constraint, and a land-use plan forms a compromise between what is optimal for public transport and what might be optimal under other criteria. For example, provision of more open space might point to a lower gross residential density, needs of public transport to a higher one. In the following discussion the situation is viewed purely from the operator's viewpoint, and in practice concepts suggested would be modified to meet other constraints.

Operating costs incurred for specified service levels are related to the ratio of peak to off-peak demand, average speed and number of routes operated. A simple network is both easier to operate and one which permits good levels of service with minimal interchange, encouraging optional trips. By concentrating traffic on a smaller number of routes, larger vehicles may be used, or rapid transit systems replace conventional buses, with savings in labour cost. The major limitation on such simple networks is the maximum walking distance and/or availability of other feeder modes to reach stopping points. A higher net residential density would permit a given population to be concentrated within a smaller area and hence served by a simpler network. This density argument extends the list already presented in this chapter.

Simplification of networks could also be encouraged by locating complementary land uses along major routes. For example, if schools, offices and shops were located along the same primary routes the need to operate separate peak-hour services for schools and works traffic might be eliminated. By combining different types of trip along the same route, a better standard of service could be justified, and hence a higher probability of a journey at the desired time being available.

Peak to off-peak traffic ratios could be reduced by centralizing to a similar degree trips of different types. In major conurbations employment may be highly centralized, necessitating long work journeys, whereas shopping and educational facilities may be sited in a number of local centres. Principal radial routes thus attract little off-peak traffic. Indeed, excessive work-trip lengths may cause an absolute reduction in off-peak travel (see Chapter 2). Within the peak period a unidirectional flow often occurs at present. If employment is sited at one end of a radial corridor, location of activities generating peak-period trips at the other end of the corridor will generate a two-way flow during the peak. Not only will additional workings in the existing peak flow direction be cut out, but empty seats in the opposite direction will be put to use.

Relocation of offices within the central area can also help to spread the peak. If the average walking time from city termini to offices is, for example, fifteen minutes, then workers due to start work at 0900 will time their arrival at termini for 0845. Construction of a major office block adjacent to a station – the Shell centre at Waterloo for example – permits those working in it to arrive on later trains although starting work at the same time as other office workers. The 'stagger' achieved is small, but perhaps sufficient to eliminate some peak-only extra trains.

The logical conclusion of most arguments above would be a linear pattern, and although no New Towns have been built to such a plan (Irvine being the closest in form) many older industrial settlements, such as the mining valleys of South Wales, approximate to this pattern. The design of Runcorn New Town achieves an ingenious compromise by forming a figure-of-eight loop for public transport, as described on pp. 95–6.

The opportunity for comprehensive redevelopment of urban areas in Britain has largely disappeared, and only incremental changes (or changes in existing uses of buildings) can be expected: a new housing estate for example. However, the principles above remain valid, and could guide such redevelopment as does occur, so that in the long run a satisfactory urban form is produced.

Appendix: A technique for determining optimal interstation spacing

The components of total travel time are defined as on page 98, the notation as:

L	average line-haul trip length per passenger	(metres)
D	average interstation spacing	(metres)
s	station stop time	(seconds)
a	distance covered by train in accelerating to normal running speed, and in retardation from normal running speed (symmetrical speed/time curve assumed)	(metres)
b	time occupied in same process as (a)	(seconds)
V	normal running speed of vehicle or train	(metres/second)
F	average speed of feeder mode to station	(metres/second)
T	average feeder trip length from origin to station	(metres)

As a working approximation, take T as equal to $0 \cdot 25D$

A number of behavioural studies have suggested that passengers experience losses while walking and waiting equal to about twice the average valuation of travelling time. The component for feeder trip time could on this argument be multiplied by two if walking were the feeder mode. Waiting time is a function of service frequency and thus is not affected directly by spacing. It is therefore not considered in this calculation, but walking has been assumed as the feeder mode.

Total travel time = feeder trip time ($\times 2$) + number of intermediate station stops $\times$ station stop time + number of interstation runs $\times$ acceleration and deceleration time + number of interstation runs $\times$ time on each run at steady speed

$$= \frac{T}{F} \times 2 + \frac{L}{D} \times s + \frac{L}{D} \times b + \frac{L(D-a)}{D} \frac{1}{V}$$

In the expression as shown stop time at the station where the passenger boards the train or vehicle is included, since normally he would arrive before the train or vehicle stopped. The values of a and b are calculated for given rates of acceleration and maximum running speed.

In this example the following values are assumed:

L = 5000 metres	T = 0·25D metres
a = 144 metres*	b = 24 seconds*
V = 12 metres/second	F = 1 metre/second
s = 20 seconds	

* Based on a constant acceleration/deceleration rate of 1 metre/second/second

Inserting the values into the equation above we obtain

$$\text{Total time (TT)} = \frac{0·25D}{1} \times 2 + \frac{5000}{D} \times 20 + \frac{5000}{D} \times 24 + \frac{5000(D-144)}{D} \frac{1}{12}$$

$$= 0·50D + 100\,000D^{-1} + 120\,000D^{-1} + 417 - 60\,000D^{-1}$$

$$= 160\,000D^{-1} + 0·50D + 417$$

Differentiating with respect to D we obtain

$$\frac{dTT}{dD} = -160\,000D^{-2} + 0·50$$

By setting the value of this expression equal to zero we can obtain the value of D for which total time is minimized.

$$0 = -160\,000D^{-2} + 0·50$$

Hence $0·50 = 160\,000D^{-2}$

$$D^{-2} = \frac{0·50}{160\,000}$$

$$D^2 = \frac{160\,000}{0·50} = 160\,000 \times 2$$

$$D = 565·6 \text{ metres}$$

The values inserted are typical of an urban railway fed entirely by walking trips, an acceleration rate similar to that of Victoria Line stock and station stop time an average for sliding doors. In practice, a calculation of this type need not be made to within limits of less than ±100 metres, since curvature, location of entrances, etc. will affect site availability, and stations themselves are over 100 metres long.

In the case of bus operation, stop time can be represented as a constant, which for a one-man bus is about four seconds, plus a time per boarding passenger. The latter ranges from about two seconds on systems with simple fare scales and no change-giving up to about six seconds. The boarding time related to the number of passengers could be regarded as a constant total and only the four-second period be included in the optimal spacing calculation. In the long run, however, stop spacing will itself affect demand, and hence total delay caused by boarding passengers. (Widening the stop spacing would cut out some short trips, but encourage more long-distance ones, and vice versa.)

References and further reading

Newell, G. F. and Vuchic, V. R. 'Rapid transit interstation spacings for minimum travel time', *Transportation Science*, **2**, 303–9: optimization of interstation spacing considered on more complex criteria than the approach adopted here.

Pampel, F. (1971) Paper 1(c) of the Union of International Union of Public Transport Congress, Rome.

Peat, Marwick, Mitchell/DoE/Merseyside PTE (1976) Summary Report on Merseyside Interchange Experiments.

Peat, Marwick & Kates, with Millward, C. (of Merseyside PTE) (1973) 'Passenger transport interchanges – theory and practice on Merseyside' *Traffic Engineering and Control*, **14**, 575–80.

Research Projects Ltd (1969) *Modal Choice in Greater London*, provides data on feeder trips to London.

Wagon, D. J. and Collins, P. H. (1973) 'The design and location of urban public transport interchanges', a paper presented at the PTRC annual meeting, University of Sussex (and at the Nineteenth Round Table of the European Conference of Ministers of Transport). Gives a valuable review of literature on interchange design.

Tetlow, J. and Goss, A. (1968) *Homes, Towns and Traffic*, 2nd edn, Faber, for a good general background to British urban planning and its relationship with public transport.

Traffic Research Corporation (1969) Merseyside Area Land-Use Transportation Study (MALTS), *Technical Report no. 24.*

Tripp, H. Alker (1942) *Town Planning and Road Traffic*, E. Arnold.

An approach to public transport network planning derived from land-use/transportation studies is that using generalized cost, a single measure reflecting both direct expenditure and time lost in travel; for simplicity cost and time have been treated separately in this volume. The basic approach is outlined in:

Parker, G. B. (1975) 'Routeing strategy for urban passenger transport services', a paper read at the Sixth Annual Symposium on Operating Public Transport, University of Newcastle. An example of its application may be found in the report of a study in Coventry by the Local Government Operational Research Unit, Report C.149, *Planning Urban Bus Routes*, Reading 1974.

Dial-a-ride services

This subject has been extensively documented. The most comprehensive source is a set of papers produced for the First British Dial-a-Ride Symposium, Cranfield Institute of Technology, 1974. The Sale scheme is described in *Coaching Journal*, **43**, no. 4 (1975).

Note

Since this chapter was written, the Hampstead Garden Suburb D-v-R service has been replaced by a fixed-route minibus service. However, the new D-v-R service in the Solihull area – operated by West Midlands PTE – has established a record level of use, at over 1000 passengers per day.

6 Pricing and costing

Introduction

Although this book is not a work of transport economics, the concentration of most recent texts in that field on cost-benefit analysis and long-term issues has led to neglect of basic questions of costing and pricing. Since a clear understanding of the latter is essential for public transport planning, an outline is given here.

Costs

Public transport operators' costs can be placed in the following categories:

1 *Crews operating vehicles and trains.* In the case of two-man bus operation this category constitutes over half of total costs, for rail, a much smaller proportion, depending on service frequency, track costs, etc.

2 *Fuel and energy.* On stage bus services and railways, which pay no fuel tax, this accounts for about 5 to 10 per cent of total costs. For some operations, however, such as high-acceleration suburban trains, or express coaches (which still pay fuel tax), it can be up to 15 per cent.

3 *Labour cost of maintenance.* As vehicles, control systems, etc. become more complex, this tends to rise; at present it constitutes 10 to 15 per cent of total bus operating costs, and a greater share of rail costs (including track maintenance).

4 *Labour cost of control systems.* Very small (2 or 3 per cent) for bus operations, being confined to salaries of inspectors, and where in use, controllers of radio and TV systems. On railways, signalling costs can form a very high share, due to the labour-intensive nature of block signalling systems (25 per cent or more).

5 *Costs of materials (other than fuel), spare parts, etc.* is affected by

particular types of rolling stock or track. About 5 to 10 per cent of total costs.

6 *Rental of land occupied by depots, tracks, etc.* Usually very low, especially for railways. However, opportunity cost could be high where more valuable alternative uses exist (e.g. railway land in inner areas of large cities).

7 *Depreciation of vehicles, infrastructure, plant, etc.* At present about 10 per cent of total cost for both buses (almost entirely vehicle replacement) and railways. For the latter, average vehicle life is much longer, and depreciation related also to track, signalling, etc. Depreciation has often been historically based, and thus provides inadequate funds for replacement, unless new assets are employed more intensively. This is often the case on the railways. In the bus industry the introduction of new bus grants has partially filled the gap between depreciation provision and the cost of new vehicles.

8 *Non-wage costs of labour.* National insurance, sick pay, welfare facilities, etc. About 5 per cent of total costs, but can be greater where operation is very labour-intensive.

9 *Salaries, expenses, etc., of management.* In the case of the bus industry, this is only about 3 or 4 per cent of total costs. In the railways, however, management and administration accounts for about 15 per cent of the total.

10 *Insurance premiums of vehicles, plant, etc.* About 2 per cent of total costs.

In addition to the above operational costs, in which depreciation has been included, payment of interest upon existing investment is required of privately owned operators, and to a lesser extent, publicly owned concerns. Much of British Rail's capital debt has been written off. Following the 1968 Transport Act its outstanding capital debt was reduced from £1562 million to £365 million. However, the rate of interest paid was increased substantially, so that annual interest payments fell by only £25 million to £41·5 million in 1969. The extent to which even this reduced figure has been 'lost' in the global subsidy under the Railways Act 1974 is not yet clear.

The National Bus Company was established in 1969 with a capital liability of £97·6 million on which interest is paid at 4·92 per cent. It has succeeded in meeting interest and depreciation charges from revenue in most years. But it is now faced by a requirement to pay off the original capital in instalments from 1975, of £10 million per annum. This may have to be met by taking out new loans at higher interest rates. The concept of an organization paying off its capital also applied to many municipal undertakings established by taking over tramway companies. The cost of acquisition was capitalized and paid off from a 'sinking fund'. Many municipal operators succeeded in this, but in consequence built up few reserves for new investment. Many today are dependent entirely on loans from their controlling authorities in order to purchase new vehicles. The notion of paying back original capital invested (except in the sense of a 'pay back' period over which dividends to shareholders equal original investment) is an unjust anachronism imposed on NBC and the Scottish Transport Group.

Major variables in operating cost

Operating cost in the bus industry can be related to three main variables:

1 *Time*. Interest payments on capital, depreciation, management and wage payments are related to the passage of time rather than mileage operated or seats provided.
2 *Mileage*. Fuel, tyres and some maintenance costs are related to mileage directly.
3 *Peak demand*. Changes in peak service provision create needs for changes in the number of vehicles, crews, etc. These in turn affect depreciation, depot costs, wages and salaries. Additional staff employed for the peak hour may often be paid a guaranteed day, irrespective of the amount of time actually spent on duty.

As Moyes and Willis have pointed out, the traditional practice of bus operators in allocating all costs to a single total which is then divided by mileage to give 'average cost per vehicle mile' obscures these major differences. Only recently has it been accepted that the average cost per mile in rural areas may be very much lower, since average speeds are higher. A bus can cover twenty miles in one hour instead of ten or twelve, virtually halving wage costs per km run (this argument is expanded in Chapter 7). The very high cost of peak extras is not yet fully appreciated. The Bradford Bus Study indicates a fixed cost of over £30 per day for an additional bus (to cover depreciation, depot accommodation, regular maintenance inspections, guaranteed shift payments to crew). Marginal costs per km run thereafter are confined to fuel, tyres, and some maintenance – about 6p per km. The problem of allocating maintenance costs has not been resolved. Regular inspections every two or three weeks, plus work for annual DoE inspection are time-based and also labour-intensive, but the probability of parts being replaced is related to mileage.

On the above figures, an additional bus which runs only during the peak periods will incur a cost per mile of £1·50 compared with average costs for a whole fleet of about 45p per mile. A vehicle in service for a guaranteed shift period but no more would incur an average of about 35p per mile. A bus which ran in service for a longer period would have a still lower average cost per mile. But it must be remembered that evening work causes bus driving as a job to be 'unsocial' and hence aggravates staff shortage (requiring more overtime work) and/or creates the need for a premium wage. A 'shadow price' could be imputed for evening and weekend work to reflect this cost. Sunday work – and some on Saturdays – is already paid at higher rates.

In the case of railways, the proportion of total costs related to mileage run is even smaller. Except in cases such as heavily loaded commuter services in London and the south-east, additional peak loads may incur low marginal costs, since they can be accommodated by adding cars to existing trains, or more standing passengers. In addition to the categories of staff, mileage run and peak train costs defined as for buses, costs also vary with:

1 *Track mileage.* This is partly a function of route mileage, but also peak demands, i.e. whether single or multiple tracks are required.
2 *Train weights and speeds.* Track maintenance costs increase as weight of trains rises, and/or maximum speeds increase.
3 *Form of station.* Usually related to traffic density, and ticketing systems, from unstaffed 'paytrain' halts to fully staffed intercity terminals.
4 *Length of day during which services operate.* Supervisory costs are much higher than for bus operation, and most signal boxes are worked by at least two shifts. Hence restriction of services to certain periods of the day and/or week can reduce costs substantially.
5 *Spacing between peak-period trains.* This affects the number of block sections and hence signal boxes. The latter may be affected also by location of junctions, level crossings, etc. under manual operation, since visibility and the effort of working chains, rodding and levers limits the distance from a box at which facilities can be operated (see Chapter 8).

Most costs related to a particular part of the rail network can be regarded as fixed in the short run (about one year, a period within which few major timetable changes occur). In the long run, track and signalling costs can be varied substantially by resignalling or rationalization of track layouts.

Present techniques of cost allocation

The National Bus Company and CIPFA systems

Following criticism by local authorities of subsidy claims for rural services on an 'average cost per mile' basis in 1970–1, NBC set about producing a more realistic method, which has been described by Beetham. The classification of time-based, mileage-based and peak-vehicle-based costs discussed above was adopted. Time-based costs are mainly crew costs. Administration, depot costs and depreciation at replacement cost are related to number of vehicles required for peak service.

By this method, higher average speeds on rural services can be reflected in a reduced cost per mile estimate, and the cost of additional peak-period workings illustrated. There is still some averaging implicit, however, in that each depot is defined as a 'cost centre'. A common proportion of overtime to normal rate working is assigned to each route based on the depot average, and each route bears a share of depot overhead costs. The latter is sensible: in many rural areas the majority of services working from a depot may be subsidized, and were these services to be withdrawn, the depot could probably be eliminated altogether. However, allocation of wage costs is more critical. Overtime working may vary greatly from one route to another according to nature of the service required, crew availability at outstations, etc. As already indicated, marginal costs of off-peak operation may be very low where a peak vehicle is operated by a crew paid for a guaranteed day shift. The NBC system may overstate substantially the cost of additional off-peak mileage by vehicles already employed in peak service.

The NBC system was adopted as a basis by a working party under the Chartered Institute of Public Finance and Accountancy. The resultant method (the 'CIPFA formula') is now being used by NBC and its application to other operators officially encouraged. It has been disputed by some local authorities as a result of sharp increases made in subsidy requests following its initial application in 1974.

The municipal and PTE sector of the bus industry has yet to adopt a common formula. Differences arising from variations in average speed are of minor importance, but peak-based costs are critical. The impact of depreciation at replacement cost may also be heavier, since mileage per vehicle per annum is lower than for NBC operations. Independents, especially those working rural stage services, tend to work implicitly on a marginal costing basis – for example, the realization that a poorly loaded market-day service may none the less cover marginal costs of fuel, wages and tyres. One function of county transport co-ordinators at present is to assist such operators in costing and subsidy estimates.

The 'Cooper formula'

Unlike the National Bus Company, BR did not disclose full details of the system, in general use up to 1975, which took its name from a method of cost allocation devised by management accountants Cooper Bros in conjunction with senior BR officers. It was used to estimate grants for 'socially necessary' services under the Transport Act 1968, and is still used in determining subsidies paid to BR by PTEs and local authorities. A picture of the formula can be built up from references to its application in certain cases.

It was applied on a route-by-route basis (in the last year of its national effect, to groups of services). Costs allocated included direct costs of fuel, maintenance, rolling stock depreciation, crew wages, signal staff and station costs. Two main problems arose:

1 Allocation of costs between grant-aided services, intercity services and freight services over common sections of track. Gross ton-miles were used as a basis (i.e. tare weight plus load for freight trains; passengers themselves weigh very little relative to the weight of the rolling stock, this serving as the 'gross' figure). The homogeneity thus assumed in ton and/or passenger-miles was unreasonable. Higher standards of track maintenance and signalling are required for the greater weight and speed of intercity services. This affected proposals to increase services. The marginal cost of extra off-peak multiple-unit mileage may be very low, since track, station and signalling costs are already incurred. However, the effect of allocating an average estimate per train mile for the above to the additional passenger-miles generated could result in the additional off-peak service not covering allocated costs. Marginal revenue could exceed marginal cost considerably, contributing to net revenue, but operation would be discouraged.

2 Allocation of station and signalling costs between routes. Allocation of station costs according to number of passengers boarding and alighting (or ticket sales, or train calls) similarly imputes homogeneity where it does not exist. In 1969 the Newcastle to Carlisle service was allocated terminal costs of £67000 per year, contributing total costs of £525000 per year. At both termini, the complexity of track layout and station facilities is accounted for largely by intercity services. The Newcastle to Carlisle trains are multiple units, requiring no reversing loops, and operated as 'paytrains'. Terminals comprising a single platform and shelter would suffice. It is the intercity services which require booking offices and interchange facilities.

Under the framework of the Railways Act 1974 many costs are regarded as common to the system as a whole, and a form of marginal costing may be applied to variations on the existing pattern, resolving some of the problems outlined above. However, the Act also presumes that a certain loss is inescapable on the system, whatever its size – on which arguments no detailed proofs have been published – and fails to allocate costs publicly between specific routes. It is thus very difficult to determine which routes are losing money or establish clear incentives to management.

Pricing

Intercity pricing

On the railways, discrimination according to ability to pay and social preference has always existed in the form of first- and second-class travel. The practice of offering cheap excursion and day return facilities is also long-established, and over many routes most tickets fall into these categories. The discount on season tickets is less rational in view of the low elasticity of demand for work trips and high costs which they incur.

Until 1968 standard single and return fares on a mileage scale (incorporating some taper effect) were applied to the whole BR system. This practice continues in most European countries. However, following report 72 of the Prices and Incomes Board in 1968, 'selective pricing' was introduced, in which the rate per mile was varied also according to the quality of service and elasticity of demand. Fares between London and Manchester were increased substantially, reflecting the high service quality and dominant market position. On the London to Sheffield route fares were reduced, in view of the lower service quality and competition from the parallel M1 Motorway. The intent in both cases was to maximize net revenue.

Recent pricing policy has included the introduction of a wider range of concessions, related to trip purpose and user characteristics. If one considers a standard price P_1 as shown in Figure 6.1 it is

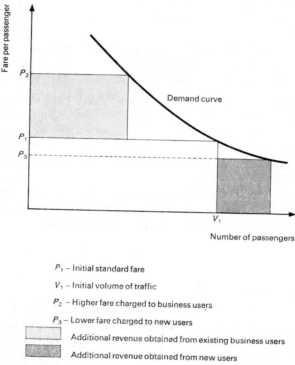

P_1 – Initial standard fare

V_1 – Initial volume of traffic

P_2 – Higher fare charged to business users

P_3 – Lower fare charged to new users

☐ Additional revenue obtained from existing business users

■ Additional revenue obtained from new users

Figure 6.1   Revenue benefits from discriminatory pricing in intercity rail travel

evident that some users obtain substantial consumer surplus (i.e. would be willing to pay a higher fare), others obtain small surplus, while a third group might travel by rail if fares were lower. If the market can be segmented, so that low fares cannot be taken up by those willing to pay existing or higher prices, total revenue can be increased without any change in service quality. This rationale has been followed by BR to a greater extent than most other European railways, with beneficial results.

The group with the highest surplus is also that least sensitive to cost: business trips on weekdays, for which intercity rail offers a high quality of service. Substantial increases, well above the trend, have been made to ordinary fares on this argument. Weekend and day return fares have tended to increase less rapidly, especially where coach competition is important, since these relate to trips such as shopping and visiting friends, demand for which is more price-elastic. Major components of the intercity market are defined in Chapter 8.

On many routes weekend return trips themselves form a peak in demand, necessitating additional trains on Friday and Sunday evenings. The high cost of this operation is not, one suspects, considered fully at the present time.

Extension of rail travel to groups not previously travelling, with the hope that existing revenue will not be 'diluted', has taken the form of 'Supersave', and later 'Economy return' tickets, aimed mainly at potential coach travellers (see Chapter 8), and now incorporates a national policy of half-fares for students and pensioners carrying appropriate passes.

There has been also a realization of the very low marginal cost of excursions which can be operated by high-quality rolling stock, used for weekday business services but idle at weekends. The long-distance day excursion market is not fully penetrated by car or coach travel, due to the discomfort of road travel over long distances, and limitations on driving hours. A number of very cheap excursions have been operated (notably from London), and their number is tending to increase. Provided that a new market is being created and trips on regular services are not diverted, this further increases total revenue.

An important consequence of selective pricing is that by increasing total revenue (the shaded area in Figure 6.1), it may be possible to retain a service which on standard pricing would have failed to cover total costs. The nearest approach on other European railways is some concessions to groups such as pensioners, and supplements on high-speed trains, some of which are first-class only.

Over shorter distances on BR, day returns account for much of the demand, but their application is very arbitrary. On 'paytrain' services a simple fare structure applies, generally without returns. Tapering of fare by distance is less marked. Although simplifying operation, such fare scales probably deter day return trips. A stimulus has been given in East Anglia by offering books of ticket coupons at a discount of 10 per cent.

Express coach services

A simple average-cost pricing structure applies, with some taper by distance. A standard pattern of concessions for return fares, etc., was introduced by National Travel in 1975. Basic day return fares are equal to single fares plus 10 per cent, period return single plus 80 per cent. Weekend summer traffic forms a marked peak, providing a semi-captive demand but higher costs (cf. the comment on weekend rail services above), and basic single fares are then increased by 25 per cent, to which the same relationships as above apply for returns. Service quality is rarely high enough to attract high-income business users who are less sensitive to price. A survey conducted by National Travel in 1974 showed the major trip purposes by rail and coach to be:

Purpose	*Percentages*	
	Coach	Rail
Visiting friends and relatives	40	33
Holidays	30	24
Business	1	16

Supplementary fares for higher quality are rare, but the higher average speed on the motorway service between Bristol and London introduced in January 1972 then justified an addition of 25p.

The ability of operators to introduce complex schemes is restricted by the need to submit detailed applications to the Traffic Commissioners. Potential for higher fares on coaches to enable an 'up market' move into a higher quality/higher revenue role is considered in Chapter 8.

Rural services

As in the case of express coaches, opportunities in pricing policy are fairly limited. However, there is evidence that price elasticity by number of trips made may be somewhat higher than that for urban public transport (below), about -0.6 instead of -0.3. This may indicate possible effects of fare reductions made in order to assist lower-income groups. In so far as shopping trips may be more price-elastic, price reductions (or at any rate, stabilizations) may be justified commercially during shopping hours. Results of such concessions by NBC companies in south-east England in 1972–4 were discouraging. Operators and their staff did not find the inconvenience worthwhile, especially in view of delays to one-man operation and in holiday areas. Standard all-day pricing has been resumed in most areas. However, a case does exist for cheap day returns over longer-distance routes, as already practised by the railways. Even if the percentage discount is no larger than for short trips, the absolute reduction in fare will be much greater, and more readily perceived as a 'bargain'. It is believed that off-peak day returns offered by Midland Red from 1971 resulted in a small overall revenue increase, and extensive 'shopping returns' are now offered by the Oxford company.

Urban bus and rail pricing

As in costing, crude averages have formed the basis for many years. Typical fare scales consist of a minimum fare, above which the rate per mile tapers off. Repeated fare rises since the early 1950s on increasingly crude scales have caused short-distance fares to increase more rapidly than those for long distances, and thus accentuate the taper effect. Although arising largely by accident, this bias was, until the latest round of sharp increases early in 1975, not altogether irrational. Each passenger boarding a vehicle delays other passengers already on board, especially if one-man operation applies. Short trips in the peak period create exceptionally high losses if extra vehicles are required.

As indicated in Chapter 2, the average elasticity of demand by price for urban bus trips is low, about −0·3; that is, although some reduction in traffic will take place when fares are increased, total revenue will none the less rise. Similarly, fare reductions are unlikely to create sufficient extra trips to cause an increase in total revenue.

Within this pattern different sectors of the market respond in different ways. Journeys to work are both a necessity, and one for which the ability to use a car, if available, may be limited by parking and road space constraints. The elasticity of demand by price is thus low, probably around −0·1. So far as the bus operator is concerned, a price increase can normally take place with little passenger loss, although to the urban planner concerned with social costs and benefits, the losses resulting from even a small transfer to private car could be significant.

Several studies have established much higher elasticities of demand for shopping and other optional daytime off-peak trips, in the region of −0·7 to −1·0. Although a general cut in fares may not be worthwhile to the operator, substantial extra traffic could be generated.

E

If an increase in fares were required, it could be sensibly concentrated on peak demand in order to minimize losses in traffic. Work
by Tyson (1973) suggests that a reduced off-peak fare introduced in
Greater Manchester in 1970 (offered between 1000 and 1200 hours
and 1400 and 1600 hours) was probably worthwhile to the operator.
Work by Buckles (1974) on the Stevenage 'Superbus' experiment
suggests an elasticity of demand for shopping trips of about -0.8

Little is known of elasticities at evenings and weekends. While the
potential for attracting extra trips by fare reductions is probably
limited (service quality at such times being low, and limitations on
car use virtually nil), existing demand by low-income groups could
be elastic. 'Family' tickets as offered on some Sunday-only services
in National Parks could be worthwhile.

The usual concept of elasticity is a short-term one. There are
grounds for arguing in urban transport in particular that there may
be a *long-term* elasticity also, that is, a general 'image' of public
transport as cheap or expensive. It is noteworthy that operators who
retain high levels of traffic, such as Leicester, retain fare scales based
on small increments, and make relatively small increases at each
change in fare scales. Operators taking a short-term view, making
sharp increases on coarser scales, have in the long run lost more
off-peak traffic. In the case of urban railways the 'long run' may be a
situation in which homes and jobs can be relocated in response to
fare changes, whose short-run effect is very inelastic.

Some off-peak fare experiments on urban railways have indicated
higher elasticities than on buses. Moran has quoted elasticities of
about -2.0 arising from selective off-peak fare reductions on
Merseyside electric suburban routes. There may be several reasons
for these: the absolute amount of money involved is greater, for the
same percentage change (cf. rural buses, above); whereas the choice
of destinations within a given travelling time by bus is limited, a low
fare on an urban railway could enable a shopping trip to be made to
the conurbation centre instead of a local shopping centre.

Relating prices to costs

Although price discrimination by users' demand characteristics may
be a valid base for pricing policy, it is also important to ensure that
total costs should be related to total revenue. Traditional average
cost pricing does this, by definition, but often involves cross-subsidizing heavy losses on some services by surpluses from others.

I have shown that additional peak demand can often be met only at very high cost, well above the average for the system as a whole. Revenue per vehicle-mile is also higher, of course, but only in the case of a long-distance peak-period run is it likely to exceed direct cost. The situation is shown in Figure 6.2, and could apply, for example, to rail commuting into London. Fixed costs (rolling stock depreciation, depot facilities, terminal costs and shift payment to crew) are incurred irrespective of distance covered. Marginal costs of energy and maintenance increase gradually with mileage. Revenues increase more rapidly with mileage, although not in direct proportion, due to the taper effect on fare scales. Above a certain point, probably around 35 to 50 km (20 to 30 miles), total revenue exceeds direct costs. A similar calculation can be performed for buses, in which the breakeven point is lower, at about 25 to 35 km (15 to 20 miles). (In these calculations, rail fixed cost is assumed to be £65 per day, bus £30 per day, rail average passenger load 200, bus 50, and fare scales about 2p per kilometre.)

The growth of such long-distance traffic on the Southern Region on routes such as Bournemouth to London has increased net revenue considerably. Short-distance peak trains are now being displaced from London termini to make room for more profitable long-distance services. This does *not* necessarily establish that such traffic is profitable in terms of covering all costs, including track, signalling and administration.

Off-peak traffic is likely to generate revenue above direct costs, except in cases of very low demand during evenings and Sundays.

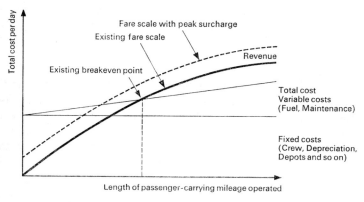

Figure 6.2 A breakeven chart for long-distance commuter travel

Quite apart from likely effects on total revenue, a strong case can be made for higher fares during the peak period simply to reflect costs. A particular danger at the moment is that of meeting demands for half-fares for schoolchildren to be extended to match the higher school-leaving age, or even beyond to cover those in higher education. Schoolchildren already incur heavy losses. If the full cost of school travel were brought home both to parents and to planners of new schools, walking and cycling could be encouraged and long-run costs to public transport reduced.

A differential peak/off-peak pricing policy to reflect costs would also be more equitable. Off-peak traffic levels are higher among groups such as those without cars, the elderly, and in areas of high population density. It is unjust that they should subsidize the highly peaked trip demands of more affluent areas, and travel by schoolchildren who could use other modes.

Economic theorists have proposed 'marginal cost pricing' by which the optimal use of existing capacity would be encouraged by pricing at marginal cost. If a facility is underused the marginal cost will be very low: an extra passenger will incur virtually no direct costs. In the peak marginal cost may be very high. Additional vehicles have to be provided, and perhaps track and terminals.

Any pricing system involves a certain amount of averaging in order to make it workable. As a practical rule one can suggest an approach to marginal cost pricing, where the marginal cost is markedly different from the average cost, for example, higher prices in the peak period. In the off-peak, and for operations such as excursions, the marginal cost can be taken as the 'floor' below which prices should not be set, unless subsidized for a specific reason (such as a basic facility in a rural area).

Conclusion

The approach suggested in this chapter has been one of splitting the public transport market into sectors defined by costs and user characteristics, and then applying average cost pricing in each market. Variations, to discriminate between users ability to pay, may be introduced where practicable; mainly in the intercity sector, in which high price per ticket increases sensitivity to price.

References and further reading

Costing

Beetham, A. (1973) 'An approach to operational costing in the bus industry'. Second Seminar on Rural Transport, Polytechnic of Central London, November.

Travers Morgan and Partners/West Yorkshire Metropolitan County (1974) Bradford Bus Study, *Interim Report on Costing of Bus Operations.*

Chartered Institute of Public Finance and Accountancy, London (1974) *Passenger Transport Operations: Recommendations on a standard financial statement and a route costing system.*

Moyes, A. and Willis, E. (1974) 'Route costing and the rural bus problem', a paper presented at the Institute of British Geographers' Annual Conference, Transport Group Symposium, University of East Anglia.

Pricing

Baum, H. J. (1973) 'Free public transport', *J. Tpt Econ. Pol.*, January, pp. 3–19.

Buckles, P. (1973/4) *The Stevenage Superbus Experiment*, PTRC Summer Annual Meeting paper L9, July 1974 (also presented at a Symposium on Promoting Public Transport, University of Newcastle, 1973).

Cobbe, R. (1974) 'Public transport demand', unpublished M.Sc. thesis, Polytechnic of Central London.

Collins, P. H. (1972) 'Analysis of the effect of September 1969 fares revision on the work journeys', *LT Report R181*, June.

Daly, A. J. and Gale, H. S. (1974) 'Elasticity of demand for public transport', *TRRL Report 68UC.*

Fairhurst, M. H. and Morris, P. J. (1975) 'Variations in the demand for bus and rail travel in London up to 1974', *LT Report R210.*

Golob, T. F. *et al.* (1972) 'An analysis of consumer preference for a public transportation system', *Transportation Research*, **6**, 81–102.

Goodwin, P. B. (1972) 'Some data on the effects of free public transport', a paper presented at the PTRC Urban Traffic Model Research Seminar.

Grey, A. (1975) *Urban Fares Policy*, Saxon House.

Hedges, B. and Prescott-Clarke, P. (1974) *Fares Elasticity Experiment*, *SPCR Report no. 226*, December.

Hovell, P. J., Jones, W. H. and Moran, A. J. (1975) *The Management of Urban Public Transport: a marketing perspective,* Saxon House.

Kemp, M. A. (1973) 'Some evidence of transit demand elasticities', *Transportation*, **2**, 25–32.

Kemp, M. A. (1974) 'Reduced fare and fare free urban transit systems', *TRRL Report 37UC.*

Smith, M. G. and McIntosh, P. (1974) 'Fares elasticity interpretation and estimation', *TRRL Report 37UC.*

Tyson, W. J. (1973) 'The effects of two differential pricing policies in demand for transport in the SELNEC Area', paper read at the PTRC Annual Meeting.

Prices and Incomes Board, *Reports:* 56 (Cmnd 3561) of 1968, 112 (Cmnd 4036) 1969 and 159 (Cmnd 4540) of 1970 all refer to London Transport fare proposals; 72 (Cmnd 3656) of 1968 and 137 (Cmnd 4250) of 1969 refer to British Rail proposals.

Readers not familiar with basic concepts of economic theory such as 'margin' or 'elasticity' are advised to consult a basic textbook, such as: Lipsey, R. G. (1973) *Introduction to Positive Economics*, 3rd edn, Weidenfeld & Nicolson.

Additional Note

In addition to work on elasticities of demand related to passenger *trips*, it is becoming possible to identify a separate, higher elasticity for passenger-*miles*. Recent work in London Transport (Fairhurst & Morris, above) suggests a passenger-*miles* elasticity approaching -0.5, in contrast to -0.3 for a typical passenger-*trips* elasticity. Within a limited budget, passengers may respond to fare increases in part by cutting out trips altogether, with walk or bicycle modes substituting over short distances, but also by reducing the length of remaining trips made, e.g. by substituting a local shopping centre for a regional one. Current research work at the Polytechnic of Central London is examining this hypothesis. Preliminary results are also consistent with Fairhurst's hypothesis of an increasing elasticity as average fare rises, since at higher fare levels bus fare normally comprises a greater proportion of generalized cost per trip.

7 Rural transport planning

The market background

It is in rural areas that public transport accounts for its lowest market share, about 15 per cent of all motorized trips. The estimate is critically dependent on whether school or 'works' services restricted to particular groups are included. In urban areas such trips take place mostly on the scheduled public network, but in rural areas are often made by contract and restricted licence services. For example, in 1970 the Department of the Environment survey in Devon found that only 12 per cent of all trips were made by public transport if the definition were confined to scheduled public services, but 23 per cent if work and school services were included.

Whereas use of intercity rail services increases with income, and middle- and high-income groups make selective use of urban public transport, especially for journeys to work, use of rural public transport is confined almost entirely to 'captive' groups such as schoolchildren and those of low income without access to cars. In a survey stratified by three levels of income, Burton (1972) found in a thinly served area of north Cornwall that public transport accounted for 17 per cent of trips reported. In the highest income households no journeys to work by public transport were recorded, but a significant share of shopping trips (15 per cent) were so made. This reflects the fact that in one-car households there is rarely a car available for the housewife on weekdays. In the lowest income group of three groups studied, 11 per cent of journeys to work were made by public transport, and no less than 38 per cent of shopping trips.

An overall average share of motorized trips of 15 per cent by public transport was observed in mid-Wales by Wragg (1974), but here also motorized shopping trips displayed a stronger attraction to public transport, 18 per cent of their total being so made.

Against this unfavourable background, in which further decline is likely, it should be noted that there are areas which are neither 'urban' nor 'rural', which have rarely been studied systematically, and yet which display much higher levels of public transport use. These include the coal-mining areas and belts of semi-urban development such as that along the south coast between Brighton and Portsmouth. Their implicit inclusion in the 'rural' category as a result of transport studies concentrating solely on extreme urban and rural stereotypes could result in serious misunderstanding of public transport's role.

A crude estimate of National Bus Company demands in different rural regions, by M. Donnellan and the author, indicates the trip rates on public scheduled services shown in Table 7.1.

Table 7.1   *Passenger trips on public scheduled services*

Planning region	*Passenger trips per head of population 1971*
South West	73
South East	84
East Anglia	47
East Midlands	79
West Midlands	85
North	191
North West	38
Wales	89

On a similar basis, Scotland displayed an average trip rate of 130 per head, and Northern Ireland 55. Passengers carried within areas served by PTEs and municipal fleets – and the relevant catchment populations – have been excluded in this calculation. Also excluded are passengers carried by most independent firms, as assignment of populations to their catchment areas was not practicable. There is thus some understatement of public scheduled service trip rates in regions where independents run many stage services, such as East Anglia. Also excluded are most trips made on school and works contract services.

The average rate for England and Wales is about eighty trips per head per annum, but markedly higher in the North (Northumberland, Cumbria, Durham, Cleveland). In so far as NBC serves many towns of less than 100 000 people, the averages given are somewhat above the purely 'rural' level, but major differences are accounted for mainly by the presence of mining and semi-urban areas, generating over 100 trips per head per annum.

The existing network

Railways

These generally provide interurban rather than local branch line services. Typical speeds of diesel multiple-unit (dmu) operation are about 30 mph (50 km/h) including stops, at a direct cost of about 70p per mile. Averages of up to 50 mph (80 km/h) may be provided by semi-fast locomotive-hauled trains over intercity routes. Typical service frequencies of six to ten trains per day sometimes form regular interval hourly or two-hourly patterns. Where provided, rail services generally take most public transport demand for trips of over 16 km or 10 miles (for example, of winter weekday trips between Norwich and Lowestoft, about 25 per cent are by rail, 5 per cent by bus). This may vary according to quality of service and access to stations. Track maintenance and signalling costs are high – about £10000 per mile per annum for double track. Total losses estimated under the 'Cooper formula' (Chapter 6) may easily exceed total revenue.

'Stage carriage' bus services

These are conventional bus services, operating at fixed fares and times, and usually open to all members of the public. The existing network was established during the 1920s, its relative rigidity since 1930 being attributable in part to effects of the Road Traffic Act (see Chapter 1). Contemporary maximum speeds (20 mph, later raised to 30 mph, 50 km/h) resulted in abnormally slow schedules (average speeds of about 15 to 20 mph, 25 to 32 km/h), many of which remain. In some cases, effects of traffic congestion and one-man operation have taken up this slack; in others scope still remains for acceleration.

The network consists partly of local services from small villages or suburbs into market towns and regional centres, but primarily of interurban services which often deviate from main roads to serve intermediate villages. The extent of this practice depends very much on the regulatory patterns and management attitudes of the 1920s and 1930s. For example, two parts of Lincolnshire display radical differences. Kesteven, the area to the south-west of Lincoln, is

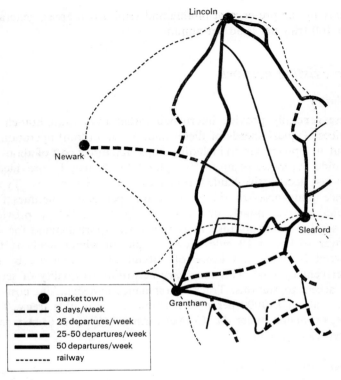

Figure 7.1 The rural bus network in south-west Lincolnshire (Kesteven) in 1969

covered almost entirely by variations of interurban routes to serve villages. A well balanced pattern thus appears, as shown in Figure 7.1 and the frequency distribution, Figure 7.3. The network in the Wolds north-east of Lincoln Figure 7.2, comprises trunk routes along main roads plus infrequent local services to other villages. The first pattern was established under one major operator during the late 1920s, the second by piecemeal acquisition of minor operators after the 1930 Act, without change being made to interurban routes.

It is noteworthy that since the frequency distribution was estimated (1969), services in the Wolds area have suffered much more severe cuts, in part due to lower population densities and a hostile local authority, but also to the fact that many villages never enjoyed an adequate frequency which would stimulate bus use.

The strength of the interurban network structure is that by com-

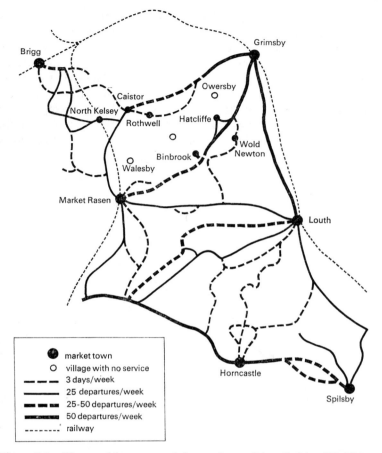

Figure 7.2 The rural bus network in north-east Lincolnshire (Wolds) in 1969

bining 'local' (village to town) and 'interurban' trips over the same route a higher frequency can be offered or higher load factor attained than would be the case in catering for each demand separately. The weakness is that journey times between major towns are often far too long, especially in relation to potential direct routeings. In the late 1920s such times were adequate, alternative railway routes often being slow or sufficiently more expensive to encourage use of the slower, but cheaper, bus. Increasing car ownership has inevitably hit such traffic, but even to non-car owners such interurban bus trips are often unattractive, as real value of time has risen.

Typical costs of bus operation are related primarily to crew hours worked, that is to time rather than distance (see discussion in Chapter 6). Costs associated with peak vehicle demand (depreciation, depot facilities, guaranteed shift payments) are also important; direct mileage costs (fuel, tyres) relatively small. The use of 'average cost per mile' estimates until recently resulted in exaggerated estimates of rural bus costs (the same time-based costs being spread over twice the mileage covered by urban services in the same period), and a tendency to withdraw off-peak mileage, whose marginal costs

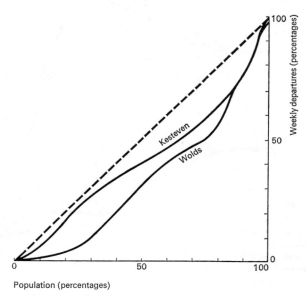

Figure 7.3 Relative frequency distributions of bus services in Lincolnshire (1969)

were in fact very low. However, some cuts, such as those by Midland Red in 1970–1, were associated with cuts in peak vehicle demand and number of depots, so that mileage per vehicle increased.

Rural services operated from isolated villages into market towns are usually less efficient than interurban routes, often involving 'dead' mileage between urban depots and rural termini to cover first and last trips. In this situation the village-based independent may score over the larger operator, working with the peak flows and providing a shorter working day for his staff. Outstations (garages for no more than five or six vehicles, without maintenance facilities) may be the best solution for the larger operator. Eastern Counties, serving thinly populated Norfolk and Suffolk, is a noted user of this practice, in which a local driver is made responsible for supervision of the vehicles.

Some shorter rural routes are often extensions of town services, running perhaps every half hour to adjoining semi-suburban villages, and may be worked conveniently from urban depots.

Other bus and coach services

Other operation in rural areas is of two major types:

Express services. Both long-distance operation and many relatively short market-day, seasonal and 'works' services restricted to employees of specified firms fall into this category, although a number of shorter services have been converted into the 'stage carriage' category as a means of qualifying for fuel-tax rebate and new bus grant. Long-distance express services rarely operate more than twice daily (see Chapter 8) but can provide valuable facilities in some rural areas if suitably timed. In some cases, local passengers are carried on express routes following elimination of poorly used stage services over the same roads (for example, between Oxford and High Wycombe on the Oxford–London service).

Excursion, private hire and contract services. These include traditional locally advertised excursions (at fixed fares, but operating according to demand), club outings, and school and 'works' services on which separate fares are not payable. The traditional seaside excursion demand has fallen, most weekend leisure trips now being made by car. However, a demand for shopping excursions remains, and growth of long-distance touring has compensated for decline. Such tours are often based on surprisingly small catchment areas and often reflect passengers' adherence to a well-known local operator. Steady growth has taken place in regular contract work, usually provided by PSVs hired from independent operators, or NBC, sometimes by non-PSVs owned by the employer or education authority. The latter may be secondhand PSVs nearing the end of their life, or purpose-built utilitarian types, on conventional chassis but spartan interiors, and often unsatisfactory entrance design (an aspect criticized by the Working Party on School Transport in 1972). Contract services may be operated by PSVs without road service licences being held for specific routes, provided that all costs are met collectively and not individually (the latter including not only direct ticket sales, but also deduction from wages).

Opportunities for improvement

The local demand

Growth of the rural bus network in the 1920s and 1930s was based primarily on shopping and leisure demand, especially at weekends. This situation is largely reversed: the decline of rural cinemas has wiped out much evening traffic, and for general leisure trips at weekends the entire family is present to make use of the car (non-car-owning households in rural areas are largely confined to elderly and very low income groups). On the other hand, the continued decline in agricultural employment, coupled with growth of employment in urban areas and shift of urban population, has created a demand for journeys to work. Many rural bus services in 'thin' areas, such as east Lincolnshire, did not feature trips arriving in market towns before 0900 until after World War Two, and examples may still be found of rural bus services working on several days of the week not providing such a facility. Potential exists here.

More than one member of a household may be in employment, for example a teenage son or daughter, and have working times or destinations that do not match those of the head of the household. The clearer perception of car operating costs (especially for relatively long trips) may produce comparisons favourable to bus use, especially over routes with good quality, limited-stop services. As high-frequency operation is usually out of the question, timing of the service is critical.

Shopping trip totals by public transport have tended to remain relatively stable, since despite the rise in car ownership, few households own two cars and thus on Mondays to Fridays the housewife does not have a car available. This does not imply an entirely 'captive' demand for public transport – the number of shopping trips may tend to fall as bulk buying of household goods, often making use of a car at weekends, becomes important. Local village shops may also substitute for day-to-day needs, or mobile shops be used. The last two forms, however, are expensive and this, coupled with a desire for more social activity, may lead to a wish to make relatively frequent trips into the nearest town if a cheap and reliable service is offered.

A picture thus builds up of an opportunity to provide a high-frequency service from about 0800 to 1800. Taking peak demands as determined by school and work trips, vehicles and staff will be available at low marginal cost in the off-peak. Full-time staff may receive a guaranteed eight-hour day, and some labour costs additional to peak-only workings be negligible. A basic service from 0800 to 1800 hours could be maintained largely by single-shift working, eliminating unattractive 'split shift' duties (one independent employs drivers for a twelve-hour day, including breaks, on a four-day working week, a pattern more convenient to both him and the drivers). Evening and Sunday services have in many cases already been abandoned.

The effect of a high frequency during shopping hours as illustrated by Hillman (1973) is shown in Table 7.2.

Table 7.2 *Housewives' bus trips and frequency of bus services* *Percentage reporting:*

Service headway	Once or more weekly	1–3 times monthly	Less than monthly
5–10 minutes	47	22	31
15–20 minutes	40	17	44
30–60 minutes	33	18	49
More than hourly	19	19	63

This would suggest that a change in headway from 'more than hourly' to '30–60 minutes' would cause an approximate demand increase of 50 per cent. If 'more than hourly' is taken to mean a bus about every two hours (a common rural frequency), then provided additional costs of doubling off-peak frequency do not exceed 50 per cent of present total costs, expansion of service frequency will be justified commercially.

Examples of such change include services operated by Court Line of Luton and the Tillingbourne company into Guildford. Both featured improved frequency during shopping hours, and no evening or Sunday service. The former, like other Court Line operations, was rather ambitious, and has since been reduced in intensity. The latter, aided by a moderate local authority subsidy, continues to be well used. A survey early in 1975 showed that typical weekday loads for shopping exceeded the total of those for work, and that over half the shoppers made the same trip three or four times a week, indicating the development of off-peak traffic.

Major problems arise in the case of:

1 Villages whose populations are too small to support a good weekday (Monday to Saturday) stage service frequency.
2 Provision of evening and Sunday services for those without cars.

In the first case, it is rare to find no stage service at all. Very often a market-day/Saturday service has operated for many years, using vehicles otherwise employed on school or works contract at peaks, hence independent operators often provide such services. Direct costs are confined to mileage costs, plus the driver's pay – even this may be small, as staff are employed part-time, or undertake cleaning and maintenance of vehicles as well as driving. Nevertheless, some decline has occurred in such services, especially on Saturdays when cars are available. Furthermore, they offer very limited choice for trips other than shopping or personal business. In many cases, small villages are served on all weekdays by non-public school or works contract services, as described above. School services are already under the control of county authorities, and only an internal change within their organization is required to bring school contracts under the same control as stage service subsidies. The merging of school and public services does create some problems, however:

1 Lack of spare capacity. Many school buses are not only filled to normal seating capacity, but by use of the 'three for two' rule, to 50 per cent more. Given the physical size of most secondary school pupils, more capacity may be needed to handle existing flows, let alone additional passengers. (This problem may be less severe in areas of declining population. The availability of high capacity 75/80-seat double-deckers of the early 1960s on the secondhand market permits replacement of smaller vehicles now in use.)
2 Restriction of existing services to school pupils only eliminates handling of tickets and cash, reducing journey time and permitting use of non-PSVs. (In practice, opening of services to the public would involve only a few fare-paying passengers on each trip, schoolchildren carrying passes. In so far as non-PSVs, driven by part-time staff, are now in use, it is not clear why lower standards of safety should be acceptable for schoolchildren than for adult passengers. Adoption of full PSV standards for school buses would improve entrance layouts, as well as permitting integration with public services.)
3 Additional services would be required during school holidays to maintain continuity – for passengers using the service to get to

work, for example. (However, vehicles and crews are generally idle at such times, except in the summer peak, and only a small subsidy would be required.)

Similar comments apply to 'works' services, except in so far as those operated by non-PSVs are probably inappropriate, and that many others vary in their times of operation according to season, overtime working, etc. However, a strong case exists for converting those operated as stage services on restricted licence, which receive fuel-tax rebate and new bus grant. Such services might provide for journeys to work (to employers other than the one originally operating the service) over routes which have some stage services, but with a morning journey-to-work run in only one direction – to the larger of two towns on an interurban route, for example. The existing 'works' service could provide a link into the smaller town. A conversion of this type has occurred at Wellington, Somerset.

Post Office services

The other major form of existing operation that can be modified to provide a basic weekday public service is the Post Office Corporation (POC) network. Existing mail deliveries in medium-density rural areas generally comprise an outward run at about 0600–0700 from the Post Office, usually in a market town, via a devious loop route, returning at about 1000. A second delivery run may operate around midday, and a late afternoon collection run depart about 1630 (note that frequencies are lower in low-density areas, one or two runs per day only).

Most POC conversions to date (over one hundred now operate) have consisted simply of permitting fare-paying passengers to travel on the post runs, replacing vans by twelve-seat minibuses. The marginal costs are very low; the minibus receives a 50 per cent new bus grant, thus its net cost is little more than that of a new van. Additional fuel costs are offset by fuel-tax rebate as a result of the service coming into the 'stage carriage' category. Running time may be increased marginally, depending on local circumstances. By slight rescheduling of existing runs, a fairly fast direct journey can be provided from the larger village(s) on the loop route into the market town for about 1030, and out again at about 1630 (as between Ockley and Dorking, for example). Shopping and personal business trips are thus catered for, but with a very long stay in the market town. Of the POC bus conversions already introduced, the midday

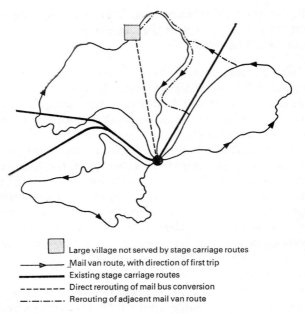

Large village not served by stage carriage routes
Mail van route, with direction of first trip
Existing stage carriage routes
Direct rerouting of mail bus conversion
Rerouting of adjacent mail van route

Figure 7.4 Potential rerouteing of a mailbus service for a morning journey into a market town

run continues, offering much greater flexibility to the passenger.

Further development of POC services is possible if there is some willingness to amend delivery and collection times to suit passenger needs. In some cases routes could be adjusted, so that one route took some devious delivery runs from an adjoining route, permitting direct 'fast' runs between some points, for example from a large village with a poor stage bus service at present into the nearest market town. Figure 7.4 indicates such a possibility. Routes could also be made more direct by installing delivery boxes at the ends of narrow lanes leading to isolated houses instead of requiring the postman to travel to the door. The increasing demand on some services, on which flows now exceed 1500 trips per annum, could justify larger vehicles, seating about twenty passengers.

Minibuses

Some scope exists for using minibuses on conventional services, but usually where the demand is very low in any case, not more than fifteen passengers on any one trip, and a subsidy therefore provided.

A reduction of about 15 per cent on average operating costs can be obtained. One example is the service operated by a local coach proprietor on behalf of the local authority in Haddington, East Lothian. Minibuses do not provide commercially viable opportunities, except in specialized markets, operated by small firms with low overheads, and at higher-than-average fares. Thus the Mountain Goat services in the Lake District cater primarily for tourists, and Thames Weald for low-density interurban traffic in the prosperous South East Region.

The surprisingly small difference between minibus and full-size operating costs is due to the high proportion of labour cost (especially drivers' pay) in both cases. However, in some cases, the greater manoeuvrability of a minibus may permit a round trip to be completed in less time, giving more substantial savings. Thus on the North Downs service from Orpington to Croydon, an hourly headway was maintained by a sixteen-seater but not by a full-size bus.

Non-scheduled, evening and Sunday services

The poor load factors of evening and Sunday operation, aggravated in rural areas by the need to walk and wait on unlit roads, make conventional operation a poor proposition even in relatively high-density areas. Conversion of school buses is of little help (except in one case, below), nor that of works services. Due to insurance limitations, POC vehicles cannot be used other than for mail purposes.

Where cuts are imposed, it is probably best to maintain a clear-cut pattern: no service after about 1830, but one or two well advertised *late* journeys – around 2230 to 2300. In parts of Lincolnshire, for example, late trips appear to have continued successfully despite elimination of other evening services. This is particularly noticeable around Boston and Spalding, from which midnight runs are operated over some routes on Saturdays.

The decline of mass entertainment has eliminated much of evening travel to and from town centres. However, there has been a growth of community activities such as adult education, often taking place in the early evening, and creating a demand for mid-evening homebound trips. Schools may often form the location for such activities, and schoolchildren themselves are involved in similar after-school activities. The combined demand could justify special services, perhaps operated by buses used on schools services during the day.

Co-ordination may be required to ensure common 'closing times'. In thinly populated areas, activities could be concentrated on one or two evenings per week to justify bus operation. Their timing could also coincide with hospital visiting hours, and a pick-up be made at the local hospital(s).

A recent attempt to develop sharing of facilities is the 'community transport' concept. A number of voluntary welfare groups, so far mostly based in cities, have begun to co-ordinate use of minibuses and other vehicles which they own, so as to make the best use of available resources. To some extent the same applies in rural areas in the use of ex-PSVs owned by churches, youth clubs, etc. More could be done, although the limitation still remains that such facilities serve members of organized groups, and not necessarily socially isolated individuals.

Another possibility is that co-operative schemes (see below) could provide evening and Sunday services, financed by subscriptions from those who would consider the facility useful, although making only occasional use of it. Many evening and Sunday trips follow a very diffuse pattern – visits to friends and relations for example – for which conventional bus networks are ill-suited even where still provided. Demand-actuated services could be most appropriate, probably using minibuses. Their growth has been restricted by emphasis on calls by phone (many low-income non-car-owners do not have telephones), and the licensing system. However, many dial-a-bus services in urban areas operate also in response to 'standing orders' (see Chapter 5), placed in writing or in person at a control office.

In order to attain a satisfactory load factor, about fifteen to twenty calls per vehicle-hour are required, a density unlikely from any rural area outside peak periods. Demand-actuated rural transport is more likely to take the form of selective diversion of scheduled services, or prescheduled minibus workings to suit individual demands. There is very little reason to believe that the latter could be commercially viable, but it might provide a better level of service in respect of diffuse trip patterns for the subsidy available.

Diversions of existing scheduled services via villages not more than a mile or so off existing routes can be made at very low cost within existing timings. The mileage costs of such diversion are only about 6p per km, covered by the revenue from only one additional passenger. Diversions could be made on telephone request, written order or verbal request from a passenger boarding at a terminus. Many rural bus services already include diversions off potential direct routes, which on some runs pick up or set down no passengers. The waste (and frustration to passengers already on board) could be minimized by making such diversions dependent on specific requests. In other cases a rural bus route may be found that traditionally adheres to the main road, even though its interurban traffic has long since been lost to improved rail or coach services. In such cases, selective diversions could create additional local facilities at virtually no cost. Potential for such diversion in the Weymouth–Wool area of Dorset has been established in a recent survey. An independent operator introduced such a system between Droitwich and Worcester in February 1975.

Regulation and licensing

Development of new types of services has been inhibited by the licensing system (for example, in the rejection or severe restriction of some dial-a-bus proposals). In attempting to meet this problem the legislation that was in progress through Parliament until dissolution in February 1974 would have replaced one extreme with another. As part of a Road Traffic Bill it was proposed to lift virtually all licensing requirements from vehicles of nine seats or less, giving an artificial incentive to operate abnormally small vehicles, a reduction in safety standards, and little assurance of reliability of service. There is little reason to believe that regular timetabled operation of minibuses on a commercial basis would have been encouraged, due to high labour costs. Instead, the effect would have been to legalize existing minibus and car-sharing schemes, and probably divert traffic from remaining regular and viable stage services. In the long run a lower overall level of service would have been likely. An amendment proposed shortly before dissolution would have restricted the lifting of control over minibuses to areas more than a specified distance from a regular bus service stop, or in cases where a regular service ran less than daily, only to those days on which the regular service did not run. The amendment also stipulated that minibuses only would be permitted, not for hire or reward, and that passengers would be pre-booked. Under the Labour Government elected in February 1974 minibus proposals were dropped entirely.

A case can be made for the liberalization of conventional PSV operation, rather than the provision of an artificial incentive to operate very small vehicles. Operators with proposals for new services could be permitted, subject to the approval of a route on safety and traffic engineering considerations, to introduce such services for a limited period (say, three months). For this period, the operator would be obliged to provide the full advertised service in his application, and traffic trends would be monitored by the operator, local authority or regulatory body. In cases in which wasteful competition could be shown retrospectively to have occurred (for example, duopolistic competition for peak traffic), restrictive conditions could be applied to the service licence. In other cases, the operator himself might wish to modify the service in the light of his experience, or the local authority to integrate the service with others in the area. By such means, new operators could be encouraged without excessive risk to established services. The licensing system in Northern Ireland could form a valuable precedent, in which routes, vehicles and staff are licensed, but not specific journeys or fares.

Co-operative organization

Another general approach to rural problems is for local people to work together in providing voluntary support for a service. By this I do not refer to 'car-sharing' (a euphemism for patronage of those without cars by those with them, often of higher income), a mode which may be better than nothing, but which involves inconvenient arrangements between the passenger and lift-giver. Most such schemes cater for hospital visits, occasional journeys to friends and relatives, etc. rather than regular work or shopping trips, and may require the lift-giver to wait at the destination of the passenger before returning. Local authorities sometimes support such schemes financially, either as a substitute for subsidies to conventional bus services, or to serve the needs of semi-disabled people who find conventional bus services of little value. As a general solution, car-sharing could involve higher subsidies than those to conventional bus services: mileage rates paid for business use, for example, already exceed marginal mileage costs of bus operation.

A better prospect in the long run may be the operation of subscription schemes, whereby local residents who feel that they benefit from the provision of a bus service contribute a regular fixed payment to ensure its continuance, although perhaps making few trips. The rationale that public transport services provide a back-up facility has been put forward to justify subsidy, but rarely tested.

For some years a weekly market-day bus in Oxfordshire has been supported on this basis, and a larger scheme was introduced in Lincolnshire in January 1976. For the passenger, the subscription guarantees provision of a service, and if travelling frequently, a lower cost. For the operator, removing the need to handle cash and tickets on each trip reduces administrative costs, and payment of subscriptions in advance improves cash flow. In contrast to car-sharing, such schemes would enable scheduled operation, meeting full safety standards, to continue, and full-time employment to be maintained. The planning of such a scheme and collection of subscriptions involves considerable voluntary effort, but the interest generated in the service within the local community may itself be of value. The major problem arising is that individuals make trips of greatly varying frequencies. In the case of once- or twice-weekly services this would not be too serious, and most subscribers would feel that value for money was being obtained. A daily service would serve a wide range of needs, and differential rates, or public subsidy, would be necessary. A facility for occasional passengers is also desirable.

Travel within small towns

Public transport services within small towns of less than about 20000 population are usually provided by the same operator(s) as rural and interurban services into them. Extra trips to provide an augmented service over rural/interurban routes entering the town may provide for most local demand, rather than separate self-contained networks. Services in such towns have generally expanded in recent years – in Northallerton and Gainsborough, for example – despite trends in the bus industry as a whole. Continued outward growth has for the first time placed housing beyond comfortable walking distance of town centre shops and employment. The high fares charged for short trips on steeply tapered fare scales can result in such services being viable with surprisingly small passenger loads. However, sharp fare increases in 1975 may well have pushed some short-distance fares to the point where walking or cycling is substituted for bus travel. The costs of such services, which involve low average speeds and a high proportion of layover time, have only been fully appreciated recently, following adoption of costing systems in which time-based costs are predominant (see Chapter 6). Moyes and Willis (1974) have shown that a surplus of £5000 per annum shown on an average cost basis for town services in Aberystwyth was reduced to about £1000 on a more accurate costing system. Further growth of services within small towns now appears unlikely, except perhaps for shopping trips, for which walking and cycling are less attractive alternatives, and which can be provided for by using spare peak vehicles from rural/interurban services at low marginal cost.

At times, or in areas, of low demand, minibus operation may be appropriate for self-contained services within small towns, especially where manoeuvrability is valuable. The service operated within Abingdon by City of Oxford Motor Services is one example.

The traffic problem within small towns is not usually such as to justify severe restraint of journeys to work by car, or high subsidies to extra peak-hour buses. However, some historic towns have suffered from the effects of car park construction and road building adopted to deal with growing traffic, and environmental grounds could justify restraint. Park-and-ride services could operate from peripheral car parks, although the importance of shopping traffic could discourage the interchange thus imposed. If cars were to be restrained by high prices for parking in the centre, then another option would be to strengthen existing local bus services to larger suburbs or villages, in an attempt to obtain voluntary car to bus diversion of the entire home to town centre trip.

Conclusions

Despite the sharply increasing subsidy demands, total rural bus subsidies remain very small. Even a marginal diversion of resources from highway expenditure in 'shire' counties would permit existing service levels to be maintained, and perhaps improved. Means also exist of improving service quality and reducing costs as suggested above. A moderate standard of Monday to Saturday daytime service, sustained by work and shopping demand, can be attained by efficient operators without prohibitive subsidy. The major problems lie in respect of evening and Sunday services, which rarely cover costs, and the high costs of school services, either in terms of special contract services, or losses to stage service operators carrying schoolchildren at low fares.

The bus industry could do more to plan positively for rural demand, as the Eastern Counties company has shown. Potential exists for better interurban services, improved off-peak shopping services, and networks which take full account of current passenger requirements rather than serving those of forty years ago. Publicity has often been poor in the past, and better efforts by operators, sometimes with the aid of comprehensive timetables published by county councils, are now becoming more common.

In the short run, pricing policy is also critical. Rural demand, though inelastic, is more responsive to price than is urban bus demand: a higher proportion of trips relate to non-work purposes, and their frequency is thus optional. The absolute expenditure per trip is much higher, due to greater length, and incomes of those in rural areas who use buses often very low. Recent evidence suggests a price elasticity of about -0.6, that is, of the same order as mileage elasticities for urban bus travel. Distinctions now made in government policy between 'revenue support' and 'specific service' subsidies may not be valid in the rural context. From the operator's viewpoint, the higher elasticity, particularly of shopping trips, may justify greater efforts to sell cheap day return tickets than is now the case.

References and further reading

References on rural public transport are somewhat scattered, due to the lack of systematic work in this area until recently. A general background can be obtained from papers relating to Conferences. The Annual Seminar on Rural Public Transport held at the Polytechnic of Central London since 1972 has presented a number of useful papers, those in 1972 including R. BURTON's survey of bus services in Cornwall, an analysis of subsidy policy by W. J. TYSON, several general reviews of the problem, and appendices on minibus services, the Haddington Rural Bus Service and bibliography. The 1973 papers include reviews by A. BEETHAM on NBC costing practice, by J. S. MADGETT and POST OFFICE SERVICES on Market Research work by the Eastern Counties company. Those for 1974 relate to recent survey techniques, services in National Parks and pricing of school traffic, and for 1975 to limited-stop surveys, pricing policy and developments in Devon.

Proceedings of a Conference held at the University of East Anglia in March 1974 are available in Regional Studies Association *Discussion Paper no.* 5, 1974, including papers by A. MOYES ('County Council approaches to rural bus subsidy'), S. TRENCH ('Subsidy criteria'), J. S. MADGETT ('The operator's viewpoint'), and D. R. MILLS ('Rural population structure related to transport').

Data has been drawn in writing this chapter from unpublished papers read at the Institute of British Geographers' Transport Group Symposium

at the University of East Anglia in January 1974, including those by
R. WRAGG ('Rural transport in Wales'), and A. MOYES and E. WILLIS ('Route
costing and the rural bus problem'). One paper from this Symposium has
been published, that by A. G. HOARE ('Some aspects of the rural transport
problem among Norwich commuter villages', *J. Tpt Econ. Pol.,* **9** (1975),
no. 2, 141–53) in which attitudes towards existing service quality are
related to characteristics of respondents and villages in which they lived.

Other unpublished work from which material has been derived include
M. HILLMAN (1973) 'Travel needs of individuals', a paper read at the Public
Transport Fares Symposium, TRRL, November (see Table 7.2); M.
DONNELLAN (1974) 'Population change and the National Bus Company'
(unpublished M.Sc. thesis, Polytechnic of Central London); and a survey
of passengers on Tillingbourne services into Guildford in February 1975
by R. COX.

A recent example of a local study proposing useful service improvements by marginal changes at low cost can be found in *Public Transport
for Rural Communities*, published by the Planning Department of Hertfordshire County Council, March 1975.

News coverage of rural public transport is very scattered. References
appear in *Motor Transport* (weekly), *Omnibus Magazine* (bi-monthly
'Rural Scene' feature), *Coaching Journal* (monthly, particularly in respect
of independent operators) and the railway journals, cited in Chapter 8.
The most detailed study published to date is that by G. REES, R. F. W.
WRAGG, *et. al.* (1975), *A Study of the Passenger Transport Needs of Rural
Wales*, Welsh Council, Cardiff.

8 Intercity public transport

The market background

It is in the intercity sector that the highest quality of public transport service can be found, and perhaps the clearest evidence of voluntary diversion from car to public transport (while it is true that public transport commands a high share of journey-to-work trips in large cities, this is associated with constraints on road space and parking that effectively prevent all those with cars making free use of them). The 'parkway' stations opened by British Rail in recent years, notably that at Bristol, offer undoubted evidence of cars being abandoned by their users in favour of a rail journey. On many routes, there has also been an improvement in service quality, if not sufficient to attract car users at least to generate substantial extra traffic from those without cars. Unlike the urban situation, in which substantial improvements cannot be made without large-scale public investment, or subsidy of labour-intensive bus operation, intercity modes have benefited substantially from new technology. By offering commercially viable opportunities, they have attracted private investment, and investment by profit-oriented public bodies such as the airlines and National Bus. An increase in average vehicle size and speed brings a twofold improvement in labour productivity. For example, in the immediate postwar period, an express coach was limited to 30 mph average, and seated not more than 32 passengers. Today the limit is 50 mph (80 km/h), or 70 mph (110 km/h) on motorways, and average capacity has risen to about 48 seats: an improvement in labour productivity at constant load factors of 150 per cent (one could add the effects of one-man operation, but this has been general for many years on express services). In air transport, the change has been even more dramatic, from the 26-seat Viking averaging about 200 mph (320 km/h) to 1-11 and Trident jets seating about 120 people, achieving about 500 mph (800 km/h), a potential improvement in productivity at constant load factors of about 1000 per cent.

On the railways, there have not been any marked changes in seating capacity (about 350 per train), but increases in average speed from about 50 mph (80 km/h) to 75 mph (120 km/h), coupled with much quicker turnround of stock have improved utilization of rolling stock on all-year service, by about 100 per cent.

Demand

Growth in incomes has stimulated intercity demand, and higher speeds have enabled a greater mileage to be covered within a fixed time budget (see Chapter 2). However, on many lower-quality services this has had the effect of rail and coach being perceived as inferior goods, to be supplanted by the private car. Coach operators have compensated for this by continuing to develop the market for cross-country travel, and demand from groups without cars available (such as pensioners). Many cross-country rail services have, however, declined in quality, either as the result of connecting multiple unit services replacing locomotive-hauled 'through' trains (for example, over the Portsmouth to Cardiff route, transfer at Bristol now being necessary), or complete closure of direct routes (such as Oxford to Cambridge). Intercity rail has lost some traffic to domestic air services, but this has been outweighed by growth of traffic captive to rail, and now, increasing air fares. The problem of declining inter-urban public transport, especially railways, in the medium-distance and cross-country sector, will be discussed later.

Two main divisions can be drawn within the long-distance market:

The business market

This market comprises trips made by businessmen, on Mondays to Fridays, usually at their employer's expense. The demand is highly sensitive to timing of arrival and departure (being sharply peaked in morning and late afternoon), and total travel time. Most trunk rail services to London feature fast trains, sometimes of the luxury stock (such as the 'Manchester Pullman'), offering arrivals in the capital at about 1000, and returning at about 1700 hours. Similar timings can be observed on many air services. By and large, only rail and air are considered as alternatives for the longer trips, rail and car for the shorter. A survey carried out by the University of Leeds in 1968 on major intercity rail and air flows found that only 6 per cent of the business travellers on the London–Glasgow rail service considered the car as an alternative, whilst 31 per cent of those on the London–Birmingham service did so.

Another feature of this market is a tendency to use taxis or hire cars at terminals, thus minimizing feeder trip time. For example, the Leeds survey found that 40 to 60 per cent of the business travellers used such a mode from their destination station, compared with 35 to 45 per cent of non-business travellers. High car availability was also noted, about 80 to 90 per cent of all travellers on rail and air, indicating the free choice available. Another characteristic of business trips was a much higher probability of travelling first class, in any given income range.

The pricing of first-class travel by rail is partly a matter of reflecting the higher cost of facilities provided – a wider seat pitch, for example – but by and large it is a case of pricing by ability to pay, and hence obtain a greater surplus over direct costs. In the case of British Airways it has been argued by the former chief economist of BEA, Richard Graham, that the average first-class traveller incurs costs about twice those of the typical economy-class passenger, a greater differential than exists between the fares.

In short, the business market has a *high elasticity of demand by time, but a low elasticity by price.*

The non-business market

Here, the time and price elasticities are almost the reverse. Many of the trips are optional – visits to friends and relatives, shopping trips, excursions – and most are paid for directly by the travellers. A decision whether or not to make a trip is thus influenced markedly by price. Time may be less critical, especially in the timing of specific trips. It is not necessary to make trips for specific business meetings, or hours of work. Apart from some entertainment trips, most non-business trips are not tied down to a specific event. Total travel time may still be significant, especially if travel itself is regarded as unpleasant or uncomfortable.

Another feature of this market is that the trip destination and mode may be considered together. Whereas a business traveller aims for a specific destination and then selects his mode, optional trips may often be suggested to the travellers by the advertising of operators – for example, BR's stress on day trips to London, or coach operators' inclusive prices for visits to stately homes and wild-life parks.

Optional trips are likely to be made by groups rather than by individual passengers. The car is more likely to be considered as an alternative, and used if available. In the Leeds survey, only 30 to 50 per cent of the rail non-business travellers claimed to have a car available. The perceived costs of fuel are divided between several people, whereas public transport fares are usually payable separately by each passenger. A higher proportion of passengers than those in the business market (in the Leeds survey, 40 per cent compared with 11 per cent) are likely to be travelling with members of the same family.

Another factor affecting the destination of non-business trips is the location of friends or relatives. Work by Lansing (1968) in the USA has suggested that the past location of residence of trip makers is important. While living in other towns or cities they may have set up relationships which continue. In a society which is highly mobile both in occupation and location, many such relationships may be established. Travel to such destinations is also encouraged by the practice of staying at the homes of friends or relatives, rather than at greater cost in hotels. In other cases, notably of long-distance tourism, hotel capacity can set a limit on the trips that can be made.

Existing intercity market split by mode

In Britain, the split for trips of over 100 miles (all purposes) in the late 1960s was:

	%
Private car	70
Air	2
Rail	15
Coach	13

Source: National Travel Survey 1965/6

A similar distribution is quoted by the British Tourist Authority for trips to their principal destination of those taking a holiday of four or more nights from home within Britain.

Although the private car is dominant, its importance is less marked than within totals for all lengths of trip (about 80 per cent of passenger-miles). Rail is known to have the largest share of trunk intercity markets where day return travel is important – up to about 70 per cent in the case of Manchester and Liverpool to London.

The rail share is similar where heavy commuting levels are found, as from Brighton to London, but otherwise much lower over medium-distance links (such as Norwich to Ipswich), probably around 20 to 30 per cent. Air travel accounts for the majority of trips only in the case of the longest journeys, such as London to Glasgow, although if sleeper travel is included, rail can often approach air totals in such cases. Express coaches account for a relatively small share of trunk intercity flows to and from London, and between other major cities (apart from the north-east of England), but account for the majority of long-distance public transport for summer excursions and tourist demand in rural regions such as the West Country. Cars account for the majority of medium-distance and cross-country journeys, over which public transport does not offer an attractive alternative.

Modal split

Data on intercity flows, other than those by air, are very scanty. Rail and coach operators are under no obligation to publish data on specific flows, and occasional public statements – in traffic courts, for example – are often ambiguous. The following table indicates approximate total flows per annum in the early 1970s, which should be taken as orders of magnitude only:

Table 8.1   *Flow: total single trips (both directions), thousands of passengers per annum*

London to	Air	Rail	Coach
Glasgow	700	650	400
Edinburgh	550	600	150
Tyneside	250	650	500
Birmingham	—	1250	250
Northampton/Nottingham/ Leicester	—	1200	400
Manchester	300	2000	250
Bristol	—	500	300+
Sheffield	—	300	400
Leeds/Bradford	150	1100	400
Liverpool	150	1500	

Over longer routes, such as London to Glasgow, air offers a substantial time advantage. Flying time of about one hour contrasts with rail centre-to-centre time of five hours. The length of feeder trips will of course depend on individual user's origins and destination, but in general airports are less accessible, placing an additional penalty of about thirty to sixty minutes over the feeder trip time by rail. The air/rail modal split is largely a function of income, in which higher-income travellers use the faster mode (see Chapter 2), especially if on business. Despite the much longer journey times, coaches show up strongly on such flows. For the low-income traveller, the difference in fares becomes substantial, and the trip forms a convenient overnight run (most London–Scottish coach traffic being at this time). Over routes of about 200 to 250 km, such as London–Manchester, total travel times by air and rail are similar. Virtually all centre-to-centre traffic goes by rail, many of the air trips being 'interline' trips via Heathrow or Gatwick on to international air services to destinations not served frequently or directly from provincial airports. Over links of about 150 km, such as London to Birmingham, air travel is negligible, and coach travel a surprisingly small sector of the public transport market: as a higher proportion of the centre-to-centre trip is made within built-up areas, the speed may be relatively low, and the absolute difference in coach and rail fares not significant to most passengers. Car flows are probably important over such links, but there are virtually no statistics available.

Conventional railway technology

Motive power

The reasons for the abandonment of steam traction, completed in 1968 in the case of British Railways, are well known. They included poor availability of locomotives, a low power:weight ratio, high costs of maintenance and a thermal efficiency of about 10 per cent. However, it should be noted that in some cases steam continues to be important, as in India where unskilled, low cost labour can maintain steam locomotives more easily than more complex types. The commonest replacement is diesel traction, offering a thermal efficiency of about 30 per cent. Motors ranging from about 500 to 4000 horsepower (775 to 3000 kW) are linked with the final drive by two forms of transmission:

1 *Diesel-electric:* the diesel engine drives a generator, with final drive via electric motors under series-resistor control (see Chapter 4): a reliable system, but with weight penalties.

2 *Diesel-hydraulic:* offering lower weight, this system was adopted by the German Federal railways, and later by the Western Region of BR. However, high maintenance costs and the non-standard nature of the equipment has lead to the phasing out of most locomotives so designed.

Lower-powered units – notably multiple-unit passenger stick – feature direct mechanical transmission (the multiple-unit system is described in Chapter 4). They were built in large numbers as part of the modernization plan of 1955, and continue in service on short-distance and cross-country services; some long-distance sets, notably the 'Trans-Pennine' units, built with mechanical transmission, have not proved very satisfactory. The Southern Region operate a number of diesel-electric multiple units, in which a generator compartment is provided in the body of the motor car, but they are of rather obsolescent design. A batch of diesel-electric multiple-unit stock based on the Mk II intercity coach was recently delivered to Northern Ireland Railways, and could form a precedent for the rest of Britain.

The major alternative to diesel traction is electric. References have been made in Chapter 4 to early development of direct current systems in urban areas. Intercity electrification in Europe began on a significant scale in the 1920s, primarily in countries such as Italy and Switzerland which could substitute hydroelectric power for imported coal. In most systems a 1500 volt dc current was supplied via overhead wires, requiring no rectification on the train, but necessitating substations at frequent intervals. Adoption of a 3000 volt dc, as in Italy and Sweden, permitted substations at intervals of up to about 40 km. The 1500 volt system was recommended in Britain by the Weir Committee of 1931, and the first line thus energized, that from Manchester to Altrincham, was converted that same year. The LNER adopted it for Manchester to Sheffield and East London schemes, although the war prevented completion until after nationalization in 1948.

The greater part of pre-1948 electrification took place on the Southern Railway, which extended its 650/700 volt dc third-rail suburban network to Brighton in 1933 and Portsmouth in 1937. Postwar extension by BR has continued to use this system, reaching Bournemouth in 1966. This route is the fastest using low voltages, but is limited to 90 mph (140 km/h).

A major user of the 1500 volt system before the war was the French railways, who electrified several main lines, including Paris

F

to Bordeaux. Postwar reconstruction and expansion was based on use of 25 000 volts (25 kV) ac current, which permitted much wider spacing of substations, and use of standard industrial frequency of supply. Substation costs were greatly reduced, and more powerful locomotives permitted. This system was adopted in Britain from 1957 when the first part of the Euston–Manchester scheme commenced, the Styal suburban line in Manchester. Delays due to lack of finance postponed completion, but in 1967 the entire network came into use, comprising the Euston to Liverpool and Manchester routes (via Crewe and via Stoke), the Birmingham loop, and suburban lines. The 1974 electrification from Crewe to Preston and Glasgow linked with the Glasgow Blue Train system inaugurated by BR in 1960, electrified at 25 kV and 6·25 kV ac (the latter over sections with limited clearances). A similar mixed voltage was applied to existing east London lines, and extensions thereof. In Britain only the Manchester–Sheffield line now remains at 1500 volts dc.

Control and signalling

Reference has been made to the introduction of the block system and track circuits in the urban context (Chapter 4). In Britain the block system became general in the late nineteenth century. While providing a high degree of safety, it was limited in several respects:

1 If a train is stopped because of a derailment, blockage, etc. between signal boxes there is no automatic indication to the signalmen and it is necessary for the train crew to protect the trains with emergency lamps located at the likely braking distance for trains on other tracks.

2 Not all movements consist of steady flows in one direction, and many shunting movements, reversals, etc., require use of additional ground level signals, hand signals from the box, etc. Many minor accidents occur in this situation.

3 The system is very labour-intensive. To a limited extent it can be varied to suit traffic density – for example, intermediate signal boxes can be switched out at night and adjoining block sections combined – but in most cases a full shift-working pattern of crews is needed for each box.

4 A rigid block system limits line capacity. From Figure 4.3 it can be seen that in many cases trains will be spaced at more than the safe braking distance, and thus potential capacity is not being utilized. If a more sensitive indication of maximum speed can be

given to the train, this wastage can be reduced. In theory, a continuous indication of safe maximum speed can be given to the driver ('cab signalling') which would permit optimal use of line capacity, since all trains could then operate at no more than the safe braking distance. A further limitation upon manual block systems is that boxes are often sited adjacent to junctions, which do not necessarily follow a regular spacing related to braking distance.

During the 1930s the original mechanical signalling and interlocking systems were superseded by electric or pneumatic operation, permitting one signal box to control complex track layouts around major stations and eliminate some minor boxes. Such systems were installed at Cardiff and Portsmouth, for example. Colour light signals began to replace semaphores. This principle was extended under the Modernization Plan of 1955 in the form of 'power boxes' controlling sections of route over many block sections. Use of track circuits permitted the control of numerous block sections without high labour costs. Route-setting switches permit routes to be set up over several successive block sections by a single operation. Indicator boards display track sections currently occupied by trains. Subsidiary local boxes controlling movements in stations or goods yards can be incorporated in the overall system. An early example of such a scheme is the Manchester Piccadilly box, replacing twenty-seven conventional boxes on the Manchester–Crewe route. In many cases economic justification for such schemes may rest on labour cost savings alone. The recent area resignalling at Feltham, Middlesex, enabled a reduction in signal staff establishment from 155 to 34 men (although it should be borne in mind that some increase in level crossing keepers was required).

A move towards indicating train speeds more accurately came with the introduction of four-aspect colour light signalling during the 1950s and subsequently, usually coincident with area resignalling. As before green indicates that section(s) are clear for running at maximum speed, red indicates stop. A single yellow denotes continuation at a speed no higher than that from which the train can slow down to stop at the next signal, a double yellow a speed from which the train can slow down to stop after the next signal (itself showing single yellow). Close headways can thus be operated despite high maximum speeds, as signals may be placed at closer intervals than that required for braking to stop from maximum speed. Experi-

mental work is continuing into means of continuous train detectio
and speed indication.

A major limitation on signalling is the very high cost of remainin
labour-intensive conventional boxes which cover many secondar
and freight routes, and the cost of construction of new area scheme
The level of safety imposed on the railways is exceptionally hig
relative to that required of road systems, and imposes high costs no
attributable to managerial policy. Several means exist of reducin
signalling cost on secondary routes. In the case of a short branch
line the 'one engine in steam' principle can apply, that is, only on
train is operational at any time and thus no collision can occu
between moving trains. Few passenger routes of this type no
remain, but one such is the branch from New Holland to Barto
in South Humberside. In such cases no signalling costs are incurre
save for the box at the junction with the rest of the network.

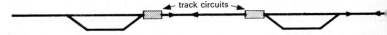

Figure 8.1 Tokenless block working

A number of single-track control systems exist, in which the ove
riding principle is that only one train has authority to occupy
section at any one time. The Victorian system was based on th
token, a device which had to be carried by each train of which on
one existed for each section of track. Hence only one train could b
operational at one time. Tokens were exchanged at passing loop
In some cases, a number of trains might be sent in the same directic
before any train was due to return (outward journeys on a seasic
excursion branch, for example). In such cases, the *key-and-tabl*
system was operated. A key carried by each train was used to turn
lock in the signalling equipment at the end of the single trac
section. This equipment was linked electrically to similar equipme
at the other end, from which another key could be released only aft
the first key had been inserted at the end reached by the train. A
improvement adopted on long single-track routes is the *tokenle*
block system (Figure 8.1). A short track circuit is sited at each er
of the section. Following completion and breaking of the fir
circuit, the second must be similarly completed and broken befo
another train can enter the section. This eliminates the need to slo
down or stop trains in order to exchange tokens or tablets.

On many secondary routes in France and Ireland, the practice of operating single- or double-track secondary routes by telephone has been found quite satisfactory. A telephone message from a station indicates that a train has arrived, and that a second train may follow from the preceding station. The Central Wales Line is worked in this fashion, but such methods are not common in the UK.

A development of single-track control systems is CTC (Centralized Traffic Control). Track circuits and telephone messages from a wide area are fed into a control centre, which by controlling train movements is able to make the best use of available passing loops, double-track sections, etc., to maximize line capacity. Heavy flows can thus be handled, as on the northern lines of the Swedish state railways, carrying several million tons of iron ore each year.

Track structure and route alignment

Conventional rail track is primarily a flexible structure, in which the highly concentrated train weight (axle loads of up to 25 tonnes bearing on small areas of steel wheel/rail contact) is distributed first through rail and sleepers and then through ballast (a layer of stone chippings) to sub-base, embankment, viaduct or tunnel structure. On major routes ballast is up to 60 cm (24 inches) deep, and sealed by an impervious layer (such as heavy-duty polythene sheet), so as to direct water into adjoining side ditches (Figure 8.2). Modern British track now follows continental practice, using flat-bottomed rail fixed to sleepers by clips. Concrete sleepers are replacing wooden ones, with savings in maintenance costs. The major problems related to conventional railway track are:

The need to cope with heavier axle loads – usually met by increasing the cross-sectional area of the rail (different types are referred to

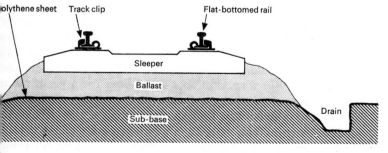

Figure 8.2 Modern railway track structure

by weight. A heavy-duty rail weighs about 120 to 150 lb/yard or 60 to 70 kg/metre). Problems also arise in the distribution of weight through ballast and sub-base.

2　Drainage – the ballast may become clogged with oil or ice, regular cleaning, now semi-automated, is desirable, but requires closure of a track for a short period.

3　Rail joints – conventional track consisted of sections about 50 to 70 ft (16 to 25 metres) length. Joints are made by fishplates, flat metal plates below the rail head, affixed by bolts through the flange. Due to the need to provide for expansion and contraction of rail, these bolts fit into oval-shaped holes. Failure to tighten bolts, or repeated rail movement, can led to rails becoming loose and star-shaped cracks developing around the bolt holes. Such factors are believed to have caused the Hither Green disaster of 1967, in which over fifty passengers were killed. Most main routes are now fitted with continuously welded rail (cwr), reducing both accident risks and maintenance costs. Rail joints are formed by overlapping tapering of adjoining rails (illustration). Contrary to the impression to be gained from school textbooks, expansion in hot weather does not create serious problems.

4　Radii of curved sections – due to centrifugal force, frequent re alignment is necessitated by outward movement of curves laid in ballast (the New Tokaido Line in Japan is a noted example). If a train takes a curve at a speed beyond the safe limit, then it may climb the outer rail. The last major accident due to this cause in Britain was at Eltham, Kent, when an excursion train approached a curve limited to 20 mph (32 km/h) at about 65 mph (100 km/h) This danger can be partially offset by super-elevation – raising the outer rail relative to the inner, analogous to the banking of a racing track. The difference in rail heights is directly proportiona to the square of the maximum speed, and inversely proportiona to the radius. In practice, it is necessary to allow for slow running or stopping of trains on a super-elevated curve. In order to retain stability of trains and prevent excessive wear on the inside rail super-elevation is limited to a maximum of about 15 cm (6 inches) This effectively imposes an upper speed limit for a given radiu and realignment of tracks is thus needed to attain high speeds An attempt to avoid this need is made in the design of the Ad vanced Passenger Train (APT) in which the body of the train i tilted in response to curvature, in order to achieve additiona super-elevation, improving comfort and stability.

5 Pointwork and crossings. In contrast to various monorail proposals, it has the merit of permitting merging and diverging movements with few moving parts. However, in order to minimize risk of derailment, pointwork is usually set in a trailing direction with respect to major traffic flow. When this cannot be achieved, and the points are said to be 'facing' the train, speed limits are often necessary, combined with interlocking to ensure that the switch blade is set firmly against the running rail before a train is signalled to approach the points.

In an attempt to reduce high labour cost of maintenance, some rigid track is now constructed by use of a slip-form concrete paver as used for motorways. As yet, its use is mostly experimental, its high cost offsetting maintenance savings except in tunnel and restricted clearance sections. Expansion joints and resilient pads around track clips are incorporated.

The alignment of track has been discussed already in respect of curvature: not only does this create a need for super-elevation, but also adds to rolling resistance, especially on four-wheel stock. Gradient has been the other major limitation. From the earliest days of railway construction, a slope of about 1 in 70 to 1 in 100 has been a desirable maximum on main lines. On replacement of steam, especially where by electrification, gradient has become much less critical. Conventional gradient limits largely dictate the need for tunnels and viaducts. The former are becoming even more costly to maintain, and in some cases have been 'opened out' on rebuilding, as on the London–Sheffield line near Chesterfield. The excellent construction of Victorian viaducts has however enabled them to carry weights well in excess of original design loads. Even after a route is closed the routine maintenance of the structure may, at current discount rates, cost less than demolition.

Construction of entirely new routes rarely takes place in Britain. Most work is on new goods-only routes, such as those to power stations and quarries. Where a new high-speed passenger line was proposed, from the Channel Tunnel terminal to White City, London, opposition on grounds of noise and visual intrusion was very strong. The environmentalists' picture of railways as less offensive than roads in these respects is coloured by the fact that most railways in built-up areas have been *in situ* for a long period, which has seen several generations of households in adjacent property. The noise levels have thus been accepted as normal. Similar opposition is now strong in respect of the Tokaido line in Japan, and plans for a national network of such routes (the Shin Kansen network) have been cut back partly as a result of such pressures. The French and German railways, however, are going ahead with some new high speed routes.

Rolling stock

The basic layout of main line passenger stock has for many years been that of two-wheel bogies supporting a frame of about 19 metres (60 ft). Within the body, the traditional layout of compartments seating six or eight passengers (a total of forty-two or fifty-six per coach) has been replaced by open-saloon stock, with centre gangways, and seats placed in groups of four to give a total capacity of sixty-four (second class). This eases access for cleaning, ticket inspection and refreshment sales. Fluorescent lighting and more attractive, easy-to-clean materials have become general.

On BR a major change came with the Mark II intercity stock, introduced in 1966. Here, integral construction of frame and body reduces weight and adds to longitudinal strength. Later versions of Mk II stock incorporate double-glazed windows, an internal speaker system, and smaller windows to reduce the visual impact of high speeds. The latest Mk III stock incorporates these features in a greater length (23 metres), of modular construction. This stock forms the basis for the HST (see below). The number of doorways has been reduced, and those at the ends of each coach made wider to aid passengers carrying luggage. A more traditional layout of doorways adjacent to seating does remain on electric multiple-unit stock for semi-fast services.

A major adaptation to suit high speeds is the replacement of vacuum braking, whose power is limited by available atmospheric pressure, by compressed air systems. Modern freight stock is also vacuum- or air-braked in order to permit operation at speeds similar to those of passenger trains. By running different types of trains at similar speeds, better use can be made of track capacity (see below).

Capacity and flow

Basic characteristics are in principle the same as for urban railways described in Chapter 4. In general, minimum braking distances are greater, acceleration rates lower and hence minimum headways somewhat wider.

A major difficulty arises where trains of different speeds are mixed over a common route: intercity passenger, freight and local passenger, for example. If trains set off from terminus A at a minimum headway of three minutes, their paths can be represented by parallel lines of the same angle, as in Figure 8.3. (The angle of inclination to the horizontal is proportional to speed, becoming greater as speeds

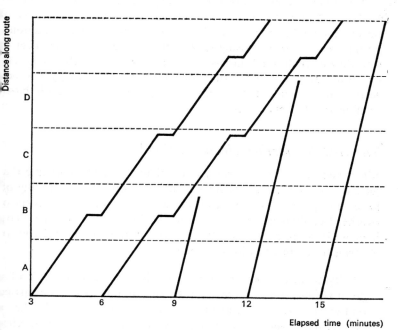

Figure 8.3 A simple timetable graph, illustrating the 'mix of speeds' problem on an urban section of main line railway

increase.) If all trains follow the same sequence of stops the minimum headway can be maintained over the whole route. If, however, a non-stop train sets off at 9 minutes after the first train, it will enter the same block section as the first train at C. Not until 18 minutes after the first train has departed can a non-stop train run without running into the same block section as a preceding train. The paths from A at 12 and 15 minutes are unused.

One means of reducing this wastage is to group similar trains in batches, or 'flights', so that empty paths occur only when one batch of trains follows another. This is the practice on the Euston–Rugby

line, for example, over which the basic off-peak service is grouped
into a half-hour period in each hour, running at five-minute intervals
between trains. Other paths are then available for slow trains, special
workings, etc. In the peak, some trains called at Watford. In order
not to create wasted paths, all trains now do so during certain
periods.

A graphic timetable of this type can be used for scheduling purposes in several ways. On a single-track route both directions of
movement can be superimposed (i.e. lines sloping in both directions;
where they intersect, passing loops will be necessary). The effect of
introducing additional high-speed trains can be illustrated. The
constraint that not more than one train should occupy a block
section at one time can be observed easily by marking off block
sections on the vertical axis.

The case for further electrification

Many people, including professional planners, tend to assume that
justifying electrification schemes is mainly a question of trading of
lower energy costs against the interest and maintenance costs of
overhead equipment and substations. In fact, only since the sharp
increase in oil prices in late 1973 has this been a factor in favour of
electrification. Justifications include:

1 Ability to attain higher speeds with locomotives or stock of
  given weight, since fuel, generators, etc., do not have to be carried
  on the train. A class 47 main line diesel-electric locomotive has
  power:weight ratio of 18 kW/tonne, a class 87 25 kV ac electric
  locomotive 27 kW/tonne.
2 Ability of a dc electric motor to withstand and produce output
  well beyond continuous rated capacity for considerable periods
  of time: for example, 100 per cent overload for fifteen minutes.
  Power thus obtained enables gradients to be surmounted without
  speeds being reduced, and rapid acceleration to recover from
  intermediate stops with little loss of time. This also has an impact
  on line capacity (see the argument concerning urban railways in
  Chapter 4). Electrification can thus be an alternative to building
  additional tracks, or a means of reducing track mileage yet
  handling the same load. (This can enable overhead electrification
  to be carried out. In some parts of south-east France double-track
  routes were replaced by single track on the centre of the former

trackbed, taking advantage of the height at centres of arches, tunnels, etc., to locate overhead wiring.)

3 Since fewer components and much less vibration are typical of electric locomotives in comparison to diesel, availability is higher and maintenance costs lower. Indeed, this can often be the most important cost difference. For example, in 1967 it was stated that operating costs for two similar locomotives of BR were such that energy costs per mile of the electric locomotive exceeded those for the diesel (10p to 6p), but that the much higher maintenance cost per mile of the diesel (19p) offset those for both the electric locomotive and related overhead supply (9p): a net saving of 6p per mile.

Manufacturing costs of electric locomotives are about 25 per cent lower than those of similar diesels. The life of electric stock is also longer, and availability (percentage of days per year available for service) also higher: in 1971 availability of a class 47 diesel – one of the most reliable and commonly used types – was 77 per cent, that of a class 86 ac electric, 86 per cent. The higher quality of service, especially for passenger traffic, generates additional demand at the same price level (i.e. in economic terms, there is a shift *in* the demand curve rather than *along* the curve). An estimate of benefits from electrification based solely on existing traffic levels is likely to understate the commercial return. The recent shift in fuel costs has strengthened the case, the cost per mile for diesel and electric types now being similar. But remember that electricity is a secondary power source. The net thermal efficiency of an electric locomotive is about 25 per cent, but around 30 per cent for a diesel-electric. Only if fuel used to generate power is substantially cheaper per thermal unit (e.g. coal instead of oil) will there be a net saving (see Chapter 10).

Overhead wiring schemes of the 1950s and early 1960s were undertaken in Britain with little experience. Use of lighter equipment, such as the current Mk IIIa type, together with better programming of work enabled a reduction by 1972 of 29 per cent in the real cost per track-kilometre (at 1972 prices, to about £15 250). Aluminium wire has replaced copper. On slow lines and sidings a single strand of wire is now deemed adequate.

Reductions in energy consumption can be made by use of thyristor control (see Chapter 4) and regenerative braking. In braking, a dc motor can act as a small generator. Where heavy trains make regular stops, or operate over long downhill sections, net energy needs can be reduced substantially. On the Sheffield–Manchester 1500 volt dc route coal trains across the Pennines generate substantial current on downhill runs. Such braking can also be used on urban systems, but has less value, since the power generated tends to come in short bursts at irregular intervals, and thus cannot be used effectively. The adoption of 25 kV ac electrification has unfortunately restricted the possibilities of regenerative braking since the motors work on rectified dc current. As energy costs increase, there may be a case for high voltage systems on dc.

High-speed conventional railways

The maximum speeds attained on conventional diesel or electric systems are about 160 km/h (100 mph). Up to 200 km/h (125 mph) is permitted on some sections of the French and German systems, but at high energy and maintenance cost. British Rail offer a similar maximum speed in the form of the High Speed Train (HST), which comprises six or seven Mk III coaches with a streamlined power and baggage car at each end, each with a 1865 kW (2500 hp) engine and diesel-electric transmission. A power:weight ratio (for the power cars) of 25 kW/tonne is thus obtained. While incorporating many modern features, the design is essentially a stopgap measure for routes which have not been electrified and require higher speeds to offset motorway competition, such as London to South Wales.

Another means of obtaining high speed within conventional design is the gas turbine engine. The Canadian 'Turbotrain', based on aerospace technology, has not yet proved reliable, but the French railways have evolved a more practical design based on conventional rolling stock. The ETG and RTG turbine trains were first introduced on the non-electrified Paris–Caen–Cherbourg route in 1970, and on cross-country routes from Lyons in 1974. They are generally limited to 160 km/h, but offer much higher acceleration and power: weight ratios than conventional diesel traction. RTG units are now being operated on the 'Amtrack' system in the USA. A streamlined unit, the TGV, has been built to run at up to 300 km/h (190 mph) on suitably aligned new tracks. A new passenger route is now being built between Paris and Lyons to be operated either by gas-turbine or electric multiple-unit high-speed stock.

The boldest attempt to make use of existing rail networks is the Advanced Passenger Train (APT). By lightweight construction, a very high power:weight ratio is obtained. In order to negotiate existing curvature, the train incorporates a pendular suspension, that is, a suspension system which automatically tilts the train's body in response to the rate of lateral acceleration, thus compensating for lack of super-elevation needed for high speeds. A more powerful braking system is required in order to maintain stopping distances provided within the existing signalling system. The first APTs to enter service will probably work the London–Glasgow run, using the 25 kV ac electric supply, an earlier proposal to power APT production trains by gas turbines having been abandoned. As a result of the pendular suspension, it is necessary to provide compensatory tilting of the pantograph so that contact with the wire can be maintained. The anticipated maximum speed on conventional track is 240 km/h (150 mph). In view of the extensive publicity given to the design, no further details are given here.

A problem of all high-speed conventional trains is the low utilization of track capacity due to the mix-of-speeds problem outlined above. It is ironic that at a time when freight services and suburban passenger trains have been accelerated to approach existing intercity passenger train speeds, a disparity will again arise.

New modes for high-speed movement

It has been suggested that a 'gap' exists in the range of modes available, in the speed range of 240 to 640 km/h (150 to 400 mph), for trips of about 480 km (300 miles): for example, to give a trip of one hour from central London to central Manchester. Until recent experiments in the USA, it was thought that at such speeds steel wheel on steel rail support systems would be impractical. Some separation of train and track would be necessary to avoid effects of high friction and oscillation. Estimates by Barwell (1968) indicate that a given wavelength of oscillation has a much greater effect on passenger comfort and health at high speeds and high acceleration rates.

The first approach to this problem was to apply the hovercraft principle, in the form of the British Tracked Hovercraft and French Aérotrain. An air cushion of about 1 cm sufficed to give the necessary clearance. In contrast to conventional rail track structure, in which weight is concentrated over a very small area, the distribution of forces from the vehicle's movement thus obtained permitted a simple and cheap boxlike structure. Two major problems arose:

1 Power supply to the vehicle – the Aérotrain used a turbine or jet engine, with fuel on board. Noise levels and energy consumption would have made this quite impractical in common use. The tracked hovercraft used a onesided linear induction motor (lim), the train picking up current from a contact rail at the track side. Full-speed test runs were never possible, and the need to maintain continuous physical contact with the rail while the craft itself ran on a cushion at over 200 mph would have been critical.

2 Control of lateral movement – a vertical guide rail would suffer severe buffeting. The tracked hovercraft track consisted of an 8 ft box section, partially enveloped by the sides of the vehicles, on to which cushion pads like those on the underside were affixed. The limited clearance both vertically and horizontally resulted in very large radii being required in both planes when running at full speed: the minimum horizontal radius of about 5 km would have created severe problems of alignment in built-up areas. At the time of the tracked hovercraft's demise in January 1973 designs were being studied which would have largely eliminated this problem by use of short protuberances from one end of the vehicle only, instead of the entire length of the vehicle, enveloping the track.

Other problems common to all monorail-type systems would have been the operation of pointwork at high speeds, and connection of single cars into trains. The abandonment of British efforts in January 1973 and the Aérotrain in July 1974 are not surprising in retrospect, although the hasty decision by the British Government at a time when further ideas were being developed seemed shortsighted to say the least. At the time the total research and development budget was only about £3 million, a fraction of the expenditure for a single type of aircraft.

The alternative form of suspension is magnetic levitation, in which magnets on the vehicle repel similar poles in the track. Track costs are clearly very high, and so are the costs of electric energy unless the magnets can be cooled to a temperature just above absolute zero ($-273°C$, $0°K$). This process, known as cryogenics, has been developed using liquid helium, and enables a high magnetic force to be sustained with a very small current. It would clearly be necessary to incorporate a refrigeration unit on the vehicle in order to maintain such levels. This in turn would impose weight and cost penalties. A solution to alignment problems (akin to those of tracked hovercraft) suggested by Cranfield Institute of Technology is that a train could be built to operate within existing rail loading gauge, running on existing track from city termini. On reaching open country, the train would then transfer to magnetic levitation track, and accelerate to full speed.

German companies have progressed farthest in levitation to date. A proposal by Krauss-Maffei to build an experimental route in Toronto was dropped in 1974 when the West German Government withdrew financial support for research.

In view of the present urgent need to reduce energy consumption of existing modes, it appears likely that work on very high speed ground transport will receive low priority. There is little evidence of urgent need for new infrastructure over the few routes which might justify it in the long run. Existing rail revenues contribute to a system which caters for a wide range of movements and whose financial position would be affected badly by removal of the most profitable traffic. Existing contrasts between the high service quality on trunk intercity routes, and medium-distance or cross-country routes would be heightened. In any case, travel times on trunk routes are being reduced by continued improvement of conventional railways, and higher frequency, short waiting time air services such as the London–Glasgow 'Shuttle'.

The railway system

Figure 8.4 shows the current BR network, indicating electrified routes and those designated 'intercity' (generally those with loco-motive-hauled services to London or other major centres). The network of the South East Region is exceptionally intensive, even in relation to density of population. Areas experiencing significant population growth (East Anglia, East Midlands, West) are poorly served, especially in respect of trips not based on London. Dating from the 'Beeching' era a line-by-line approach to closure of inter-mediate stations remains. In the south-east, virtually all halts and village stations (often staffed) have been retained. In other areas stations are now being reopened to serve large villages or nearby market towns deprived of rail connections, often with local authority assistance. The most notable example is Alfreton and Mansfied Parkway, serving towns of over 50000 population, which for some years did not receive a rail service.

Of the 29000 million or more passenger-km generated on the

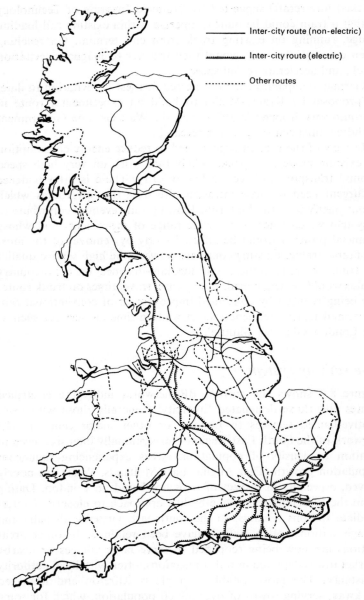

Inter-city route (non-electric)

Inter-city route (electric)

Other routes

Figure 8.4 The British mainland rail network in 1975

BR system each year about 45 per cent are classified as intercity, accounting for about 40 per cent of total revenue. Average trainloads of 150 passengers generate revenues usually covering direct costs, but many fixed costs such as maintenance of high-quality, high-speed track are largely attributable to intercity demand. Growth in traffic has averaged 3 per cent per annum. The rural branch and cross-country lines generate less than 10 per cent of total passenger mileage and revenue, but often act as important feeders to the intercity system: the Exeter–Barnstaple line, for example.

Cross-country intercity services are now developing, with major cross-platform interchange at Birmingham between services from Manchester, Liverpool, Yorkshire, Bristol, Reading, etc. A noted feature of the British network is the use of 'regular interval' time-tabling. Almost universal on the Southern and other commuter services, it applies also to most main lines, hourly or two-hourly headways being typical. This is in marked contrast with other European systems, especially France, and attributable to the relatively short distances between major cities. A single return run at peak times achieves poor utilization of both stock and crews, and additional off-peak services at low marginal costs can be offered to potential passengers at reduced fares, as outlined in Chapter 6.

Express coach services

Long-distance express coach services between major centres first became practicable in the late 1920s. Following wartime disruption, a fairly stable network has been maintained since around 1950, with substantial improvements over longer routes, especially where motorways exist. Traditional seaside excursion traffic has declined, especially day trips, for which the family car is more convenient. There has been some growth in demand for services used by those travelling to stay for several days or more in a resort, especially where railway branches have closed. All-year-round traffic has continued to grow, although largely dependent on groups, such as old-age pensioners, with low incomes and without access to cars. Traditional interchanges such as Cheltenham have been supplemented by those related to the motorway system (such as Aust, adjacent to the Severn Bridge).

Comment on vehicle design is made in Chapter 3. British operators have been reluctant to invest in very high quality vehicles such as those favoured by the Greyhound network in the USA and some

European operators, limiting their investment to about £20 000 per vehicle. A private hire demand for 'executive coaches', fitted with swivel chairs, tables, bar, television, etc., exists in most large urban areas, but is marginal in contrast to total demand. Typical 'heavy-weight' coaches such as the Bristol RE and Leyland Leopard differ little mechanically from stage service buses. They can thus be operated and maintained from the same depots, permitting an extensive network without excessive 'dead' mileage from a few specialized bases. The practice of NBC vehicles being painted in 'National' colours has limited this flexibility, but most coaches remain the property of regional operating companies and are used on local private hire work.

Despite improvement, coach travel retains a low-cost/low-quality image. Improvement is required, particularly in refreshment and station facilities. All too often a coach stop is identified in time-tables as a high street shop – difficult to find, and without shelter or information. A more enlightened attitude on the part of local authorities – who seem to regard coaches as a nuisance rather than part of the public transport system – could help in providing shelters and stopping points sited for good interchange with local transport.

The coach industry itself has done little to invest in facilities. Victoria, London is grossly inadequate for peak traffic, with passengers and vehicles mixed in a dangerous and confusing fashion. The corresponding station at King's Cross barely merits the title, and the few coach stations in other cities, such as Birmingham, Newcastle and Manchester, are often poorly sited in respect of local public transport services.

The network structure

A map of all express coach services would be difficult to update, and largely meaningless in that many of the services are of very low frequency, or, over short distances, restricted to certain groups. Figure 8.5 indicates all services operating daily (or Mondays to Saturdays inclusive) all-year-round. A comprehensive pattern may be observed, with notable concentration on Cheltenham and major cities. In Scotland, the SBG has tended for many years to operate long distance internal services as stage carriage routes. Some of the faster services, filling an 'express' function, have been included.

Even the daily services, however, are mostly infrequent. Many operate only once or twice each way. In the case of Cheltenham and other interchanges they may form a well-connected pattern at

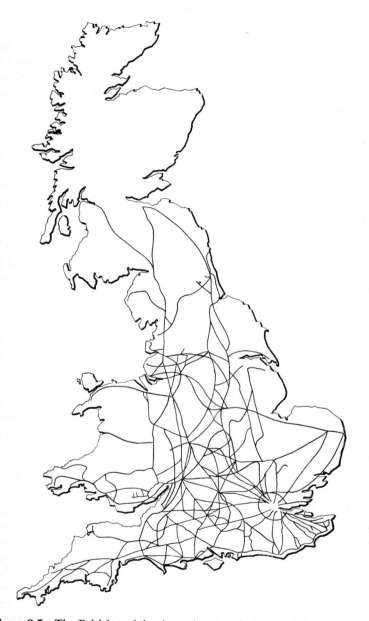

Figure 8.5 The British mainland coach network (1975); daily services operating all year round

common interchange times (over forty services departing from Cheltenham at 1430 on summer Saturdays). Other routes carry little more than day return facilities to major centres. This is not to deny their usefulness – many are better timed than more frequent rail services, for example – but their potential role for connecting minor towns en route is restricted, and it is surprising, given the low direct costs and capacity of each vehicle, that more frequent services are not offered.

Figure 8.6 shows those services operated all-year-round at least four times in each direction (a frequency generally sufficient to permit day return trips from either end, plus midday trips en route for more remote points). This map shows also limited-stop bus and coach services, such as those operated by Ribble in Lancashire, which may fill a similar function. In contrast to Figure 8.5, it displays not so much a network as a series of links concentrated around major cities, although the London–Bristol/South Wales services are a noteworthy exception. Few of these services link major centres which are not also directly connected by rail though express coach routes which are paralleled by railways may none the less serve a valuable function by providing better local accessibility.

The motorway network has had a marked effect on reducing journey times, notably over the M4. It also has a critical effect on costs in that a journey routed in part over a motorway may be shortened so that a return trip is possible within the maximum driving hours now allowed. Were the time required any greater, a relief driver would be required and the service be no longer viable. One example is the Ipswich–Bristol Saturday service operated by Grey-Green of London in conjunction with National Travel.

Regulation and finance

The legal definition of 'express carriage' does not accord with the general conception of 'express coach' in that any timetabled service on which the minimum fare is 10p or more is so defined (see Chapter 1). Many services have been converted into 'stage carriage' operations by inserting fare stages of less than 10p, thus entitling the operator to fuel-tax rebate and new bus grant. In some cases this has been done openly with the consent of the Traffic Commissioners as a means of enabling continuation of services which would otherwise not be viable. A recent example is the Liverpool to Manchester airport route.

Figure 8.6 The British mainland network of coaches and limited-stop interurban buses operating at least four times per day all-year-round (1975)

This confused definition makes the published statistics of passengers carried almost meaningless. For many years the 'express' total in *Passenger Transport in Britain* (see Chapter 1) has been around 70 million. But in 1971, for example, the average fare recorded was only 28p: a rough estimate of the total long-distance passengers would be about 20 million per annum.

Coach and rail competition

The treatment of coach and rail services in Britain is highly inconsistent. The railways receive large subsidies whereas express coaches qualify for neither fuel-tax rebate nor new bus grant. The railways may object to an application for new or modified coach service, but they may amend timings and fares, often in a manner designed to compete with the coach, without reference to any similar procedure. Recent decisions both by the Traffic Commissioners and, on appeals, by the Secretary of State have been more liberal than in the past, overruling railway objections in authorizing improved coach services from Newcastle, Scarborough and Buxton to London in 1973–4. It is now accepted that coach and rail largely serve different markets, and that improved coach services are likely to generate new traffic rather than divert it from rail.

Nevertheless, there is an area of overlap, primarily over trunk routes between major centres where a substantial low fare market exists. The major example is Tyneside to London, over which coach and rail hold similar shares of the market. London to Bristol and South Wales is approaching a similar position, but trunk routes to the north-west (Birmingham, Manchester, Liverpool) are dominated by rail despite motorway improvements. Rather than limit coach services, present policy gives an incentive to BR to offer low fares. Regular interval operation on trunk routes results in many spare seats in high-quality rolling stock outside the peak. If the railways can offer these seats to coach travellers at a similar fare (perhaps a little higher in view of the higher rail service quality), without diverting passengers who would otherwise pay full fares, they can obtain substantial net revenue. The marginal costs are negligible.

The first attempt to create such diversion was the 'Highwayman' service of 1970. A slow train, of old stock, ran between London and Newcastle once a day at very low fares, attracting extremely high load factors in summer. However, an additional slow train on inter-city tracks may impose high costs due to its effect on route capacity (see above). The Highwayman was superseded by the selling of existing empty seats on off-peak trains by 'supersave', and now 'economy return' fares. These are priced at about half standard rate, but are subject to three weeks' advance booking. In this fashion BR have imitated some features of the coach market. However, while it is usual to book in advance for coach travel, most offices now accept bookings almost up to the time of departure, and the period stipulated for pre-booking by rail appears unrealistic. Since early 1975 BR have also offered half-fare pensioners' passes, in another attack on the coach market.

Future of the coach system

The British network is probably the most intensive in Western Europe, the Europabus system being severely restricted by regulatory systems which favour rail. The extent to which EEC regulations inhibit development (especially by limits on drivers' hours) remains to be seen. Suggestions that the USA Greyhound network should be imitated, except in so far as comprehensive national marketing has advantages, make little sense. For all its fame, the US coach system accounts for little more than 2 per cent of all intercity traffic, compared with express coaches' share of 13 per cent in Britain. Motorway access to city centres is rarely available, and unlikely to develop.

Once temporary financial difficulties of some of National Travel's subsidiaries are overcome, stable profits and steady growth can be expected, although the financial position does not permit any risk-taking such as introduction of high-frequency services over routes now served once or twice daily. Continued growth of new towns, and regions such as the West Country and East Midlands, which are poorly served by rail, can be expected.

In the long run, trunk services and semi-fast services may be segregated more clearly, the former on motorways, the latter incorporating limited-stop bus facilities and licensed as stage services. The system of pre-booking now used incurs high labour cost, and while permitting high load factors and efficient allocation of additional vehicles at peak periods and on trunk routes, is very costly in relation to revenue from medium-distance trips. It may be cheaper to move to direct sale coupled with retention of standby vehicles and crews to duplicate workings if required. British Airways' London–Glasgow Shuttle service is justified on such calculations, and if it is worthwhile to operate standby jet aircraft and high-paid crews, then surely a similar trade-off exists between coach charting and standby coaches? Removal of the need to book ahead would also encourage optional travel.

Another opportunity lies in co-ordination with rail, not to divert existing coach passengers, but to create new high-quality links attracting the business market. A good example is the half-hourly Reading–Heathrow service connecting with Western Region trains from Bristol, South West and South Wales. Similar links could connect growing towns poorly served by rail with trunk intercity routes to offer end-to-end timings not available by either mode at present (for example Luton to Stevenage, for Yorkshire, Tyneside, etc.).

The medium-distance interurban problem

Although services in the intercity sector have generally improved, many minor rail services have been withdrawn, and cross-country trips made more difficult. In many areas, stage carriage bus services provide the only link, at very low speeds (25 to 33 km/h, 15 to 20 mph) and over devious routes. Paradoxically, it is becoming easier to travel long distances to major centres than over distances of thirty to forty kilometres. The car users will normally find cars convenient over such distances, although if the intercity image were applied to high-quality medium-distance services, they might transfer voluntarily. It can be argued that for the non-car-user, the problem is marginal in contrast to essential local transport needs for work, shopping, etc. However, there are strong reasons for concern:

1 Hardship to existing users if present loss-making services are cut.
2 Additional road congestion and accidents resulting from additional car trips.
3 'Cascade' effects: decline in revenue on remaining services if feeders are closed, and the stimulus to additional car ownership within medium-sized towns (up to 200 000 population) within which existing public transport is adequate. Once owned, cars may be used at perceived marginal cost, adding to congestion within those towns.
4 Regional development and employment.
5 A distribution of population in which development is concentrated into towns of about 100 000 population may be optimal. Such towns provide adequate support populations for most

facilities, but without high peaking or lengthy work journeys (evidence is produced in Chapter 2, and policy implications considered in Chapter 10).

6 The need for access, as of right, to increasingly centralized communal facilities. As counties replace smaller authorities for many functions, and hospitals, school, etc., are based on larger catchment areas, it is important to ensure that people without cars are able to enjoy the same rights as those with cars.

Note that these arguments suggest a certain level of service, not necessarily a large subsidy. In many cases it may not be necessary, but we should be prepared to offer it to bus and coach services where they fill these functions.

Within the bus and coach industry, clear potential exists:

1 To expand existing express coach services offering a frequency of at least four trips a day, in such a way that they provide a useful range of timings over intermediate sections. The Norwich–Newmarket–Cambridge–London service of Eastern Counties/National Travel is a good example. A less cumbersome pre-booking system would be desirable than that which exists on most express services, perhaps direct payment to the driver as on London–Oxford services. From the operator's viewpoint, conversion of a service from 'express' to 'stage' category (subject to Traffic Commissioners' approval) enables cost savings. Unfortunately many existing express coaches operate only once or twice daily.

2 Conversion of existing stage services to limited-stop, average speeds thus rising from about 25 to 40 km/h (16 to 25 mph), with associated reductions in time-based costs, as well as improvements from the passengers' viewpoint. Most existing limited-stop conversions retain about one stop per mile, and overlap remaining local stage services. Hence a comprehensive public transport service is retained, albeit at a lower frequency for some passengers. In more thinly populated areas the local service might be provided by post-van or school bus converted to carry fare-paying passengers (see Chapter 7). Two recent examples investigated by the Transport Studies Group of the Polytechnic of Central London illustrate the problems and benefits.

Between Newcastle and Morpeth four buses per hour are operated by NBC, one of which runs limited-stop along the A1 road from the southern edge of Morpeth into Newcastle. The other three buses per hour via minor villages sited on the old A1 road. Conversion of one of these slower buses into another limited-stop run, creating a regular thirty-minute limited stop headway enables it to run to a large housing estate within Morpeth (whence many trips to Newcastle previously required a feeder trip within Morpeth), within the same running time. The intermediate villages retain a good service into Newcastle from other converging routes. The rail service operates only eight times per day from a poorly sited station.

Between Brighton and Portsmouth an intensive belt of coastal development is well served by both bus and rail, albeit at low speeds. In January 1975 the local NBC operator converted two connecting half-hourly bus services into a single hourly limited-stop through route, cutting interurban travel time by about 25 per cent. Additional local services partially compensated for frequency reduction and elimination of intermediate stops. From the operator's viewpoint the scheme was a success, enabling cost reductions and attracting substantial new interurban traffic. However, this role was largely filled already by the heavily subsidized rail service. Since the urban/rural distinction is not as sharp as in the first example, many points within urban areas found their stops on the interurban route removed, and some large villages had their service reduced to an hourly frequency. Given the change that has now occurred, the logical development would be a reduction in rail service, the railway concentrating on longer-distance traffic.

Where less frequent existing interurban bus services are paralleled by railways, one may find that nearly all remaining interurban traffic has passed to the railway. This is the case between Wareham, Dorchester and Weymouth for example. The bus may still be routed along the main road. In such cases advantage may be taken of the slack which often exists in rural timetables to offer selective diversions to nearby villages, as discussed in Chapter 7.

At high volumes of traffic, road and rail upgrading may be alternatives for interurban flows in rural regions. A preliminary study suggests that investment in an upgraded rail link may provide net benefits as high as for a parallel road scheme, if the railway can be made sufficiently attractive to offer comparable door-to-door journey times. As fuel costs rise, diversion of car trips produces substantial resource savings. Opportunities are discussed further in Chapters 9 and 10.

References and further reading

Barwell, F. T. (1968) 'Problems of support, guidance and propulsion involved in high-speed transport systems'. IRCA, UIC Symposium, Vienna.

British Tourist Authority, London *The British on Holiday* (annual survey).

Alston, I. (1974) 'HSGT with repulsive magnetic suspension', a paper read at University Transport Studies Group Conference, January 1974 (see also Cranfield Centre for Transport Studies *Report no. 5*).

Claxton, E. (1974) 'Electrification reaches Glasgow', *Railway Engineering Journal,* July, pp. 32–6.

Clemow, C. J. (1972) 'Planning for railway electrification', *Inst. Elec. Eng. Jnl*, **119**, 431–40; discussed in **119**, 1628–40.

Evans, A. W. (1969) 'Intercity travel and the London Midland electrification', *J. Tpt Econ. Pol.,* **3**, 69–95.

Fellow, T. G. (1974) 'High speed surface transport', *Rly Eng. Jnl,* **3**, no. 2, 4–13.

Jones, S. (1973) 'High speed running with special reference to the advanced passenger train', *Inst. Tpt Jnl,* **35**, no. 2, 49–61.

Lansing, J. B. (1968) 'The effects of migration and personal effectiveness on long distance travel', *Transportation Research,* **2** (December), 329–38.

Leake, G. R. (1973) 'Some characteristics of rail and air passengers on domestic inter-city routes in Great Britain', *Traffic Eng. and Control,* **14** (April), 581–5.

Perren, B. (1972) 'SNCF experience with turbotrains', *Modern Railways,* **29**, June, no. 285, 224–6.

Sephton, B. G. (1974) 'The high speed train', *Rly Eng. Jnl* (September) pp. 22–41.

Stanley, P. A. and White, P. R. (1973) *A Review of Medium-density Inter-urban Public Transport*, Discussion Paper no. 2, Transport Studies Group, Polytechnic of Central London. (Details of further working papers in this field are available from the author.)

Transport and Road Research Laboratory (1970/71) *Report of the Working Party on Inter-City Transport*, vols 1 to 3, 1970/71; reissued 1973 as *TRRL Reports SR1, SR2, SR3*. Long-term forecasts for high-speed modes over trunk routes, including APT, Hovertrain.

Little detailed analysis of demand patterns, or any aspects of the express coach industry, has been published. Rail developments are well covered in *Modern Railways* (monthly), *Railway Gazette* (monthly) and *Rail International* (quarterly). The express coach industry has its own journal, *Coaching Journal* (monthly) and is covered in other bus and coach publications, notably 'Express Scene' column in each issue of *Omnibus Magazine* (bi-monthly).

9 Policy in the short run

Introduction

Although making some proposals of my own, I have aimed to provide a basic description of major elements in current British policy, and likely trends over the next four or five years. Long-term considerations are outlined in the final chapter.

Organizational structure

> We trained hard, but it seemed that every time we were beginning to form into teams we would be reorganized. I was to learn later in life that we tend to meet any new situation by reorganizing; and a wonderful method it can be for creating the illusion of progress while producing confusion, inefficiency and demoralization.
>
> PETRONIUS ARBITER, Rome, *c* 55 AD.

As related in Chapter 1, numerous changes have been made in organizational form in an attempt to combat problems faced by public authorities and transport operators. Some of the change has been both inevitable and desirable. The establishment of PTAs and later of Metropolitan Counties has permitted integrated planning of conurbation rapid transit networks. Replacement of separate grants for different transport activities by allocations under the Transport Policy and Programme (TPP) system is slowly encouraging a positive role in public transport by authorities whose previous interest was solely in highways. But such changes are only valid if they cause the level of service offered to passengers, or the use of scarce resources, to be improved. PTAs did little to stem decline in bus use, and may even have accelerated it. Local authorities now employ more planning officers than ever before, but new construction of houses and roads has fallen markedly.

Any change in organization is justified only if it permits the introduction of new techniques and attitudes which increase the organization's ability to achieve its primary objectives. There must always be some adaptation to change, which may necessitate the removal of existing officers. One means of so doing is to redefine roles. Rather than sack a manager whose policies are outdated, it is less painful in the short run to retitle his role as 'consultant' and appoint someone else effectively to replace him. In the long run such compromises merely add to the weight of bureaucracy, and make radical change even more difficult.

The latest attempt to solve problems by reorganization is the proposal of a group of academics, trade unionists and politicians under the aegis of *Socialist Commentary* to create a National Transport Authority, replacing some functions of the Department of the Environment, within which road and rail authorities would produce accounts on a comparable basis. There seems to be little that could not be performed by existing organizations. In practice, only marginal changes are likely during the next few years, and it is in specific operating and planning techniques that useful change may occur.

The railways

The greatest change is that likely to be forced on the railway system as a result of the annual deficit of about £500 million (almost half of total costs) now generated. An unpublished document prepared by the Railways Board in 1974 claimed that much of the deficit was inescapable, whatever size of network were operated. This case was accepted implicitly in the Railways Act of 1974 which replaced existing specific grants with a global subsidy. New constraints on public expenditure limit such a policy and cutbacks seem likely. These could take the form either of severe reduction in network size, or change in operating methods so as to reduce labour costs. Dr Pryke (Pryke and Dodgson, 1975) has estimated that over 40 000 staff, over 20 per cent of the present total, could be removed without significant effect on service quality. A less extreme approach to safety by the Railway Inspectorate could permit more unmanned level crossings and much lower signalling costs. A change of this type is preferable to one of cutting the network. As argued in Chapter 8, medium-distance and cross-country links are of increasing importance as the national population becomes more dispersed. A limited network would cater only for intercity and commuting traffic, directing the benefits of rail subsidy even more firmly to higher income groups (see Chapter 10).

Some internal change in organization might be precipitated by a general reduction in staff, as fewer non-operating staff would be required to administer the system. Unfortunately the proposed rationalization of regions, divisions and areas into territorites and areas was abandoned early in 1974. A general upheaval of railway organization would serve little purpose, and probably distract attention from necessary technical change. However, where other organizations are willing to take over operations, notably the PTE rapid transit scheme on Tyneside, they could provide the oppor- tunity to change operating techniques.

Domestic air services

In airline operation government policy has not yet moved fully into a 'no subsidy' position, but pressure exists to impose economic charging for navigation facilities, and expenditure on new airports is relatively low. The duplication of regional airports within England and Wales may be resolved if current plans of the Civil Aviation Authority (CAA) to designate a limited number of regional airports for development can be enforced. Such airports may serve wide catchment areas, and hence justify direct flights to the Continent. Such concentration is likely to extend the length of feeder trips, and perhaps to reduce 'interline' traffic on domestic routes (i.e. trips to major airports such as Heathrow or Gatwick at which connection is made with international flights not available from provincial air- ports). Increased fuel costs affect short-haul operations more radically than long-haul, and the gap between rail and air fares which narrowed in the 1960s is now widening again. Even drastic increases in rail fares to match current costs would do no more than equal likely air fares. Barring the unlikely introduction of wide- bodied jets on domestic routes, few opportunities for reducing cost per seat kilometre exist which do not also entail a reduction in service quality. In many ways the future of domestic air sevices would appear to lie with cross-country routes, especially those with sections over water, which offer marked advantages in speed and quality over corresponding ground routes. Worked in many cases by independent operators with low overheads, these routes also have potential for economies of scale, in that relatively small aircraft are now in use.

The bus and coach industry

In the express coach industry, the creation of the National Bus Company has enabled the setting up of comprehensive planning and marketing via its subsidiary National Travel. The small profit margin, lack of government financial support and perhaps some conservatism in management make it unlikely that any dramatic changes with their associated risks can take place. However, a large number of minor network changes are producing considerable improvement in cross-country links, and emphasis is shifting from the traditional seasonal role to a good level of service all the year round. Given likely fare increases on the railways, and the effect of fuel costs on private car and air travel, the coach industry is well placed for growth.

The benefits from formation of NBC to local bus operations are less clear-cut. Some basic research has been sponsored that would not have occurred otherwise. The potential for co-ordinating orders for new vehicles so as to obtain economies of scale and bargain effectively with manufacturers has been limited by the poor record of the manufacturing industry (see below), necessitating purchases of non-standard vehicles. The central function within NBC is fairly limited, and apart from the above roles, confined largely to setting financial targets to subsidiary companies. There is little action taken on matters such as scheduling techniques or network structure. While many features of each company's network are unique, some techniques now employed usefully by more progressive subsidiaries – such as the market research of Eastern Counties or United Automobile – are not actively disseminated to other companies. Given a financial target, a poor company will react by cutting mileage (or increasing subsidy requests!) faster than a fall in patronage, a progressive one by reshaping services to meet demand. The centre seems unwilling to ensure that the latter will prevail, save by movement of senior officials by promotion between companies.

The poor performance of some NBC subsidiaries has intensified demands by local authorities now paying high subsidies for indifferent services to operate them directly. Councillors in Hertfordshire and Bedfordshire, for example, have made such proposals. In addition, existing municipal bus services, now controlled by district councils, remain confined to arbitrary boundaries. The position could be resolved by an Act of Parliament giving general powers to county and district councils to operate bus services, either by extension of existing municipal networks or voluntary takeover of parts of NBC. Where the existing NBC operator is considered satisfactory, or the county council uninterested in bus operation, no unnecessary, harmful change need take place, but the option of substituting local authority operation for that of NBC should exist where poor services are now offered.

Despite occasional threats to their existence, notably a recent proposal to sell the Edinburgh Corporation undertaking to the Scottish Bus Group, municipal operators will probably survive at least to their present extent, as the need to control both highway planning and public transport within the same urban area becomes more evident.

In rural areas, independent operators are likely to remain important, perhaps taking over a few more NBC services (although the case for this is likely to rest on their ability to operate a given level of service with a lower subsidy than NBC, rather than at a clear profit). As a result of increased cost estimates and a reluctance to pay adequate subsidies, many rural areas now face dangerous cuts in service levels.

Financial policy

British Government policy towards transport has shown marked lack of certainty and cohesion. However, if for no better reason than the existence of external economic constraints, some decision-making has been forced in the financial sector.

The Transport Act of 1968 inaugurated a policy in which a limited amount of subsidy was accepted as desirable, for 'socially necessary' rail services, and some bus services in 'rural' areas. After allowing for receipt of these specific grants, the British Railways Board, Scottish Transport Group and National Bus Company were expected to break even, taking into account interest payments, depreciation, and in the case of NBC and STG, eventual repayment of commencing capital debt. Road freight, rail freight and intercity passenger services were assumed to meet these demands without subsidy to specific services (although in practice some intercity rail services of low quality, such as Liverpool–Leeds–Newcastle, fell into the grant-aided category from the outset). Railway revenue was increased as a result of the 'selective pricing' policy (see Chapter 6). The bus and coach industry, however, remained severely constrained by the Traffic Commissioners' powers, requiring specific approval of each fare revision.

Rural bus subsidies under section 34 of the Act were initially of little importance, but in 1971 substantial demands were made by the National Bus Company. Local authority responses varied markedly, often questioning the costing procedure, resulting in the evolution of new costing methods as described in Chapter 6. In the event, the total allocated by local authorities to NBC was little over £1 million per year, and considerable service cuts were made in 1971–2.

The 1968 Act extended the principle of infrastructure grants to public transport, and a considerable number of schemes were inaugurated, mostly related to railways in the London area over which traffic flows were sufficiently high to suggest an adequate 'social' rate of return on capital.

This fairly coherent policy operated successfully until about 1972. From that date, partly as a result of strikes and low demand from some major freight customers (notably steel), the railways failed to attain a surplus after taking into account grants for individual passenger services. The National Bus Company and Scottish Group continued to achieve small surpluses in 1973, but ran into deficit in 1974. At the same time, there was increasing public support for subsidies to services in urban areas. From 1972, West Midlands PTE and London Transport maintained stable fare scales. Many other municipal and PTE operators failed to raise fares at the same rate as inflation. As suggested in Chapter 2, the effect of lowering fares in real terms, although not spectacular, was sufficient to offset other factors, and total demand for urban bus services remained approximately constant from 1972 to late 1974. The ability to subsidize urban services was confined to those authorities operating their own services, as bus company subsidies under the 1968 Act (other than for concessionary fare schemes) related only to 'rural' areas.

The 1968 Act had placed capital grants for public and private transport on a comparable footing. However, it retained a bias in favour of capital, rather than operating, expenditure. For example, it can be argued that urban peak-hour traffic demands can be accommodated *either* by building additional roads *or* by providing additional, high-quality public transport services. The Stevenage Superbus experiment indicated the extent to which a sharp increase in demand (over 100 per cent) could be obtained by providing a high-quality, high-frequency service. Although much of the generated traffic came in the off-peak period, significant diversion from car to bus did occur in the peak, and could have been further stimulated by parking restraint. A cost-benefit study had demonstrated that the additional operating costs of such a service were less than those of constructing additional road space solely for peak traffic. Notting-

G

ham city has followed this work on a larger scale by abandoning major road schemes and offering improved public transport, especially peak hour park-and-ride services, as a cheaper alternative.

The opportunity of setting annual operating subsidies against capital cost was offered in the new transport grants structure introduced in 1975, the TPP system, as described in Chapter 1. All expenditure (operating subsidies and capital investment, roads and public transport) now falls into a common total. Although the Government no longer investigates each scheme in detail, its powers are if anything increased, as it not only allocates a grant to cover much of the cost but also holds power to approve total expenditure and most schemes involving loan capital. The introduction of the TPP system unfortunately coincided with a high rate of inflation, and desire to cut back public expenditure. Instead of public transport representing an additional expenditure, such money as could be found had to come out of a reduced total transport budget. In the Metropolitan Counties, substantial amounts – between one- and two-thirds of total expenditure – were allocated to public transport in 1975–6, and major road schemes curtailed. In 'shire' counties, public transport accounts for less than 10 per cent of total expenditure. Although the road share remains high this does not necessarily indicate substantial new construction: in many rural areas a high and largely inescapable expenditure is required for road maintenance. It may be argued that some reduction could be made: there is little point in maintaining roads to a high standard if simultaneous cuts in bus services deprive a substantial proportion of the population from any opportunity to use them.

In late 1974 government policy towards the bus industry was abruptly reversed when proposed reductions in revenue support were announced, from a current level of over £100 million per annum to £50 million (at 1974 prices) by 1978–9. This move was aimed largely at certain metropolitan authorities, such as Greater London and the West Midlands, who were allocating a substantial proportion of their TPP budgets to subsidies required to hold fares at the 1972 level. The government policy was supported by the argument that the elasticity of demand for urban bus services by price (about -0.3) was relatively low, whereas that by service frequency (i.e. miles run as a proxy, about $+0.7$) was much higher. Roughly speaking, an increase in current expenditure of 10 per cent could be used to reduce fares, generating about 3 per cent more trips, or to increase mileage (assuming a constant cost per mile), generating 7 per cent more trips. On this line of argument, expenditure on higher service quality (which might include bus priority schemes, etc., as well as higher mileage) was a better option than the simpler, cruder policy of holding down fares.

As applied to NBC and STG the policy of attempting to break even by raising fares has been very harmful. The anticipated increase in revenue did not occur to the full extent. Although in some cases the increases did little more than catch up with recent inflation, their short-term effect, when applied in late 1974/early 1975, was that of a sharp *real* increase in fares. The effective reduction in fares over the previous two years had already affected traffic levels in so far as it had compensated for a decline in average service quality. The elasticity of demand for NBC/STG services may be higher than that of urban municipal services (upon which nearly all officially sponsored work on fare elasticities has been based). In the smaller towns typically served by company rather than municipal operators, walking and cycling are feasible alternatives if fares become too high. Over rural and interurban routes, shopping and other non-work trips account for a high proportion of total demand. Overall price elasticity related to number of *trips* made may be around −0·6, related to passenger-miles even higher.

The Government's distinction between revenue support and grants for specific measures (for example, a basic off-peak service, extra peak buses to handle diverted car trips) is thus largely artificial in the case of non-urban services. In urban areas it is valid in the long run, but in the short run varying the level of fares has been one of the few means open to authorities to stimulate public transport use (shortage of spares and new vehicles has effectively prevented any significant increase in mileage run). A more cynical interpretation of government policy would suggest that the bus industry has been chosen for stringent financial measures (i.e. a *reduction* in current subsidies, not merely prevention of further growth) since it forms an easy target. The industry has not moved so far from viability that a return to breakeven principles would not have the near-unthinkable consequences that would occur in the railways, for example. The bus industry is poorly organized as a pressure group and its users, although numerous, have little political weight.

Financial policy towards the railways has been less certain. The higher service quality offered has enabled fare increases to catch up with inflation without harmful effect on total demand. However, elasticity of demand in the intercity/cross-country market appears to be about unity, so that further real increases could be self-defeating. There is one area of railway operations which could withstand a sharper increase: commuting into London. In the short run, most commuters would have little alternative but to pay up. In the long run, rail commuting might decrease significantly, but this would not necessarily be harmful. (A decrease sharp enough to result in closure of any important routes is unlikely.) The existing commuter peak results in heavy losses and poor utilization of rolling stock. It can be argued that, in the short run, substantial costs would arise as a result of price increases. Any extra car trips generated as a result would increase existing inner-city congestion. In the long run, however, it must be realized that a continuous turnover of households is taking place in the main commuting areas. At any one time fresh decisions to locate in such areas are being made on a basis of current rail fares. The problem is a dynamic one, for which the static assumptions of most cost-benefit analyses are inappropriate. Whereas the Government has taken a tough line towards the bus industry, it has taken much longer to suggest target reductions in commuter rail subsidies.

Subsidies to rail and bus services may also, of course, be lessened by reductions in cost. In the bus industry the low proportion of administrative costs and high share of one-man operation make further reductions difficult, except by directly reducing service levels. In the railway industry substantial opportunities remain for reducing manning levels, as outlined above.

Government policy towards capital expenditure has also been erratic. For the moment, the 50 per cent grant towards cost of new stage service buses continues to be paid, but the railway industry has seen violent fluctuations – often within a few weeks – in proposed investment programmes. As a result, the continuity of work necessary to achieve economies of scale in production of rolling stock, electrification, etc., has not been attained.

Operating and marketing techniques

Policies adopted by operators towards the running and selling of their services have changed significantly, although rather slowly, in recent years. The importance of current requirements, rather than those existing when services were first established, is being accepted. Repeated surveys have emphasized the importance of reliability, speed, frequency and comfort. Vehicle design now takes account of factors such as step heights, location of handrails and better suspension, in a more systematic fashion. Market-research techniques are coming into general use. Unfortunately marketing is a subject which easily lends itself to nebulous and generalized discussion. Rather than cover the whole field I shall concentrate here on one example, and leave the reader to consult texts on other aspects: recent work by Hovell, Jones and Moran (1975) is particularly useful.

The passenger transport industry is almost unique in that the customer is involved with the process of production. Whereas most goods or services are produced in one specialized area and then sold through a limited number of outlets such as shops, cinemas and bars, much public transport 'production' is sold direct. Most bus journeys and many rural train journeys are paid for on the vehicle. Even the urban/intercity rail, and coach industries possess a very large number of sales outlets. Coupled with the wide range of fares for different types of trip and destination, this presents both passenger and operator with much expense and inconvenience. Simpler systems may both reduce operating costs and stimulate additional travel.

As a first stage one may improve the presentation of information, so that questions are eliminated at the stage of purchasing a ticket. (There are few things more irritating than to queue to board a one-man bus while a passenger interviews the driver on the fare scale, timetable and location of stop for the return trip!) This process extends most widely in the intercity sector. Both rail and, to a lesser extent, coach operators, have developed travel centres in which a wide range of information is available prior to booking a ticket. Sales of package holidays and other travel facilities help to cover costs. Information on intercity services is now more accessible. Since 1974 British Rail and National Travel have published comprehensive national timetables. Pocket-sized time and fare cards are widely distributed. Credit cards may be used for purchase of rail tickets, and coach bookings often made up to time of departure. The only significant handicaps remaining for the intercity travellers are the lack of co-ordination between coach and rail services, and ill-defined nature of many coach pick-up points, as discussed in Chapter 8.

For the short-distance traveller severe problems remain. Since the number of services and range of destinations is far greater than in the case of the interurban network, publication of national, or even regional, timetables is often impractical. Since the value of each fare

paid is much less, advertising of specific fares, even to major destinations, is rarely worthwhile. But such difficulties do not excuse the
erratic and inadequate efforts of many operators. Limited standard-
ization of timetables was achieved by a bus operators' committee in
the 1960s, and a pattern incorporating twenty-four-hour clock,
common page layout and coding, has been adopted by NBC and
STG companies. In some cases, usually with the assistance of county
councils, independents and municipal operators appear in the same
format, together with rail and express services. Northumberland,
Durham and Devon offer good examples. Little effort has been made
nationally to ensure a consistent effort. Municipal timetables (if
issued) follow a different format, and some independents appear
reluctant to disclose any information at all!

As one-man operation has become widespread, many operators
advise passengers to 'have the correct fare ready' when boarding.
Unfortunately they do little to make this possible. Some, such as
Hull and Leicester municipalities, have made a practice of displaying
fares to major destinations at each stop, but few have followed this
lead. Simplified fare scales do exist, although in practice the most
frequent users (generally those in the peak) will become familiar
with fares charged, and possess the correct change. The problems lie
in the *knowledge* of the fare to be paid (whether it forms part of a
simplified or complex scale is not directly relevant), and the need
to handle money.

Apart from purely rational objections to the delay and inconvenience now resulting from cumbersome fare systems, there is an
important subjective aspect: a passenger who has difficulty in finding
the right fare may feel that he or she has been made to look foolish
in front of others, and thus be reluctant to use the service in future.
Handling money and ticket may be none too easy for the passenger
(especially if carrying shopping or small children), and the operator
has to count and transport a large quantity of low-denomination
coins or tokens. Considerable advantages can be gained by eliminating the operation altogether.

Season tickets and free passes are one example: payment (if any)
is made infrequently at a booking office, and tickets inspected on
request during travel. Whether a season ticket should offer a substantial concession on ordinary fares, as in the case of railways, is
debatable: the user will find such a system more convenient in any
case, and if travelling in the peak period, will have little choice other
than to pay full fare. For most bus passengers, however, such

systems are not available. The wide variety of origins and destinations and limited number of staffed offices, make railway-type season tickets impractical. Two solutions emerge:

1 Issue prepaid multi-journey tickets, either for a specific denomination of fare (such as Merseyside's 'Bus Economy Ticket') or used in a zonal fares structure, in which one or more tickets may be used for a single trip according to how many zones are traversed. Such systems give useful savings in boarding time, but tend to offer savings to the peak-hour user.
2 Issue weekly or monthly unlimited travel tickets, the price of which is related to the typical value of tickets purchased by a peak-period traveller during that period. For example, someone making a trip at a single fare of 12p would make about twenty trips to and from work per month, a total purchase of £4·80. The ticket generally consists of a card, bearing its value, expiry dare and a polaroid photograph of the holder. Following their use in Stockholm since 1971 they have been introduced in several British and European cities.

At first sight, the weekly/monthly system would appear to conflict with the case for peak/off-peak and other market-based pricing policies outlined in Chapter 6, but provided there is a fairly close relation between the monthly cost and total cost of peak-period journeys that would otherwise have been made, such tickets do reflect operators' costs quite well. Many costs are geared to a high fixed peak, and marginal costs of extra off-peak trips often very low. The passenger similarly pays a fixed sum for peak usage, and then makes additional off-peak trips at zero cost. The major problem arising in Britain has been the slavish imitation of the Stockholm system: the latter was applied to a network already receiving a high subsidy and was intended mainly as a means of simplifying ticket handling. A flat rate for the whole region was acceptable. In Britain the use of a flat rate, coupled with pricing aimed at a breakeven policy, has led to high rates being charged for such monthly tickets. They attract only the longer-distance peak traveller, who obtains a substantial saving, but not the inner-city resident. The market penetration of the system is limited (hence its ability significantly to reduce bus boarding times), and serious inequities arise in that the longer-distance traveller is usually better off.

In Hamburg the monthly ticket system has been adopted on a zonal basis, the price paid being related to the number of zones within and across which a passenger wishes to travel regularly. A relationship between trip length and monthly fare, albeit coarsely graded, is thus established. In the latest and most ambitious monthly ticket, the *Carte Orange* of Paris (including Metro, city bus, suburban rail and independent bus operators), the city region is split into five concentric zones, with price varied accordingly. The initial impetus from Sweden does not seem to have been followed by observation of other European experience by British operators.

Some other current issues

Many other aspects of current policy deserve attention, but in a volume such as this space is limited and comment made on some matters rapidly outdated. The following list identifies some critical issues, progress in which readers may follow from the technical press.

Shortage of new vehicles and spare parts

The inability of the public transport industry to meet desired service levels is largely due to this factor at present. The major British bus manufacturer (the Leyland group) is running two years behind on delivery dates, and availability of spares is also poor. Older vehicles have been retained in service beyond their normal life-span and many transfers of vehicles made between fleets in order to maintain fleet strength. The resulting additions are often non-standard, aggravating spares and maintenance difficulties. Body-builders have been unable to make full use of their workshops due to late delivery of chassis.

Shortage of maintenance and operating staff

Although less severe as unemployment rises, this factor also has inhibited operation of advertised services. Shortage of maintenance staff is now less critical, as redundancies occur in the motor industry (although problems remain in obtaining the wider range of skills required for more complex modern vehicles). Operating shortages remain serious, particularly in some large cities. The railways have been affected less seriously than the bus industry, but some posts associated with inconvenient working hours and poor pay relative to other occupations, notably signalmen on older installations in urban areas, are difficult to fill.

Working hours of staff

The road transport industry has already been affected adversely by drivers' hours limits introduced in 1970. Under EEC Regulation 543/69, total driving hours per day would be limited to eight. This would severely affect the road haulage industry and parts of the bus and coach industry (in particular, split-shift peak operation, and long-distance coach services). In theory, Britain, as a full member of the EEC, is required to enforce the regulation from 1 January 1976. If eventually enforced, implications could be favourable to rail, whose share of long-distance freight and passenger traffic might increase. The reduction in peak period bus services in urban areas would strengthen the case for early expansion of rail and rapid transit facilities, whose peak operations are less labour-intensive. There is very little firm evidence to support the supposed safety benefits of restricting drivers' hours to the degree proposed by the Commissioners. Other aspects of EEC passenger transport policy are as yet so uncertain that no clear implications can be drawn for the UK.

Regulation of the bus and coach industry

As outlined in Chapter 7, a strong case exists for liberalization of stage carriage service licensing, especially in rural areas. The Government appears, wisely, to have set itself against lift-giving as a policy, but is unwilling to ease the conditions under which new operators of full-size PSVs can enter operations except for experiments in small areas.

School transport

Schoolchildren now account for a substantial share of weekday peak-period demand for bus services, and there are numerous contract services, whose cost in rural areas greatly exceeds the subsidies now paid to public services. The tendency to plan very large schools, often with little estimation of subsequent transport costs, may now be questioned. Smaller schools based on local catchment areas may be both educationally and economically desirable.

References and further reading

Buckles, P. (1974) *Stevenage 'Superbus' Experiment: Summary Report,* Stevenage Development Corporation/Department of the Environment.

Foster, C. D. (1972) *Social Cost/Benefit Study of the Manchester–Glossop and Manchester–Marple/New Mills Suburban Railway Services,* 2 vols, British Railways Board, Midland Region, London. An example of 'static' analysis.

Hovell, P. J., Jones, W. H. and Moran, A. J. (1975) *The Management of Urban Public Transport: a marketing perspective.* Saxon House.

Huckfield, L. *et al.* (1975) Report of a Study Group on Transport Policy, supplement to *Socialist Commentary,* April.

Lichfield, N. and Associates (1969) *Stevenage Public Transport Cost/ Benefit Analysis,* 2 vols, Stevenage Development Corporation.

Joy, S. (1973) *The Train that Ran Away.* London, Ian Allan. On the economics of British Railways since 1948.

Plowden, S. P. C. (1972) *Towns Against Traffic.* Deutsch. A critique of urban transport planning practice.

Pryke, R. and Dodgson, J. (1975) *The Rail Problem: an alternative strategy,* London, Robertson.

Public Expenditure to 1979/80 (1976) Cmnd 6393, HMSO.

Tanner, J. (1974) 'Forecasts of vehicles and traffic in Great Britain, 1974 Revision', *TRRL Report LR650.*

Trench S. and Slack, J. A. (1973) 'Nottingham's new transportation policy', *Traffic Engineering and Control,* **15**, no. 4/5, 200–4.

10 Policy in the long run

The present system

Current attitudes towards the 'long run' (which I take to be a period more than five years hence) are schizophrenic. On the one hand, much of the effort in transport planning, and subsequent economic evaluation, is based on the assumption that fairly accurate predictions can be made, on a basis of existing statistical relationships, of income, car ownership and hence road travel demand; official forecasts estimate vehicle ownership as far ahead as 2010. On the other hand, most people are aware that in practice very few forecasts can be treated with certainty, and that future policy is more likely to take the course of responding to external conditions as they arise than that of setting out a clear path of planning and investment over the next twenty years.

A result of this situation is the common tendency to continue efforts at long-term planning – if nothing else, considerable inertia exists in the system created over the last ten to fifteen years – but to make little serious effort at implementation. Accurate monitoring of critical short-term trends remains inadequate, and many planners are alarmingly out of touch with current problems. There is a failure to distinguish between a minimum level of investment and construction that might be required in any case (i.e. related to lowest current forecasts of population, income, etc.) and a whole range of possible long-term options. It is all too easy to argue that since a plan relates to, say, a twenty-year time scale, a few months' difference in starting date has little effect. From this one drifts into a situation in which plans are restudied *ad infinitum* and the original objectives lost. The Greater London Council seems especially prone to this disease.

The logic of critical path analysis would suggest that for a project to succeed, the element requiring the longest completion time should be started as soon as practicable. Far from regarding short-term delays as acceptable in such cases, one should begin on basic long-term construction projects as soon as practicable, and consider subsidiary aspects of design during the initial construction period. For example, given a basic decision on loading gauge, construction of the Channel Tunnel could have begun in 1974. It was not necessary to finalize all details of rail links to London, or layout of termini before beginning work. Similarly, it is difficult to see any long-term solution to the problem of public transport in large urban areas – short of drastic change in land use – which does not involve further urban rail construction. Such works could be put in hand before the detailed design of park-and-ride systems, bus feeder networks, etc.

It must of course be accepted that the low level of public investment and high unit costs of construction at present inhibit substantial efforts. However, the system of evaluation itself may also be at fault. Quite apart from the resources it now consumes in its own right, it is based almost entirely on assessment of *benefits*. Many economists expert in the finer points of judging small-time savings, or the effect of taxation in determining net resource costs, have only the haziest idea of costs. Given alternative construction estimates of, say, £10 and £15 million for the same design, most would not be able to judge which was more accurate. Much effort is given to identifying benefits for projects already defined by engineers, little to setting targets within which costs should fall. A more satisfactory method was that used by Sir Herbert Walker as manager of the Southern Railway during its electrification programme of the 1930s. The outlines of a scheme were defined – such as the likely improvement in average speeds and peak capacity – and estimates of the likely financial returns then made. The next benefit obtained was related to the prevailing target rate of interest, and a total cost limit set for the engineer. For example, if a scheme produced a net financial benefit of £100000 per year, this could be used to pay interest on capital invested. If the prevailing minimum rate of interest desired were 10 per cent, the scheme would be justified provided that total cost did not exceed £1 million. 'Social' costs and benefits may require more complex assessment, but the same sequence could be followed.

Before proceeding to possible long-term policies, major underlying factors should be considered. Since operating subsidies are now a large share of government transport expenditure, it is necessary to examine their effect on the present system.

Who benefits from subsidies?

Following substantial growth, subsidies to public transport are being curtailed. Limitations of the local rating system have made local government more dependent on support from central government taxation revenue. It is important to know, in this situation, who benefits from subsidies – whether, for example, they include those better-off who could pay more directly – and how additional revenue might be raised. Definition of 'subsidy' is difficult, but an attempt is made in the government's 'Consultation Document' on Transport Policy. Some overstatement is made – payments for concessionary fares are payments to a bus operator on behalf of certain passengers (just as a business pays for its executives to make inter-city rail or air journeys), *not* subsidies. Similarly, bus fuel tax rebate is only in part a subsidy (insofar as motor vehicle taxation generally exceeds direct costs of providing the road system), and the railway deficit includes certain inescapable pension payments not borne to a similar degree by road transport operators. A large category of expenditure not shown is that on school transport – about £40 million in 1972 and now probably double this figure.

The main conclusion to be drawn is that subsidy tends to increase not with potential hardship should the service be withdrawn, but the existing level of service and income now experienced: higher income, higher subsidy.

For example, the only item which can be allocated almost entirely to lowest income groups, rural bus subsidy, is by far the smallest. Other grants to the bus industry, notably fuel-tax rebate, also aid for rural services and low-income bus users in general, but their proportionate effect is greatest in those areas where demand is highly peaked, and poor load factors obtained in the off-peak. These also are likely to be the higher income areas, such as low-density suburbs, generating peak loads or school or work trips, but few other journeys.

Rail subsidies are high, especially in the south-east where they relate to heavily used commuter services: the highest figure per head per annum of any facility. It may of course be argued that the loss per passenger-mile, or as a percentage of total operating costs, is less in the south-east than in other regions (a result of high volumes and long commuting trips). However, despite the image of 'value for money' thus given, what matters in terms of equity and ability to raise tax revenue is the figure per head.

While it is true that rail services in other regions – which now include intercity in the loss-making category – lose a higher share of total cost, commuting by higher income groups is of far less importance, and a wide range of the population dependent upon rail for cross-country travel.

In 1973/4 municipal and PTE bus services effectively received a subsidy of about £18 million, or about £1 per head of population in the areas served, rail services in PTE areas about £12 million, a further £1 per head in the conurbations thus served. By contrast, subsidy attributable to rail operating losses and capital expenditure in the London & South-East area was about £3, and £2 per capita in other areas. Insofar as London's own transport budget is allocated to public transport in preference to road schemes within a similar total TSG/RSG expenditure per head, this simply reflects the greater priority given to public transport in large urban areas. However, the existence of high national expenditure per head on the BR network in the South-East is debatable, benefitting high-income areas to a disproportionate extent. Rural bus subsidy in 1973/4 amounted to a mere 25p per head in areas served (taken as equivalent population to that in rural district council areas). Subsequent increases in this figure have had only a slight effect in improving the relative position, as PTE and BR losses have risen substanially. In 1973 London Transport's railways attained a surplus which offset bus losses, but here too total deficits have risen steeply. Expenditure on new bus grants and fuel tax rebate in 1973/4 was about £57 million, just over £1 per head throughout the country, and maintenance and capital expenditure on the road system £1348 million, or about £24·50 per head throughout Britain.

Estimation of subsidy on a per capita basis is to be considered preferable to the household basis employed in the National Travel Survey: the latter may be affected by variations in household size, and produce apparently surprising levels of public transport expenditure among middle- and high-income households. These are often accounted for by wives and children rather than the head of the household, and should be considered in relation to their individual disposable incomes rather than gross household incomes. A major omission from the Consultation Document is any detailed estimate of subsidies to air transport. Only operating losses on domestic services – about £5 to £10 million p.a. in the early 1970s – are mentioned. Total subsidies are substantially greater: navigation and other costs incurred by the Civil Aviation Authority not recovered from airlines (£40 million in 1974/5), effective losses on regional airports (about £4·5 million), subsidies implicit in over £200 million 'public dividend capital' held by British Airways, and support for R & D work. If fully-allocated in the manner of 'Cooper Formula' railway costs, subsidies would amount to several pounds per passenger trip, with a higher figure for domestic services (insofar as most operating losses are related to short-haul operations, and subsidies to navigation and airport facilities). One is not implying any drastic cutback in domestic air services – if operators can cut costs and attract more traffic by techniques such as the 'Shuttle' this should be encouraged. Most airports make a loss if interest on past investments is included. The British Airports Authority, controlling major London and Scottish airports, is amongst the most profitable of nationalized industries, and its surplus could probably cover deficits of other airports. However, almost half its revenue comes from trading concessions rather than from transport-related activity. Arguments concerning industrial growth and prestige in various forms have influenced expenditure by local authorities on provincial airports, which, like that on air travel, tends to benefit the better-off.

Capital grants to railways have been directed almost entirely to the major conurbations, since only in such areas does the passenger flow justify large-scale investment, and to date nearly all expenditure under the 75 per cent grants introduced in the 1968 Transport Act has been in the London area. The Fleet Line, Victoria Line to Brixton, King's Cross electrification and London Bridge resignalling have been matched only by some initial work in Tyne and Wear, Glasgow and Merseyside conurbations.

The picture is confirmed when *cross*-subsidy within the public transport industry is examined. For example, in 1972 the National Bus Company achieved a surplus of £7 million (excluding government grant in respect of price restraint). Much of the surplus came from companies such as United Automobile Services and Northern General, serving industrial areas in the north-east. In addition to financing much of the overall surplus, they helped to cross-subsidize losses by operators such as London Country, which serves an area of much pleasanter environment and higher income. It is difficult to see how such transfers can be justified politically. Within Scotland a similar pattern can be found, in which the Central SMT company serving the Lanark and Clydeside industrial area covers losses in the Highlands and north-east, also areas of better environment, and now, increasing prosperity.

Within bus operators' networks, cross-subsidy can often be observed between areas of high density rented or municipal housing and low density private housing, the latter generating much less off-peak traffic, which as already argued, is often the most profitable.

The commonly held view on both sides of the political spectrum is that subsidies benefit lower income groups, being viewed either as justified for that reason alone (left) or as a means of supporting the thriftless and irresponsible (right). In fact, the typical recipient of a large annual subsidy is likely to be a car owner, living in an outer suburb, commuting by rail and voting Conservative. Furthermore, it is the professional and managerial groups who are most likely to receive 'expenses' for private car mileage, first-class rail travel, etc.

One justification sometimes put forward in the light of these facts is that the higher income groups pay more tax, and are, in effect, receiving higher benefits in proportion. It is difficult to see how this can be sustained, save in the case of existing prices not reflecting true scarcity and requiring a similar distortion in the prices of other services to maintain the correct ratio (an argument is put forward for subsidizing public transport into congested city centres, on the grounds that in the absence of road pricing, motorists do not perceive their true costs). Provided that services can be priced at their true opportunity cost there is little reason deliberately to distort public transport prices. The question of restructuring private car costs to make them comparable in form is discussed below. The argument for taking away part of the income from the upper income groups, and in effect deciding for them how it should be spent, appears to be little more than interference for its own sake. In so far as the aim of a progressive income-tax policy is to redistribute income, the greater revenue from higher income groups should surely be diverted directly to lower income groups, through measures such as an increase in old-age pensions, or public utilities such as libraries and hospitals.

It can be argued that some of the groups who may not benefit from transport subsidies do benefit from other types of public expenditure. For example, council house tenants may generate a profitable demand for bus services but at the cost of rent and rates subsidies. However, owner-occupiers are effectively subsidized in a similar manner through tax relief on mortgage repayments. Such matters are questions for the sectors in which they arise, rather than compensation by measures in the transport sector.

Overall, a policy of charging true cost for public transport services would be both more efficient (in encouraging users to appreciate true resource costs) and more equitable. The one exception to this would be the provision of services at a basic level, used by people without cars. The minute amount now spent on rural transport subsidy could be increased several times, yet total transport subsidies cut substantially by correct pricing of intercity rail and air transport.

Attempts to cut subsidy to the absolute minimum in rural areas, which ironically are far more common than in the case of commuter railways or air travel, can easily result in greater costs in other sectors, such as out-patient ambulances and school transport. It may also be the case that inhabitants of a city or specific area are prepared to pay for a high-quality public transport system as a means of improving the quality of life in that area. For example, large-scale pedestrianization of central areas is made more effective by underground rapid transit links, the benefits from which would accrue to all users and not only rapid transit passengers. Provided that revenue is raised locally and in an equitable fashion, such attempts should be encouraged as an alternative to private expenditure on trivial consumer products.

Means of raising public revenue

Public expenditure on transport is financed in three ways, by:

1 Motor taxation: fuel tax, purchase tax, annual vehicle duty.
2 Local rates.
3 Income tax and other taxes (e.g. VAT) contributing to general government revenues.

Strictly speaking, motor taxation is to be regarded merely as another form of raising government revenue; this is certainly true of VAT on sale of cars, for example. It can be argued, however, that annual duties and fuel tax are related to use of the road system and that some proportion of revenues from these taxes could be allocated directly to the road system, much as public transport users pay fares to operators.

The existing system could be modified in two ways of benefit to public transport:

1 Converting levies on motor vehicles, so that a higher proportion would correspond to mileage run, resembling the manner in which public transport costs are perceived. If the existing annual road

tax were allocated to fuel tax, the average motorist travelling about 16 000 km (10 000 miles) per annum by car would pay an extra 10 to 15p per gallon. If motor vehicle insurance were to be nationalized – for which arguments exist on grounds of providing security to those insured – the minimum amount per annum common to all those insured could similarly be allocated to fuel tax. A 'safe' motorist would make no additional payment, but others would pay additional amounts as now to reflect differences in risk according to age, type of car, etc. If the common amount were £30 per annum, a further 7 to 12p would be added to fuel tax. Total cost of fuel would thus increase from about 72p (at the time of writing) to about 95p per gallon but *total* costs of using a private car would be no higher for the average user than previously. Someone using the roads to a greater than average extent would pay more, which is reasonable, but someone who used a car only for certain essential trips would pay less. In this respect people in rural areas for whom the car is a necessity could benefit substantially. If road pricing were introduced in urban areas to indicate scarcity of road space, then some reduction in national fuel-tax rates would be appropriate.

2 Replacing local rates systems by a local income tax, with a specific annual charge levied on those whose choice of residential location incurs substantially higher costs than average in postal delivery, road provision, servicing, etc. (as argued in Chapter 5). A local income tax would be more equitable, and produce a yield automatically correlated with inflation. Penalties now imposed on those who improve their houses (for example, by building a garage and thus removing their car from the kerbside) would be removed. About 60 per cent of local government revenue now comes from central government grants, of which the Transport Supplementary Grant is one example. 'Local control' is becoming meaningless as central government stipulates levels of service and financial aid. This trend could be reversed were local government given more flexible means of raising revenue.

Coupled with a local income tax could be the ability to deduct from gross income before application of income-tax rates, costs incurred in travelling to work by public transport. At present costs incurred by car use can be deducted relatively easily under the heading of 'business' use even though they are often calculated from the home base. In the case of public transport, claims tend to be more specific and frequent home-based trips included less easily. Acceptance of public transport commuting expenditure for deduction would place the two modes on a comparable basis. The danger of encouraging lengthy commuting trips could be offset partly by charging true costs, especially for season ticket travel, and partly by strong land-use planning.

Such a system could be adopted as in Sweden, in which transport expenditure deducted from income before levying of tax is equated to the appropriate public transport fare(s) for the trips in question, whether or not public transport was the mode actually used. This is obviously limited to those cases where public transport and private cars are valid alternatives, i.e. where, within a given distance range of origin and destination, a sufficiently frequent public transport service is provided. The majority of urban commuting trips would probably fall into such a category. In such cases, tax revenue will increase if public transport fares are reduced (since the amount that can be deducted from gross income will also fall). This increase in public revenue will assist in financing a subsidy to public transport fares, the proportion of required subsidy being thus met being dependent upon the marginal tax rate. Complete equilibrium is not achieved, but the increase in local tax rate necessary to finance the fares subsidy is less than would be the case otherwise.

In the short run, the effect of introducing for the first time an estimate of relevant public transport fare instead of estimated motoring costs would be dramatic. Existing 'casual user' allowances of as much as 12p per mile for car trips on business would be assessed as income for tax purposes. A typical public transport fare scale of about 4p per mile would be used in estimating the deduction from income before levying of tax. Hence existing expenses of, for example, £150 per annum which are now free of tax, would be included as income, and only £50 (the equivalent public transport fares) deducted from gross income. If the marginal tax rate were 33 per cent, then an additional £33 tax revenue would be obtained. In addition, such a policy would discourage use of cars in city centres, giving benefits in the form of reduced congestion.

External factors

Population

World population is growing at an alarming rate, and in consequence of high birth rates is likely to display a lower average age.

The British situation is very different. Recent population estimates have been revised downward almost every year, the contrast between the estimate made in 1965 and that in 1971 being shown in Figure 10.1. A very slowly growing total is now envisaged. Since average life expectancy remains high, an ageing structure is likely to develop. The high proportion of retired people has implications for demand: a substantial opportunity for off-peak traffic, provided that vehicle design and network structure are adapted to demand. The rising proportion of the population in the working-age groups should eliminate recruitment problems in most areas.

During the 1980s the school population will be relatively low ,per-

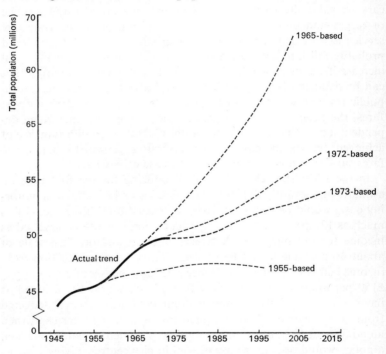

Figure 10.1   Population forecasts for England and Wales

haps relieving some peak traffic demands and the losses now associated with concessionary fares. A secondary problem arising from the age structure could be that of recruiting new management from the reduced younger age groups, and hence conservatism in policy which could make adaptations to other changes more difficult.

Population structure is also changing geographically. Areas of traditionally high public transport use, such as the north-east of England, and Scotland, are likely to remain static or decline marginally. Such growth as does occur is likely to be in East Anglia, the East Midlands, the West Country and outer South East Region. In so far as this is associated with migration to those regions (mostly by young adults) and/or higher birth rates in those regions, age structures will also differ by region. At the *intra*-regional level, movement out of inner city areas continues, with growth in suburban areas and new towns. This implies an increased demand for inter- and intrasuburb transport facilities, and possibly improved inter-urban facilities, particularly between new towns (cross-country links from Northampton and Milton Keynes, for example, are amongst the poorest in Britain for towns of such size). New investment should be concentrated in these areas and not necessarily on renewal of existing facilities at their present capacity. The London Rail Study, for example, anticipates substantial falls in peak-hour volumes on some inner London rail services.

It is to be hoped that the trend towards very low density semi-rural development will be curtailed by increasing energy costs. It is very difficult to see any way in which a good level of public transport service can be provided to such areas.

The outward movement of population from urban centres has implications for the organization of the transport industry. For example, the share of the population of England and Wales falling within the areas now served by the National Bus Company rose from about 44 per cent in 1951 to 50 per cent in 1971. Expansion of areas served by municipal bus services could be justified as a means of maintaining their catchment populations.

A pessimist might conclude that a poor future exists for public transport in the light of the above trends. However, if adaptation is made, many positive opportunities exist. Changes in age structure could improve peak:off-peak service ratios. In so far as population re-sited from existing industrial cities is located in new or expanding towns of about 100000 population, similar improvements could occur. As argued in Chapter 2, such towns, by virtue of their suitability for walking or cycling to work, create a better peak:off-peak demand ratio than conurbation cities.

Many transportation studies and trip forecasts now current were produced before the latest, reduced, forecasts of total population. Downward revision may be necessary in some cases. Such significant variation in total travel demand as does occur in the next few years is likely to be a result of variations in trip *rate* rather than population.

Energy

The case of conservation of energy is almost too well known to require repetition. Limited oil reserves, the high cost of exploiting other sources, and dangers of nuclear power generation are adequately documented elsewhere. Such arguments are generally favourable to public transport, due to the much greater efficiency in energy used per passenger-kilometre. A particularly strong case can be made for electric traction *vis-à-vis* oil in that alternative sources of power can generate electricity, and use of regenerative braking enables further reductions in net energy consumption for some movements. However, the situation is not as simple as many early advocates of public transport's advantages in this context assumed. The sharp rise in petrol prices in late 1973 and early 1974 was associated with a fall in consumption, but this was due largely to curtailment of marginal car trips, driving at lower speeds and high occupancy factors, rather than diversion to public transport. Other qualifying conditions include:

1 Actual rather than potential efficiency is important, although allowance can be made for improvement in existing load factors where extra traffic can be diverted to public transport. Typical public transport seating load factors, averaged over the whole day, tend to be around 15 to 20 per cent. This very low range does not necessarily indicate poor management. Highly peaked demand, plus the incremental alighting or loading pattern as a vehicle serves a radial corridor account for much of the spare capacity. A private car normally achieves a load factor of at least 25 per cent (one person driving in a four-seater), and typically 35 to 40 per cent. This variable is particularly important in comparing different modes of public transport, since air travel's low potential efficiency is much improved when its typical load factor of about 55 per cent on domestic routes is noted.

2 The high unladen weight of some vehicles may absorb much of the energy required for movement. This is critical in comparing rail with other modes: a typical carriage weighs about 25 tonnes, to carry about sixty seated passengers weighing about 4 tonnes. An express motor coach of about the same seating capacity weighs about 8 tonnes unladen. The rolling and aerodynamic resistance

per tonne by rail has to be less than one-third that of the coach in order to display a net energy saving at the same load factor. Again, the difference does not necessarily indicate managerial inefficiency, but partly the higher standard of comfort and safety provided on rail.

3 Primary and secondary sources of power: an electric motor is a more efficient user of energy than an internal combustion engine, the thermal efficiency of the latter being about 15 per cent (for petrol) or up to 30 per cent (diesel). However, the electric motor is dependent upon a primary generating source. Existing British power stations have an average thermal efficiency of less than 30 per cent, the best achieving only 36 per cent. This figure could be improved by measures to use existing surplus heat generated at power stations (for example, in district heating or smelting of mineral ores), and/or by reducing peaks in demand so that a steady level of generation occurs. Allowing for losses of efficiency in the primary source, existing electric traction systems in Britain display a thermal efficiency of about 20 per cent. The cost of fuel used to generate electricity has thus to be about 70 per cent or less that of diesel oil in order to offer a lower net cost per thermal unit.

At present coal fills this role, and is likely to continue to do so. Increases in labour cost of mining will probably be matched by higher extraction costs of oil from unfavourable settings such as undersea or shale deposits. If hydro or solar power can be used, or nuclear power made sufficiently safe, then reduction in generating costs may occur.

Other proposed fuels include liquefied or high-pressure hydrogen. Although offering similar weight:payload characteristics as does an internal combustion engine and its fuel tank, such a 'fuel' would require large amounts of energy for its creation, and be highly dangerous in use.

A second area of efficiency lies in the vehicle itself. Energy used in acceleration is proportional to the square of the speed attained, and *power* required is related to the rate of acceleration. Power required for steady motion is needed to overcome transmission losses (rising marginally with speed), to overcome rolling resistance (rising approximately in linear proportion to speed), and to overcome aerodynamic resistance (approximately exponential to speed). A simplistic view would suggest that the lowest possible speeds be adopted, but in practice most internal combustion engines achieve a minimum fuel consumption for a given load at about 65 km/h (40 mph). Furthermore, even under conditions of energy shortage, time-based labour and depreciation costs would probably remain significant. A very low average speed would imply a large number of vehicles to operate existing services, which would itself involve more energy being consumed in construction of vehicles.

Reduction in the number of intermediate stops or severe speed limits reduces the frequency with which acceleration is required and hence total energy consumption for a given end-to-end average speed. For the private car, linking of traffic signals may permit a steady flow. For the bus, priority at traffic signals and at other points can help, but in the long run some extension of the distance between stops might be necessary (for implications on passengers, see Chapter 5). Another implication of high energy costs for bus services would be a change in the ratio of distance-based to time-based costs, making marginal expansion of off-peak mileage more difficult to justify. Rail services are affected in a similar manner to buses, save that energy costs form a lower proportion of the whole. In urban areas, higher rates of acceleration followed by a period of coasting can enable a given schedule to be covered using less energy (this is illustrated with reference to speed-time curves in Chapter 4).

Long-run implications of high energy cost consist of a possible decline in very short trips by public transport, with transfer to foot or cycle. Long- and medium-distance trips could be depressed by the effects of high fuel costs on economic growth, but increased by the greater stimulus to car users to divert wholly, or by the nearest available park-and-ride interchange, to public transport. In so far as cars now account for the majority of travel, the overall implications to public transport are beneficial.

Is high mobility desirable?

An underlying assumption until recently was that higher personal mobility was a good thing in itself, allied with other measures of economic growth. This simplistic view has been challenged by those looking at the distribution of mobility. Despite rapid growth overall, some groups have become less mobile than before, notably those without cars in rural areas. The report of the Independent Commission on Transport in 1974 wisely replaced the concept of 'mobility' with that of 'access'. Following the logic of transport economists who see travel costs as a disutility justified only by the greater utility of the activity being reached, they argue that the *need* for mobility is dictated by the availability of objectives such as work opportunities, educational institutions and shopping. A person with a good range of facilities near at hand has less need to travel than someone in a poorly served area. In rural situations, for example, a large village with few shops may justify a heavily subsidized bus service whereas a smaller one with good local facilities may not.

In reality, individual trip frequencies follow the opposite trend. Londoners, despite the proximity of almost all facilities of an industrialized society, make substantially more interurban trips per head (especially by air) than the rest of the British population. True, this is partly accounted for by the high proportion of business and administration employment, location of friends and relatives outside the capital, and perhaps the need to get away from the urban environment from time to time. But a paradox remains. Is it that the profusion of facilities actually makes life worse? That there is too much choice? Could the same apply to mobility?

Any intelligent person can raise these questions, but few of those professionally concerned with transport planning have done so. It has been left to a well-known radical social theorist. In his book *Energy and Equity* Ivan Illich (1973) sets out explicitly the case against mobility at high speeds. These views form part of his general vision of society, in which small-scale human institutions would replace existing large and formal structures, integrating the functions now performed in bureaucratic fashion – medicine, education, industrial production – into communities. This picture is clouded by some sentimentality, especially as regards life in rural areas without industrialization. But it is much more attractive than a continuation of present trends in industrialized society, in which ever larger units control not only industrial production, but many once informal aspects of life. In material terms individuals might be richer, but life as a whole less satisfying.

Conventional economic wisdom would suggest that increased consumption leads to increased satisfaction, but this may only be true for the individual in the short run. The opportunity for more foreign travel will in the short run give a chance to see regions of different culture and life style, but as tourism increases this variety is reduced. Many leisure trips are based not on unique features of the destination, such as historic buildings or the geology, but a desire to travel a certain distance as an aim in itself. Does an 'evening out' for drinks or a meal really necessitate a 30 km drive into the country? If a sense of having spent effort in reaching a destination is all that is required, then a 4 km walk will suffice.

Illich's views, from which the above is partially derived, are expressed in the form of a polemic. In advocating change he over-reaches himself, neglecting the high proportion of urban settlement already existing, and erring by an order of magnitude in estimating peak flows of cycle traffic. A more realistic but no less radical view of society is that offered by Schumacher (1974), who shows that existing measures of efficiency can often support arguments in favour of small-scale organization. Small, integrated units permit better use of energy and recycling of materials. Some evidence has been presented in this book to suggest that the smaller urban areas, served by operating organizations of similar size, require least subsidy to attain a satisfactory level of service.

Some critics of arguments against the present inequities in mobility have read into them an implication that the same mobility per person is being advocated. While suggesting that groups such as the elderly should enjoy more mobility than they now do, and middle-class executives do not justify the importance they now receive in transport plans, there are of course substantial differences connected with age (parents with young children make relatively few journeys, and retired people do not need to travel in the weekday peak) and with personal preferences.

It is important to direct these arguments against their true targets: encouragement of high-speed intercity systems, and growth of long-distance commuting. Like many ecological or environmental arguments they may be used all too easily by those now enjoying the high level of material wealth produced by the present industrial system while living in what remains of small-scale communities, and applied only to others. A recent television programme presented by a lady novelist portrayed one of her regular visits to a traditional village in Dorset – in a chauffeur-driven car with a nanny to handle the child – which was described with genuine feeling. But the villagers appeared largely as the backdrop to church garden parties or farming activities. Amid a string of unintentionally patronizing comments viewers were informed that non-car-owning villagers enjoyed a bus service once a week to Dorchester market. And after a few days' stay she returned to London in the same chauffer-driven saloon.

Even at the present levels of centralization of employment,

shopping and other facilities a substantial increase in rural public transport provision is essential. In some urban areas services also fall below the minimum level.

Any sane individual view on transport must take account of the structure of the whole society which results from high mobility. Travel cannot be divorced from the purpose it serves. As Matthew Arnold wrote:

> Your middle-class man thinks it is the highest pitch of development and civilization when his letters are carried twelve times a day from Islington to Camberwell, and from Camberwell to Islington, and if railway trains run between them every quarter of an hour. He thinks it nothing that the trains only carry him from an illiberal, dismal, life at Camberwell, to an illiberal, dismal life at Islington, and the letters only tell him such is the life there.

(From *Friendship's Garland*)

Expand the middle class to include the car owning affluent worker, substitute telecommunications for letters, and the statement still holds.

References for further reading

Association of District Councils (1974) *A New Look at Local Government Finance* (two parts). See also other evidence submitted to, and report of, the Layfield Committee of Enquiry into Local Government Finance.

Illich, I. D. (1973) *Energy and Equity*, Calder & Boyars.

Klapper, C. F. (1973) *Sir Herbert Walker's Southern Railway*, Ian Allan. Chapter 10 refers to appraisal of electrification schemes.

Masefield, P. (1975) 'Energy for traction', *Railway Engineering Journal*, **4**, no. 2, 39–49 (summary in *Modern Railways*, **32**, no. 320, 209–10).

Office of Population Censuses and Surveys (1975) *Regional Population Projections, mid-1973 based*, HMSO.

Schumacher, E. F. (1974) *Small is Beautiful*, Abacus.

Transport Policy: A Consultation Document (1976) HMSO (2 vols).

Index

Acceleration rates: of buses, 69; in network design, 98–100; of urban railways, 76–9 *passim*

Acts of Parliament: Housing (1969), 95; Local Government (1972), 14–16; Local Government (Scotland) (1973), 22; Railways (1974), 28, 125, 189; Road Traffic (1930, 1960, 1974), 11, 12, 149; Transport (1968), 13, 23, 124, 193; *see also* Northern Ireland

Advanced Passenger Train (APT), 166, 172–3

Aérotrain, 173–4

Ailsa-Volvo bus design, 58

Air braking, 168

Air services, UK domestic, 30, 155–60 *passim*, 175, 183, 190, 206

Alexander PSV bodywork, 59

Alweg monorail system, 87

Appeals on road service licensing, 11

Area Traffic Control (ATC), 66

Automatic ticket systems, 83, 84, 89

Automatic train control, 83

Axle loads on railways, 165–6

Bedford PSV chassis, 59

Belfast, trip distribution, 43

Block section signalling, 81–2, 162–9

Brighton, 39, 43, 186

Bristol, city of, 41, 61, 62, 72, 106

Bristol PSV designs, 59, 178

British Airports Authority (BAA), 207

British Electric Traction (BET), 13

British Rail Engineering (BREL), 15

British Railways Board, structure of, 14–29 *passim*

British Tourist Authority 158, 187

Buckles, P., 130, 133, 202

'Bus Economy Ticket', 199

Bus Demonstration Project, 70

Bus Electronic Scanning Indicator

(BESI), 61

Bus operation: TV/Radio control systems, 61; traffic management, in, 62–6, 70; Station design, 66–8; *see also* network structures

Buses: new bus grants, 14, 145; design of, 54–61

Business trips, 39, 43, 127, 156–8

Busways and bus links, 68–70, 88–9

'Cab signalling', 163

Capital debt structures: National Bus Company/Scottish Transport Group 120–1; British Rail, 14, 120

'Captive' users, 30, 31

Cars, ownership levels, 41, 42, 47, 48, 50; role of, 30, 32, 38, 39, 47, 49, 150; intercity use, 156–9; *see also* 'Park-and-Ride'

Carte Orange, 200

Central Transport Users' Consultative Committee (CTCC), 165

Centralized Traffic Control, 165

Certificate of Fitness (CoF), 11, 55

Channel Tunnel, 167, 204

Chartered Institute of Public Finance and Accountancy Bus costing system ('CIPFA formula'), 123, 133

Circumferential bus services in urban areas, 91, 92

'Citybus' (Belfast), 23

Closed-circuit TV bus control, 61

'Clyderail', 19

Coaches, *see* Express coaches

Collins, P. H., 104, 117, 173

Colour-light signalling, 163, 164

'Community Transport', 148

'Commuting', 48, 131, 132, 196; *see also* works trips

Continuously welded rail (cwr), 166

'Contra-flow' bus lanes, 65

Control of bus operations, 61, 62